GOVERNOR
WILLIAM E. GLASSCOCK

AND PROGRESSIVE POLITICS

IN WEST VIRGINIA

WEST VIRGINIA AND APPALACHIA

A SERIES EDITED BY RONALD L. LEWIS

VOLUME 9

Other books in the series:

Transnational West Virginia
Edited by Ken Fones-Wolf

The Blackwater Chronicle
Edited by Timothy Sweet

Clash of Loyalties
By John Shaffer

Afflicting the Comfortable
By Thomas F. Stafford

Bringing Down the Mountains
By Shirley Stewart Burns

*Monongah: The Tragic Story
of the 1907 Monongah Mine Disaster*
By Davitt McAteer

*Sectionalism in Virginia from 1776 to 1881,
Second Edition*
By Charles Ambler

Matewan Before the Massacre
By Rebecca J. Bailey

GOVERNOR
WILLIAM E. GLASSCOCK

AND PROGRESSIVE POLITICS

IN WEST VIRGINIA

Gary Jackson Tucker

MORGANTOWN 2008

West Virginia University Press, Morgantown 26506

© 2008 by West Virginia University Press

First edition published 2008 by West Virginia University Press

Printed in the United States of America

15 14 13 12 11 10 09 08   1 2 3 4 5 6 7 8 9

ISBN-10 1-933202-35-1

ISBN-13 978-1-933202-35-8

(alk. paper)

Library of Congress Cataloguing-in-Publication Data

Tucker, Gary J. (Gary Jackson), 1940-

Governor William E. Glasscock and progressive politics in West Virginia / Gary Jackson Tucker. -- 1st ed.

p.   cm.   -- (West Virginia and Appalachia; 9)

ISBN 978-1-933202-35-8 (pbk. : alk. paper)

1. Glasscock, Wm. E. (William Ellsworth), 1862-1925. 2. Governors--West Virginia--Biography.

3. West Virginia--Politics and government--20th century. I. Title.

F241.G55T83 2008

975.4'041092--dc22

[B]

2008049809

Cover Design by Than Saffel

Cover Image: Portrait of Governor William E. Glasscock, courtesy of the West Virginia Division of Culture and History. Painted by Alphonse Jongers; Photographed by Michael Keller.

For my family

CONTENTS

FOREWORD

T HIS IS THE POLITICAL BIOGRAPHY of a governor and his times, the Progressive Era. West Virginia Governor William E. Glasscock, West Virginia's governor from 1909 to 1913, was a member of the generation that came to power and prominence around the turn of the twentieth century. The impact of the Civil War and its aftermath certainly left its imprint on the developing personalities of the young men and women of this generation, perhaps motivating them to achieve their own victories over iniquities in a rapidly changing society. During this period, a young, professional middle class developed that was composed of individuals who desired more control over their world. Perhaps the chaos and corruption of the recent past prompted many of these newcomers to attempt to bring order, understanding, and efficiency to social, economic, and political systems that had undergone remarkable stress in the transition from the pre-industrial to the industrial age. From the latter part of the eighteenth century, local economies slowly spread to the regional and then to the national level, and business enterprises grew from single proprietorships to larger partnerships. The Civil War vastly accelerated the dynamics in the marketplace resulting in the creation of large concentrations of wealth based on newly created corporate entities and ultimately economic monopolies, affecting all areas of society.

Following the Civil War, the consequences of rapid economic growth forced the new generation to grapple with its incumbent problems—city slums, inadequate public utilities, crime, political corruption and machines (bossism), and the assimilation of large numbers of immigrants and migrants—especially in the urban areas. Other major problems were centered around the out-of-control growth of giant corporations and the creation of fantastic personal fortunes (compared with real and perceived poverty of the industrial worker and farmer, and dissatisfaction among the traditional middle class, the guardian of American values). In reaction to this unwieldy growth, workers began to organize in significant numbers to deal with the impersonal forces of industry and professionals. Taking their cues from well-organized businessmen and their organizations, they joined their own respective associations. While many unions won acceptance and negotiated favorable working conditions, others did not and felt compelled to take a stand for their fair share of the economic pie. Although most Progressives were good capitalists and saw nothing wrong with financial gain, they attempted to rein in some of the more blatant aspects of industrialism through governmental regulation and a fair tax system.

Unfortunately, the tensions and strains of the new economic system often erupted in violence, such as the mine wars on Paint and Cabin Creeks near Charleston, West Virginia. The governor, who tried to referee the opponents, calling right and wrong where he saw them, attempted to walk a fine line between the protection of property and the right of workers to organize. During these bloody mine wars, there were excesses on both sides. Of course, the miners suffered many personal hardships such as the indignity of eviction from their company homes to reside in tents provided by the union, while men of property and wealth stood by their right to protect their investments under the law. Glasscock sought to protect both and often found himself the target of both sides.

In other areas of violence, remnants of slavery survived the Civil War in the form of racism displayed in the actions and attitudes of many American citizens, and often taking its ugliest form in the act of lynching. From the latter part of the nineteenth century, states in the North and the South witnessed an increase in these acts. West Virginia was not spared the horrible deed. In reaction to the heinous crime of lynching and vigilante mob action, Governor Glasscock proved to be a man of character, a firm believer in law and order, and a passionate advocate for the downtrodden. Never hesitating to muster up the police power of the state to defend the life of an individual, sometimes even placing his own personal safety in jeopardy, Glasscock won the praise of law-abiding citizens everywhere. By standing firmly against racism and mob action, the thirteenth governor of the Mountain State earned the gratitude of struggling minorities for generations to come.

Progressives, including Governor Glasscock, believed in the basic goodness and intelligence of the people, whose support would allow government to organize society in a rational way. They also felt strongly that the control of party affairs should be in the hands of the people, instead of political machines, or the bosses who acted on nineteenth century principles of the Gilded Age. In order to accomplish fairness and openness, they diligently fought for the establishment of primary elections operating under state rules to make nominations to public offices. To achieve more democracy and transparency in politics, the direct primary became an important goal for most reformers. The Progressive governors of West Virginia and like-minded politicians such as Governor Robert M. La Follette of Wisconsin made it of utmost importance in their agendas. In a sense, these crusaders viewed the primary as a benchmark for their administrations.

To ensure that public servants followed the rules of office, reformers also advocated the use of the initiative, referendum, and recall. In order to eliminate graft and corruption, they insisted upon tough corrupt practices acts and fair laws, limiting the activities of lobbyists. Only after the passage of such laws could the people register their concerns so that regulatory legislation could be passed to correct the social and economic ills of society. Glasscock agreed with most reformers that the influence of the state should be extended in two ways: "negatively, to use the power of government to limit and regulate capital and business, and positively, to use it to promote and protect the public, social and economic welfare."[1]

When it came to the economy, socialism was as unacceptable as "laissez faire" capitalism. The solution to the rapacious appetite of big corporations was regulation, a conservative or middle-of-the-road approach. Reformers soon learned from their experiences at the local, grass roots, state, and later, the federal level, that the legislature acting through the direction of a strong executive was necessary to accomplish their goals. To create a "New Order" out of pre-industrial America, fit for modern times, reformers attempted to create administrative bureaucracies to administer rules in order to provide continuity as well as fluidity for a fast changing society.[2] Speaking of the regulatory commissions, conservative U.S. Senator Elihu Root of New York, prophesied in 1916, "We shall go on; we shall expand them, whether we approve theoretically or not; because such agencies furnish protection. . . [which] cannot be practically accomplished by the old and simple procedure of legislatures and courts."[3] In order to achieve success and to create governmental channels through which problems could be solved, the public had to be informed and educated by enlightened professionals, politicians, educators, and journalists, who would bring to the light of day the wrongs for the people to correct.

---

1   Russel B. Nye, *Midwestern Progressive Politics: A Historical Study of Its Origins and Development, 1870–1958* (Lansing: Michigan State University Press, 1959), 187. Hereafter cited as Nye, *Midwestern Progressive Politics.*

2   Robert H. Wiebe, *The Search For Order: 1877–1920* (New York: Hill and Wang, 1967), passim. Hereafter cited as Wiebe, *The Search For Order.*

3   Wiebe, *The Search For Order,* 295–96.

For the younger, middle class professionals who became active in the Republican Party, it was no longer practical to recall the past glories of hard-fought Civil War battles to instill loyalty and discipline among party members, especially at the local level. Older Republicans had used this tactic to their advantage almost to the twentieth century. Democrats, who controlled state government from the mid-1870s to the mid-1890s, still struggled in their effort to become a united national force. Racial issues and the desire of southern Democrats to establish white supremacy in their region protected by a federal government caused their party to be less successful in the modern industrial world. Industrialism had changed the nation, and it would be necessary to educate the public about critical national and international issues that impinged upon their lives. Modern politicians, who were most often middle class, business-oriented, well-educated, and professional, such as William E. Glasscock, knew that the old way of doing things must change, but it was not easy to convince the older generation to break from the past and seriously consider reforms. Of course, one way of breaking the control of the "old guard" and the "Old Order" was to give more power to an educated voting public.

The different opinions engendered by these issues and others, such as struggles between the "ins" and the "outs," often led to bitter fighting within the political parties. Because of these debilitating divisions and the reluctance of conservatives to change, the many hard-fought battles often forced the political combatants to pay serious consequences. While becoming involved with state and national politics, such as Teddy Roosevelt's run for the presidency in 1912, Glasscock greatly depleted his personal finances and also severely impaired his health; however, by the end of his administration, West Virginia was definitely in the Progressive column.

ACKNOWLEDGMENTS

I OWE MUCH APPRECIATION to so many people for their assistance in writing this book. First, I give much credit to my former teacher, mentor, and friend, Dr. Otis K. Rice, now deceased, for recommending Governor William E. Glasscock as a topic for my doctoral dissertation many years ago. I was also inspired by his writings about West Virginia and frontier history. In addition, I acknowledge the professional constructive advice given by other teachers and authors of West Virginia history. They include Dr. Ronald L. Lewis of West Virginia University, Dr. Gordon B. McKinney of Berea College, and Dr. Paul Rakes and Dr. Stephen Brown of West Virginia University Institute of Technology. Through their questions and comments, the manuscript slowly took its final form, and its clarity and quality I attribute to them.

No less important, I offer my appreciation to general readers of West Virginia history who read my manuscript and gave me their impressions. It was always my intention to write a book that was not only acceptable to the professional community but also to those interested in reading about our past. They are Mr. James Dennis, chairman of the Social Studies Department of Parkersburg South High School and Mr. David Coleman, an avid reader and a true Mountaineer. I give you my thanks.

Of course, the librarians of West Virginia University, West Virginia Tech, West Virginia University at Parkersburg, the West Virginia Division of Culture and History in Charleston, the Manuscript Division of the Library of Congress, and the Theodore Roosevelt Collection at Harvard University provided invaluable service in facilitating my research at their institutions. I wish to thank all the people associated with the West Virginia University Press for their hard work and assistance in making this book a reality. I would especially like to thank Than Saffel, production coordinator and designer, and Rachel Rosolina, graduate editor, for their assistance and guidance through the publishing maze.

Finally, my family, my wife Janice, son Gary J. Tucker, Jr. M.D., his wife Carri, my younger son Brent, and my daughter Debbie, who endured endless days of listening to me ruminate about Governor Glasscock and Progressive politics, you have my love, sympathy, and appreciation. Of course, it is understood that any shortfalls or mistakes belong entirely to me.

THE ORIGINS
OF A YOUNG REFORMER

". . . the only lawyer I know who was successful from the beginning of his career."[1]

T HE CIVIL WAR AND ITS AFTERMATH, strong regional feelings, adjustments to the new economic conditions, and outright racism would all create heated political debate in nearly every political election until well into the twentieth century. One of these debates involved the creation of West Virginia. The rending of Virginia on June 20, 1863, was a momentous event for western Virginians. People like Congressman Jacob Beeson Blair of Parkersburg worked diligently to persuade President Abraham Lincoln that it was constitutionally, legally, and morally right to force the Mother State of Virginia to give birth to the new state of West Virginia.[2] Depending upon the opinions of western Virginians, this action generated intense debates and arguments for decades to come. In this setting, a future governor of West Virginia was born, the third chief executive elected to lead the newly created state in the dawn of the twentieth century.

William Ellsworth Glasscock, thirteenth governor of West Virginia, was born on December 13, 1862, on a small farm in Monongalia County (then Virginia), about thirteen miles from the city of Morgantown. Glasscock and his generation, the sons and daughters of Union and Confederate families, born during violence and despair, came of age during a period of great social, economic, and political turmoil. "Rebuild, reform, and change" appeared to be the motto for the newer generation, who were mindful of the past but had their eyes fixed on the future.

1 Jack O. Henson to Glasscock, 4 December 1908, Glasscock Papers, West Virginia University Library. Hereafter cited as Glasscock Papers, unless location is different.
2 *Dictionary of Virginia Biography*, s.v. "Jacob Beeson Blair," by Gary J. Tucker (Richmond, Virginia: The Library of Virginia, 1998), 1:539.

This generation spawned such state and national heroes as Theodore Roosevelt, an urbane sophisticate who was very comfortable in the company of the new and old rich, big city financier or western cowboy. Robert M. La Follette, governor of Wisconsin who espoused many Progressive ideas in the hallways of the Wisconsin legislature and the governor's mansion, and ultimately influenced other state and city leaders was another leading light. William Jennings Bryan was the "hayseed" editor from Nebraska who first captured the Democratic nomination for president in 1896. He also promoted ideas with roots going back to the Liberal Republicans, the Greenbackers, the Mugwumps, the Populists, and ultimately to progressive Democrats and Republicans, north and south of the Mason-Dixon Line.

From their own points of view and unique circumstances, journalists, politicians, educators, farmers, and workers all shared a vision of an America unfettered by large concentrations of power, where the individual could still achieve his goals. Bringing their ideas, hopes, and dreams with them into their positions of power, these influential leaders sprinkled their pronouncements with such terms as *progressive, new, forward-looking,* and *modern.* Those influenced by them also peppered their conversations with these terms when describing their personal and public goals for the future. They even succeeded in encouraging conservatives, hesitant to change, to test the political winds and embrace different ideas in a careful way.

The young reformers entered the new century searching for a fairer and more equitable way of sharing the wealth created by the new concentrated forms of industry. For many of the middle class, reform was necessary in order to regain social status seemingly lost to the "captains of industry."[3] Others joined the ranks of the reformers because they felt they had lost control to the machine politicians, rather than out of a genuine concern for the people. More importantly, reformers desired to make sense of a rapidly changing society in which many individuals felt a sense of loss and lacked direction because of overwhelming forces in their lives. The new generation knew that the old way of permitting passive governments to forfeit decision-making powers to leaders of industry must change. Establishing active governments with strong executive leadership, presenting programs to lawmaking bodies, and creating channels for orderly change, continuity, and stability, appeared to be a workable road map for the reformers.

---

3   Richard Hofstadter, *The Age of Reform* (New York: Vintage Books, 1955), 131–48, 166. See also Michael McGerr, *A Fierce Discontent: The Rise and Fall of the Progressive Movement in America, 1870–1920* (New York: Free Press, 2003), 68–69; and Wiebe, *The Search For Order,* 111–32.

William E. Glasscock typified the young, up-and-coming middle class professional eager to achieve an "independent position" in life. A mild reformer in the beginning of his political career, Glasscock eventually joined the ranks of the fervent Progressive leaders. Throughout his governorship, he attempted to achieve such typical Progressive legislation as the statewide primary, tax reform, anti-lobbying laws, a corrupt practices act, fair regulation of railroads and public utilities, workmen's compensation law, proper maintenance of natural resources, and efficiency and openness in governmental operations. Throughout the Progressive Era, the common denominator would be faith in the innate goodness and wisdom of a knowledgeable electorate working in unison with a powerful central government,[4] which would pass legislation and create an administrative bureaucracy that would administer and harness forces beyond the control of ordinary citizens.

As with the majority of Americans of the nineteenth century, the future governor grew up in a rural setting not a stone's throw from belching industries owned by anonymous entrepreneurs who resided in far away places. Although he was quite familiar with the bustling urban areas, Glasscock often recalled with obvious pleasure his youthful experiences on his family's farm surrounded by gentle, rolling hills. These early experiences led to a deep respect for farming and husbandry. Whenever possible, he spoke and wrote with pride about his beloved state,[5] telling his audience about the people, the productive climate, the vast natural resources, and the growing industry of the thirty-fifth state. Perhaps because of Glasscock's rural background and his obvious dedication to, and love of, his home, he often expressed a special interest in West Virginia's rugged beauty and appealing climate, maybe even to the point of exaggeration. For example, in one such speech Governor Glasscock not only extolled the wonders of his state, but also bragged that its people experienced more sunshine than the people of Florida and less snow than those in Ohio, Indiana, and Illinois.

While Glasscock knew the history, facts, and statistics of his homeland well, he lacked solid information about his own background. On several occasions, the governor expressed regret over the fact that he was unable to be more specific when tracing his ancestry. Naturally, he was appreciative when Virgil A. Lewis, West Virginia historian, informed him that the name Glasscock went as far back as the founding of

---

4   Stephen F. Knott, *Alexander Hamilton and the Persistence of Myth* (Kansas: University Press of Kansas, 2002), 98–99.
5   William E. Glasscock, *The State of West Virginia, An Address Delivered by Governor Glasscock at Seattle, Washington, July 29, 1909* (Charleston, West Virginia: News-Mail Company, 1909).

Virginia. Lewis stated that the 257th land patent granted in that colony, dated October 7, 1635, had been made to Robert Glascocke. He concluded, "this Robert Glasscock was doubtless the emigrant ancestor of the Glasscock family, of Virginia, the lineage of which, I have no doubt may be readily traced."[6] Glasscock received Lewis's letter with pleasure, since the extent of his knowledge to that time had been that "all of our people came from Fauquier County, where my ancestors resided and some to other parts of what was then Western Virginia."[7] With his interest aroused, the governor made a decided effort to gather as much information as he could on his family's past. He soon learned that his great-grandfather, John Glasscock, son of Hezekiah, had been an American Revolutionary War soldier.[8] John and his son, Charles, the governor's grandfather who died around 1840, moved from Fauquier County, Virginia, around 1800, to Pharaoh's Run in Marion County, now West Virginia. They later journeyed from there to the Benjamin J. Miller farm on Indian Creek located in Monongalia County. It was in that area that Charles married Mary Arnett, the daughter of Andrew Arnett, and the granddaughter of James Arnett, who had also served in the Revolutionary War. They lived on a farm near Arnettsville, where Charles and Mary reared their family, following such agricultural pursuits as farming and milling.

In that same sylvan area, Glasscock's father, Daniel, was born in 1828. He grew up in Arnettsville and eventually became a farmer. He was a man of distinction, active in the Republican Party and a devout Methodist. During the Civil War he was elected captain of a body of home guards. Daniel married twice. His first marriage was to a "Miss Musgrave" in 1855, which produced a son, David. Two years after the death of his first wife in 1857, he married Prudence Michael. They had nine children, one of whom was William, the future governor of West Virginia.[9]

At an early age, Ellsworth—as his close friends called him—developed an interest in education, which he maintained throughout his life. Influenced by his mother, who often read to him from the Bible, and perhaps, too, by his slight stature, which precluded strenuous activities, Glasscock devoted much time to reading and study. Upon graduation from the local common schools, he went to the Midwest, where

6 Virgil A. Lewis to William E. Glasscock, 11 May 1910, William E. Glasscock Papers.
7 Glasscock to J. H. Glasscock, 29 October 1909, Glasscock Papers.
8 S. F. Glasscock to Glasscock, 31 January 1912, William E. Glasscock Papers, West Virginia Department of Archives and History, Charleston, West Virginia.
9 *Biographical and Portrait Cyclopedia of Monongalia, Marion, and Taylor Counties, West Virginia* (Philadelphia, Pennsylvania: Rush, West and Co., 1895), 113. See also "West Virginia's Thirteenth Governor," *The West Virginia Review*, 21 (July, 1944): 11.

he had relatives, and taught school in Nebraska and Iowa for four years. Because of the harsh winters, which frequently caused him to become ill, Glasscock returned to West Virginia, where he successfully ran for the office of county superintendent of Free Schools of Monongalia County.[10] So far, life had been good to the young Mountaineer, who was blessed with a sharp mind and a willingness to work hard in order to achieve his goals, despite physical weaknesses.

Over time, Glasscock's ambitions broadened. While serving as superintendent, he ran successfully for two six-year terms as clerk of the Circuit Court of Monongalia County. During his tenure as clerk, he began to study law at West Virginia University. Classified as a special student, Glasscock took courses over a two year period to prepare him for the bar examination, which he passed in February 1902.[11] On January 1, 1903, he entered a partnership with his brother Samuel, better known as Fuller, who had already begun practicing law. Opening an office in Morgantown, the brothers built a lucrative practice, handling many corporate cases. A fellow attorney once wrote that Glasscock was the only lawyer he knew who was successful from the very beginning of his career.[12] The Glasscock brothers acted as general counsel for the Morgantown and Kingwood Railway System, which was controlled by U.S. Senator Stephen B. Elkins, whom Glasscock considered "very friendly." Their legal practice certainly added to the family larder.[13] In addition, Glasscock served as a member of the board of directors of

---

10   Glasscock to Mrs. R. A. Phelps, 10 February 1912, Glasscock Papers; George W. Atkinson, *Bench and Bar of West Virginia* (Charleston: Virginian Law Book Company, 1919), 262–63; See also the *Fairmont West Virginian*, October 5, 1908.

11   A special student classification in law was for those individuals over twenty-one who wished to prepare for the bar examination, but were not working toward a law degree. See *West Virginia University Catalogue, 1899–1902* (Morgantown: West Virginia University, 1902–1903), 142–43.

12   Jack O. Henson to Glasscock, 4 December 1908, Glasscock Papers.

13   Glasscock to S. F. Glasscock, 15 April 1909, Glasscock Papers. See also Oscar Doane Lambert, *Stephen Benton Elkins* (Pittsburgh: University of Pittsburgh Press, 1955). Hereafter cited as Lambert, *Stephen Benton Elkins*. Senator Elkins, a powerful figure in the Republican Party, had an interesting past. A native of Missouri, Elkins later resided in the Territory of New Mexico, becoming its territorial representative in the U. S. Congress. Later he was appointed Secretary of War by Benjamin Harrison and elected U.S. Senator from West Virginia from 1895–1911. He was a graduate of the University of Missouri, with an interest in mathematics and languages and taught school for a while before entering politics. He married West Virginia's Democratic U.S. Senator Henry Gassaway Davis' daughter, Hallie, and lived in West Virginia. Ironically, Elkins remained a staunch Republican while he and Davis, "the Grand Old Man" of West Virginia, invested and built interests in coal, timber, and railroads in the Mountain State.

the Bank of Morgantown. At this point in the young lawyer's life, he had met with good fortune in many of his endeavors. He made "considerable money" and was well on his way to an "independent position."[14]

The climb to economic independence was not a solitary journey for Glasscock, for others also shared in his early accomplishments. On August 15, 1888, he married Mary Alice Miller of Arnettsville. The daughter of Calvin W. Miller, she was a direct descendant of Colonel John Evan, a well-known leader in the settlement of the Monongahela Valley. Mary Alice devoted her life to her family, giving birth to three children,[15] caring for and supporting her husband during his stormy political career, and tending to his health, which was always a great concern to her. Toward the end of his life, Glasscock praised his wife for her steadfast love and gave her credit for whatever good he had accomplished.

Since Glasscock's father had supported the Union cause during the Civil War and had been a loyal Republican, it was predictable that William would also become a member of the same political party. When the future governor served on the Republican State Executive Committee from 1900 to 1908, the "political bee" stung him.[16] In April 1905, President Theodore Roosevelt appointed Glasscock as collector of Internal Revenue at Parkersburg, a position previously held by former Governor A. B. White. Without a doubt, this position arrived through the auspices of Senator Elkins, who had much respect and faith in the appointee, to whom he gave free hand in filling offices in that department.[17] Being a friend of the powerful senator had considerable advantages, but it also had its drawbacks. Later, when nominated for the governorship, Glasscock would find that one of the most persistent charges against him was that he was merely a tool of the senator. After his election as governor, Glasscock would find that the powerful party chief would temper many of his inclinations to

---

14   M. L. Brown to Glasscock, 19 March 1909. See also Glasscock to S. A. D. Glasscock, 25 February 1913, both in Glasscock Papers.

15   Of the three children, only one survived, William E. Glasscock, Jr., who later obtained a law degree and practiced in Morgantown. See *Biographical and Portrait Cyclopedia of Monongalia, Marion, and Taylor Counties, West Virginia*, 114; "West Virginia's Thirteenth Governor," 11.

16   Virginia D. Malcomson, "William E. Glasscock: Governor of the People" (master's thesis West Virginia University, 1950), 3.

17   William E. Glasscock to U.S. Senator Stephen B. Elkins, 27 April 1909, Stephen B. Elkins Papers, West Virginia University Library. Hereafter cited as Elkins Papers, unless location is different.

S. B. Elkins dominated Republican Party politics in West Virginia. Democrats charged that he personally selected the so-called "Elkins" governors. Reprinted with permission from George W. Atkinson and Alvaro F. Gibbens's *Prominent Men of West Virginia*.

reform, but time would prove that the governor was his own man and, indeed, the aged senator would realize that it was necessary to change and accommodate.

It is difficult to explain Glasscock's rapid rise to success in business and politics. In a sense, he must have been very lucky. On the other hand, he had proved himself a man of character and a popular "vote-getter." After winning several elective offices and serving as a member of the Republican State Executive Committee, he began the practice of law at the age of forty. As a skillful politician, Senator Elkins would have been remiss had he not noticed and aided William Glasscock's rise in party affairs, as he had done with so many other younger men in building the notorious Elkins machine. Perhaps the senator realized that change was inevitable and by selecting and promoting the careers of honest, intelligent, reasonable young men, with whom he also had personal business relations, he could influence decision-making policies on the state level. Similarly, it would have been uncharacteristic of Glasscock had he not, whenever practical, returned the senator's generosity.

MOUNTAIN STATE POLITICS: THE NEW GENERATION MEETS THE OLD

"... there are no [R]epublicans in heaven and ... we know there are no negroes [sic] there."[1]

L
ATE IN THE NINETEENTH CENTURY, the West Virginia economy experienced significant change. While the manufacturing and mechanical trades were on the increase, it was coal mining that had become the most important industry. A number of economic forces were responsible for this. First, since 1870, capitalists had built railroads into the underdeveloped regions of the state, extending into the rich coal lands. Money could be made by connecting branch lines with the main rail arteries of the B&O and the C&O railroads. West Virginia Democratic Party leader Henry Gassaway Davis and his "carpetbagger" son-in-law, Republican Senator Stephen B. Elkins, one of the most interesting and influential partnerships of early West Virginia capitalists, made significant investments in the state. While both men were considered honest and intelligent, they were not above using their influence in political affairs, especially in areas that would benefit the industry and labor of their adopted state and profit them.[2] Davis and Elkins made a huge fortune in constructing branch rail lines, opening the central part of the Mountain State's coal and lumber reserves, and bringing in such nationally well-known investors as James G. Blaine. At the same time, there were ever-growing markets for coal, which could be shipped cheaply over the railroads and waterways. This supplied fuel for many industries, not to mention the navy and the merchant marines.[3] Finally, because of the quality of the coal and the moderate cost

1   Robert A. Kincaid to Louis Bennett, 6 November 1908, Louis Bennett Papers, West Virginia University Library. Hereafter cited as Bennett Papers, unless location is different.

2   John Alexander Williams, *West Virginia and the Captains of Industry* (Morgantown: West Virginia University Press, 2003), 17–67. Hereafter cited as Williams, *West Virginia and the Captains of Industry*.

3   Charles H. Ambler and Festus P. Summers, *West Virginia: The Mountain State,* 2nd ed.

H. G. Davis: a powerful leader in West Virginia politics and business. Courtesy of the Otis K. Rice Collection of the West Virginia Virginia Institute of Technology, Montgomery, WV.

....

of mining it, often at the expense of lower wages, West Virginia operators were able to undersell their competitors in Pennsylvania, Ohio, Indiana, and Illinois.[4]

The growing mining industry created wealth.[5] With coal production doubling between 1900 and 1920, more people migrated into these coal-producing areas.

(Englewood Cliffs, NJ: Prentice-Hall, Inc., 1958), 430. See also Charles M. Pepper, *The Life and Times of Henry Gassaway Davis, 1823–1916* (New York: The Century Co., 1920), 90–104. See Phil Conley, *History of The West Virginia Coal Industry* (Charleston: Education Foundation, Inc., 1960) 175–201. Hereafter cited as Conley, *History of The West Virginia Coal Industry.*

4   Ambler and Summers, *West Virginia: The Mountain State,* 430–31.

5   In 1870 West Virginia produced 600,000 tons of coal. With a population of 762,794 people in 1889, the Mountain State produced 6,231,880 tons of bituminous coal. In comparison, Pennsylvania, with a population of 5,258,014, mined 36,174,089 tons; Ohio, with a population of 3,672,316, extracted 9,976,787 tons. Moreover, by 1902 West Virginia moved into second place in coal production, passing Ohio, with the Buckeye State spending a total of $8,232,183 for mining expenses and West Virginia only $4,841,796. See U.S. Bureau of the Census, *Extra Census Bulletin, No. 10,* Washington D.C., Government Printing Office, September 30, 1891, 1–13. See also U.S. Bureau of the Census, *Special Reports of the Census Office, Mines and Quarries, 1902* (Washington

Occupational growth in this sector was rapid. In 1910, the coal industry employed 64,436 workers, and between 1910 and 1920, it expanded its workforce to 102,856.[6] Indeed, the face of West Virginia had changed, and its people demanded a share of the prosperity.

Increase in the extraction of coal coupled with expansion of railroads and the Panic of 1893 led to redistribution and change in the labor force.[7] While men moved to the industrial areas seeking jobs in the mines, mills, and factories, women sought employment as clerks, stenographers, and teachers. By 1900, with the introduction of electrical motors, change even overtook the miner's faithful work companion, who toiled side-by-side, day and night, forging bonds of trust and friendship. The mule, stubborn, yet less excitable than horses, needed a tough man who knew its language. Finding it hard to change, older miners who had placed much confidence in their loyal beast of burden felt that nothing could replace the old bank mule.[8]

The transition to a more industrial economy was difficult, necessitating new attitudes, rules, and regulations not only in West Virginia but throughout the entire nation, constituting what historians commonly refer to as the Progressive period of American history. Confronted with the power of accumulated wealth and the unrestrained actions of some corporations, the workingman often felt helpless. Although it was a bitterly long process, workers organized in unions and called upon

D.C., Government Printing Office, 1905, 680.

6   U.S. Bureau of the Census, *Thirteenth Census of the United States, 1910, Population, Occupation Statistics*, Vol. 4 Washington D.C., Government Printing Office, 1914, 138–39; U.S. Bureau of the Census, *Fourteenth Census of the United States Taken in the Year 1920, Population, Occupations*, Vol. 4, Washington D.C. Government Printing Office, 1923, 1039; see also U.S. Bureau of the Census, *Fifteenth Census of The United States, 1930, Population, Occupations, by States*, Vol. 4, Washington D.C., Government Printing Office, 1933, 1041, 1732. This rate stabilized, however, between 1920 and 1930, with 109,900 males employed in mining by the latter year.

7   The word panic was often used in place of depression in the nineteenth century. The Depression of 1893, or the Panic of 1893, had many causes, but the overexpansion of the railroads ultimately led to numerous bankruptcies. The unexpected failure of the Philadelphia and Reading Railroad signaled hard times ahead. This depression was the most severe during the nineteenth century. See Carl N. Degler, *The Age of the Economic Revolution, 1876-1900* (Glenview, Illinois: Scott, Foresman and Company, 1967), 129-137.

8   Conley, *History of the West Virginia Coal Industry*, 35–36. See also Ambler and Summers, *West Virginia: The Mountain State*, 424 and Robert F. Munn, "The Development of Model Towns in the Bituminous Coal Fields," *West Virginia History* 40 (Spring 1979): 246–47. Hereafter cited as Munn, "The Development of Model Towns." On the eve of the First World War the state had 2,749 industrial units with a total investment of $175,000,000. This sum provided for the employment of 71,000 laborers, who received a total annual wage of about $44,000,000.

the government to pass social and regulatory legislation. In brief, the "common man" asked for, and even demanded, fair treatment from industry and government alike. Reformers in both parties recognized these needs and attempted to fulfill them, but they were often at odds with their conservative opponents. Social and legal change had lagged behind economic development, leading to a struggle to correct the imbalance. Thus, in a many-sided evolutionary process, progressives attempted to enact legislation to address the ills of society as well as the corporate and political abuses by establishing governmental agencies to provide rules promoting fairness, order, and stability. Intermingled with the true reformers were always anti-organization politicians who merely looked for ways to further their own interests.[9]

Under the flexible, intelligent control of Stephen B. Elkins and like-minded members, the Republican Party had steadily gained control of state politics since the "Democratic" depression of the mid-1890s. Smart, conservative, business-minded Republicans such as Elkins, who perhaps read "the sign of the times," recognized that reform was inevitable. Of course, he preferred careful manipulation at the national and state levels, knowing that it was necessary to attract money for development and at the same time mollify demands for reform. This effort to develop the state's resources and maximize profits at minimum risk, especially in the coalfields, often led to exploitation by outside forces. With the ever-increasing demand for coal to feed the needs of a growing economy, venture capitalists such as John D. Rockefeller, invested large sums of money in the process, influencing both the economy and politics of West Virginia.

In their eagerness for profit and political gain, members of both political parties were happy to comply with capitalists who resided in places like Pittsburgh, Philadelphia, Baltimore, and New York. While the people of the state eagerly approved of prosperity and increasing their standard of living, in many cases they felt they were at the mercy of the "new rich" and their political henchmen. Thus, conservatives, such as West Virginia's two future Republican U.S. Senators Stephen B. Elkins and Nathan B. Scott, the latter to a lesser degree, recognized the need for careful manipulation and accommodation. After all, in order to control policy, one must win elections.

After the Civil War and during Reconstruction in West Virginia, the fathers of the Republican Party maintained power by controlling the franchise and eliminating the votes of many former Confederates by using test oaths and registration boards. With the passage of the Fifteenth Amendment that gave blacks the right to vote, many people thought the federal government was becoming too intrusive. In addition, with

9   Williams, *West Virginia and the Captains of Industry*, 98–99.

the debate and passage of the 1875 Civil Rights Act (declared unconstitutional in 1883), which barred discrimination against blacks in public places, Mountain State whites became disgruntled. While they were willing to fight for the abolition of slavery, many were not willing to give blacks social equality with whites. These problems led to the rise of the Democratic Party to power in the state from the mid-1870s to the mid-1890s. It also forced a change in Republican Party leadership to former Civil War veterans, such as Nathan Goff, Jr., who reminded the old soldiers and their families and friends, along with grateful African-Americans, of past military victories. By waving the "bloody shirt," demanding strict party military discipline, and focusing on local issues rather than national, this new party-army political structure succeeded in reorganizing the state GOP. These efforts laid the groundwork for later party successes and ensured the leadership role of Goff until the rise of a new younger generation of Republicans[10] who would once again establish complete political dominance in the state.

About 1887, concern over the intensity of efforts to lower the protective tariff and the rising tide of populism within the Democratic Party caused Henry G. Davis to persuade his Republican son-in-law Stephen Elkins to make West Virginia his home and political base from which he could obtain a seat in the U.S. Senate. First, however, he had to remove Republican Nathan Goff from his leadership role within the state. In 1891, Elkins, who had recently become a West Virginia resident in Leadsville (later renamed Elkins) in Randolph County, wrested power from Goff and the old-line leaders.[11] In a smooth operation orchestrated by Davis and Elkins mainly at Davis's home in Deer Park, Maryland, the dynamic schemers persuaded President Harrison to appoint Nathan Goff to a federal judgeship and Elkins to fill the position of Secretary of War. They rationalized that with Elkins in control of the state Republican Party its electoral votes would be more secure. With federal and state patronage given to Elkins and denied to Goff, Stephen Elkins built a solid political base from which he achieved election to the U.S. Senate in 1895,[12] bringing along the first Elkins governor, George W. Atkinson, a former Goff supporter. By handing out jobs, making faithful followers a part of lucrative business deals usually involving coal, and employing loyal, skillful lawyers,

10   Gordon B. McKinney, *Southern Mountain Republicans, 1865–1900* (Chapel Hill: The University of North Carolina Press, 1978), 62–66. Hereafter cited as McKinney, *Southern Mountain Republicans*.

11   John Alexander Williams, "New York's First Senator from West Virginia: How Stephen B. Elkins Found a New Political Home," in *West Virginia History*, 31 (January 1970): 79–80. Hereafter cited as Williams, "New York's First Senator."

12   Williams, "New York's First Senator," 84–87.

G. W. Atkinson, the first Elkins governor, 1897–1901. He spoke out strongly against "Jim Crow" laws. Courtesy of the West Virginia Division of Culture and History.

Elkins established his base of power. This began a new era in Mountain State politics—the rise of businessmen-politicians. Overall, residents, who desired employment and economic development, welcomed the new politician warmly. W. M. O. Dawson, a future governor, but then a young editor of the *Preston County Journal*, wrote:

> Mr. Elkins is the sort of man West Virginia needs. He is not only enterprising but aggressively so, we will say. He pushes things; and he is at the head of a railroad enterprise that will do more to develop this state than any of the other now in process of building or projected.[13]

The Democracy, as many late nineteenth century Democrats preferred to be called, made the transition easy because the party was so badly divided over racial issues, hard money (gold) versus soft (silver), the tariff, industrialists versus agrarians, and especially

13 Quoted in an unfinished biography of W. M. O. Dawson written by Don Blagg, W. M. O. Dawson Papers, West Virginia University Library.

the Panic of 1893. Commenting on the 1894 mid-term election, one Democratic Party member solemnly reported, "Some of our Democrats are going Republican, they say on account of the hard times, they claim caused by the Democrats."[14] Democratic mistakes and misdeeds paved the road for the Elkins machine and the industrialists who would maintain control until the 1930s.[15] Therefore, within a relatively short period, Senator Elkins adroitly obtained a political base at the national level with the aid of his Democratic father-in-law and the West Virginia Republican Party, from which he could maintain traditional business principles such as a protective tariff, low taxes, and sound fiscal and monetary policies. Under this formula, the nation and the state would prosper, not to mention Davis and Elkins.

Continuing the practice established by earlier politicians, Elkins dispensed economic morsels and appointed men—in his case, usually young men from the rising professional middle class—to responsible, political positions throughout the state, strengthening his control. The senator did not reject free, independent thinkers, but he did expect a certain amount of personal loyalty from his subordinates, with whom he could temper excessive reforms. The process was not without challenge because with every appointment there were other applicants who were disappointed. Party discord threatened harmony periodically, especially when proposed reforms impinged upon corporate interests within the state.

During the summer of 1900, Senator Elkins focused on a second term in the U.S. Senate, carefully evaluating the competition for the fall election. Since state legislatures still elected U.S. senators, it was imperative that the Republican Party maintain a majority when it met in 1901 for Elkins to be ensured a second term. Because of events on the national level, like-minded politicians from both political parties prepared for battle when the Democracy once again nominated William Jennings Bryan. "The corpse," as Elkins called him (no doubt because of his failure to win the presidency in 1896), rankled the conservatives because of his populist rhetoric that called for wider government control over industry, the unlimited coinage of silver, and tariff reform. To many businesspersons, these policies seemed ruinous and inflationary. With West Virginia's economy at stake, and especially Elkins's and Davis's coal and lumber investments, the senator contacted politicians of similar interests in both parties.

14   D. E. Coberly to Joseph T. McGraw, 18 September 1894, Joseph T. McGraw Papers, West Virginia University Library. Hereafter cited as McGraw Papers, unless location is different.
15   McKinney, *Southern Mountain Republicans*, 200.

Elkins wrote with a sense of urgency to his friend and fellow businessman, former Democratic U.S. Senator Johnson N. Camden, that "The corpse stinks now and the whole outfit will be rotten by Nov. . . . The next twenty-five years will witness a fight in this country to maintain the integrity of property; assaults against it are coming, both in Congress and State Legislatures every day."[16] The senator's statement proved prophetic, and that belief prodded capitalists of both parties to join forces to protect their interests as they entered the new century. Republicans, of course, and many Democrats, felt secure with the GOP nomination of corporation-backed William McKinley, but they were not that sure of his running mate, Theodore Roosevelt. Roosevelt would provide many anxious moments when he succeeded McKinley following his assassination in 1901.

On the state level, Senator Elkins and his legion of newly-recruited businessmen-politicians and/or professionals turned politician prepared for the coming battles. The senator was a cautious planner and an excellent organizer, who in times of stress could maintain his emotions, or at least let others provide the fire when needed. In preparation for the campaign for the senatorship in the state legislature, Elkins knew he could count on the support of his Democratic father-in-law Henry G. Davis, or at least on his inaction. Learning that he would most likely face sometimes-reformer Democrat Joseph T. McGraw in the legislative battle, Elkins prepared to neutralize his opponent by drawing the support of fellow businessmen-Democrats. In this vein, he again sought the aid of former Senator Camden of Parkersburg, writing, "You are nearer our people than you are McGraw and Bryan . . ."[17]

As the summer of 1900 progressed, Senator Elkins's attention once again turned to shoring-up his political base in the state. With the combination of Bryan's populist rhetoric and the growing din of reformers in both political parties calling for stricter controls over the corporations, the conservatives grew anxious. Elkins sounded the alarm when he wrote to Camden in a hurried handwritten letter, "How can you as anyother [sic] businessman stand the attack on corporations doing interstate business. This takes in all our coal [,] lumber [,] iron & steel companies—indeed every corporation in the state—they must show their books. Be subject to state & gov't. espionage—let their condition be known to the public—this is simply outrageous—and the people won't stand for it."[18] Elkins concluded, "I can fight McGraw and the Bryanites—but

16   Stephen B. Elkins to J. N. Camden, 29 July 1900, Johnson N. Camden Papers, West Virginia Library. Hereafter cited as Camden Papers, unless location is different.

17   Stephen B. Elkins to J. N. Camden, 8 July 1900, Camden Papers.

18   Elkins to J. N. Camden, 8 July 1900, Camden Papers.

can't fight you & Sen. Davis with them."[19] Confident that Davis and Camden would provide passive support, Elkins turned his attention to other problem areas in the state such as Marion County, politically headed by the Democratic coal-rich Watson family of Fairmont who led the Fairmont Coal Company. Elkins wrote to Camden, "This is the most difficult County to carry in the State. I have a great many friends there, but the trouble is the Watsons stand in the way . . ."[20] The senator asked for Camden's intercession. Regardless of party affiliation, fellow conservative businessmen often placed self-interest over party allegiance.

President McKinley handily defeated William Jennings Bryan in 1900 and Senator Elkins secured another term in the U.S. Senate, serving with his junior Republican Senator Nathan B. Scott, a rich Wheeling industrialist elected in 1899. By the turn of the century, Elkins and the Republican Party clearly dominated politics in West Virginia, even more than Republicans in the Border States, where politicians intensely debated racial issues. West Virginians also elected another Elkins governor, Republican A. B. White (1901–1905), who was more progressive than the first Elkins governor, George W. Atkinson. Atkinson was an old-line Republican, a former Goff supporter, who, as governor, did have a few nice things to say about labor.

Governor White had been an early Elkins follower, supporting him in the editorials of his *Parkersburg Journal* newspaper and conducting his senatorial campaign, for which Elkins rewarded him twice with the Collectorship of Internal Revenue at Parkersburg and later, with the governorship. Little did he suspect that White would begin an earnest push for reform legislation in West Virginia. With the Elkins machine well oiled and functioning efficiently, however, the senator was prepared at a moment's notice to defend the rights of property owners and to temper the drive of his lieutenants. This was the case when, in 1903, Governor White sought to modernize the state tax structure so that big business would carry more of the financial load to the chagrin of the conservatives. Senator Elkins did what he did best. He raced to the state legislature and convinced lawmakers not to be rash in their deliberations, which resulted in the establishment of a study commission, postponing immediate action. Under stiff opposition from the "anti-taxers," White later called a special session in July of 1904 to achieve what seemed to be the impossible task of placing a tax on coal, oil, and gas leases and options. Attempts to tax West Virginia's most valuable natural resources always elicited rebuttals that it would hinder further development. Overall, however, Governor White managed to shift more of the tax burden

---

19 Elkins to J. N. Camden, 8 July 1900, Camden Papers.
20 Elkins to J. N. Camden, 27 August 1900, Camden Papers.

A. B. White, the second Elkins governor, 1901–1905. White advocated reform of West Virginia's tax laws. Courtesy of the West Virginia Division of Culture and History.

from small businessmen and farmers to larger corporations. His administration also created the office of state tax commissioner and ordered assessors to assess all property, real and personal, at true and actual value. More importantly, the legislature lifted exemptions on such items as mines, salt wells, and a variety of manufactured goods that existed since the 1870s,[21] put in place by fiscally tightfisted conservative Democrats.

Struggles over reforms would continue into the administration of Republican W. M. O. Dawson, another Elkins lieutenant, who was elected in 1904. A skillful political organizer as chairman of the Republican Executive Committee, Dawson had been very important in orchestrating Elkins's rise to power in the 1890s. For his services he was rewarded with the office of secretary of state under Governors Atkinson and White and then was further rewarded with his own gubernatorial administration. Dawson, even more progressive than his predecessor, continued to press for the reforms

21   Ambler and Summers, *West Virginia: The Mountain State*, 367–69; see also Williams, *West Virginia and the Captains of Industry*, 17–67.

W. M. O. Dawson, the third Elkins governor, 1905–1909. Dawson continued Governor White's fight for tax reform and called for the construction of a new state capitol building. His plea went unheeded and the old capitol burned in 1921. Courtesy of WV Division of Culture and History.

proposed by former Governor White. Bills dealing with water pollution; anti-lobbying laws; further tax reform; taxes on coal, oil, and gas; railroad legislation; constitutional reform; and a primary election law were defeated one by one, but passed on to the next Elkins governor.[22]

These actions prompted the conservatives of both parties to urge caution in the wake of change. Nevertheless, the Elkins machine maintained a firm grip on the Republican Party through careful strategic planning and influence with newspapers (he had made a large investment in the *Wheeling Intelligencer* and later in the *Charleston Daily-Tribune*). If all else failed, the businessmen-Republicans and their fellow businessmen-

22   Nicholas C. Burckel, "Governor Albert B. White and the Beginning of Progressive Reform, 1901–05," *West Virginia History* 40 (Fall 1978): 11.

Democrats, such as Davis and Johnson N. Camden, John D. Rockefeller's "Right Arm"[23] in the West Virginia oil industry, would unite in battle. In fact, both parties vied for the support of big money corporations; by 1900, industrialists and their political henchmen, such as Davis and Elkins, led both,[24] setting the stage for a new period in state politics and ushering in the Progressive Era.

The new Republican Party had done exceptionally well since its return to power in the 1890s, seeing three of its members elected governor from 1896 to 1904. With lingering factional difficulties, however, centering on party control and differences between the "ins" and the "outs," patronage, and, of course, the need for reform legislation,[25] the Democratic Party had reason to believe that once again it could win the seat of government in Charleston. In 1908, a vocal element within the "Grand Old Party" threatened to open the old wounds of the past. On the state level, State Auditor Arnold C. Scherr, who resented the Elkins machine and was more of an old-line Republican than a true reformer, voiced concerns of disgruntled Republicans. The "Regulars," or

23   Williams "New York's First Senator," 77. See also Festus P. Summers, *Johnson Newlon Camden: A Study in Individualism* (New York: G. P. Putnam's Sons, 1937), 172–73

24   Williams, *West Virginia and the Captains of Industry*, 107. See also Ronald L. Lewis, *Transforming the Appalachian Countryside* (Chapel Hill: The University of North Carolina Press, 1998), 212–14. Hereafter cited as Lewis, *Transforming the Appalachian Countryside*. Lewis viewed the Republican Party at this time largely divided between the conservatives or regulars who controlled party machinery and a much smaller liberal reform faction. The Democratic Party, however, was much more complex and strife ridden. On the state level, four major factions contested for control. They were (1) the Regulars, situated in the developed counties, who maintained party control; (2) the Redeemers, representing the back counties and more southern and traditional in their views; (3) the Agrarians, many of whom were reformers, supported by the farmers of the older established counties who favored railroad regulation and resisted taxation of farmers. The Kanawha Ring, as headed by Democratic Governor W. A. McCorkle, blended with the Agrarians. McCorkle, an industrialist, also vied mightily for outside investment dollars and sought to protect the corporate investors—(4) the Bitter Enders, who cut across factional lines and worried about the "New Departure" of the Democratic Party. For a more detailed description of the Democratic factions and the leading personalities of that time see John Alexander Williams, "The New Dominion and the Old: Ante-bellum and Statehood Politics as the Background of West Virginia's 'Bourbon Democracy,'" *West Virginia History* 33 (July 1972): 317–407. Hereafter cited as Williams, "The New Dominion and the Old."

25   James Morton Callahan, *Semi-Centennial History of West Virginia* (Charleston: Semi-Centennial Commission, 1913), 247. See also Carl N. Degler, *The Age of the Economic Revolution: 1876–1900* (Glenview, Illinois: Scott, Foresman and Company, 1967), 114.

conservatives, gave their support to Secretary of State C. W. Swisher, a strong supporter of Elkins and a frequent correspondent with former Democratic Governor A. B. Fleming of the Fairmont Coal Company. While conservatives had the advantage of established political machinery, each had a considerable following,[26] portending trouble when both men decided to become their party's gubernatorial candidate in 1908. Adding to the political confusion, William H. Hearne, an attorney from Wheeling, announced his candidacy, thus creating a three-way race for the nomination.

The road to a gubernatorial nomination was a long and arduous trek. The procedure resembled the presidential nominating process, with counties playing a role analogous to the states in presidential nominations. Delegates to the state nominating convention were chosen in a variety of ways with each county executive committee determining how they were selected. This placed much influence in the hands of the local party committees and, of course, provided a locus for machine politics. During the election of 1908, as in past elections, one of the most popular methods used in the nominating procedure was the indirect primary, with the county or magisterial district as the electoral unit. Following the election, the winning candidate received the privilege of choosing delegates pledged to him to attend the state convention. Seemingly democratic, the indirect primary contained elements of "smoke and mirrors," because those who controlled the local apparatus could just as easily determine the outcome through the purchase of votes and fraud. Another method was the county or district mass convention, which was obnoxious to many people because it could be "packed" by a candidate's supporters.[27]

The first sign of party disharmony appeared in Kanawha County in early 1908. Scherrites alleged that C. W. Swisher and the "Hog Combine" controlled the Kanawha County Republican Committee. This was the equivalent of the Democratic "Kanawha Ring" headed by former Governor MacCorkle and William E. Chilton. The committee decided upon a preferential primary, whereby Republican voters indicated their choice for governor. The victorious candidate earned the right to name fifty-nine delegates from the county to attend the state-nominating convention to be held in Charleston on July 8, 1908. Learning that the County Executive Committee had selected all Swisher-men as commissioners and clerks to operate the primary, Scherr and Hearne decided not to run and appealed to the State Executive Committee for fairness. To their displeasure, members of the state committee voted 8–6 to seat the

26 Lambert, *Stephen Benton Elkins*, 293. See also Williams, *West Virginia and the Captains of Industry*, 234–37.

27 *Wheeling Intelligencer*, July 6, 1908; *Parkersburg Sentinel*, July 6, 1908; *Wheeling Register*, July 4, 1908.

Kanawha County delegation, even though only slightly more than sixteen percent of the Republicans had voted in the July primary.[28]

Another incident that further divided the GOP concerned the candidacy of William Hearne of Ohio County. Hearne had boasted that he would go to the state convention with the complete support of the Northern Panhandle.[29] Since no other candidate chose to oppose him in his home county, he was assured of its fifty-two delegates. After unexpectedly losing the primary in Marshall County to Arnold Scherr, however, he abruptly and unwisely withdrew his name "in a huff."[30] In a sense, he picked up his marbles and went home. The duty of selecting the delegates to the state convention then fell to the Ohio County Committee, which selected delegates favorable to Scherr, who had previously been their second choice. An angry Hearne, still stinging from rejection, allegedly established close contact with Swisher and reentered the race determined to select his own delegates. Hearne recognized that he really stood little chance of winning the nomination, but in the Charleston convention he could play the role of power broker and, apparently, he would broker on the side of Swisher. When the county committee refused to acknowledge Hearne's representatives, he appealed to the State Executive Committee, which upheld Hearne by a vote of 10-6. This outcome led Scherr supporters to charge that the state committee was unduly biased toward C. W. Swisher. However, one Scherrite, Judge T. A. Brown of Wirt County, noted that there was some degree of fairness in that political tribunal because such well-known Swisher boosters as state committee members C. D. Elliott and W. E. Glasscock had voted against the Hearne appeal.[31]

On the night of July 7, at Charleston, when the state committee members made the Hearne decision, a clear rift was apparent in the Republican Party. The Scherr people bolted the regular convention and held their own on the following day. With the backing of a number of important state newspapers, they elected Pressly W. Morris of the *Parkersburg Journal* as temporary chairman and the powerful H. C. Ogden of the *Wheeling Intelligencer*, secretary. In addition to these newspapers, the Scherrites enjoyed the support of the *Wheeling News*, the *Parkersburg News*, and the *Huntington Herald*.[32]

---

28   *Wheeling Intelligencer*, July 6, 1908; *Parkersburg Sentinel*, July 6, 1908; *Wheeling Register*, July 4, 1908.

29   *Wheeling Intelligencer*, July 17, 1908; *Wheeling Register*, July 27, 1908.

30   *Wheeling Intelligencer*, April 13, 1908; *Wheeling Register*, July 27, 1908.

31   *Wheeling Intelligencer*, July 17, 1908; *Moundsville Daily Echo*, July 8, 1908.

32   *Wheeling Intelligencer*, July 8, 1908; *Wheeling Register*, July 8, 1908; July 9, 1908; *Charleston Gazette*, July 9, 1908.

Calling themselves Lincoln Republicans, the Scherr group drew up a list of candidates along with a party platform that called for the "primitive doctrine of Republicanism," defined as a government of the people, by the people, and for the people. It also asked for the submission of the proposed state prohibition amendment to the people of West Virginia and urged the passage of a uniform primary election law "for the selection of all candidates for office, state, congressional, county and municipal." In addition, the platform blamed United States Senators Elkins and Scott, along with West Virginia Governor W. M. O. Dawson, for the existing conditions in the state Republican Party.[33] It further stated that most of the members of the state committee, who seemed to favor C. W. Swisher, were federal officeholders and under the influence of the two U.S. senators.[34]

Squabbling within the Republican Party had become a perennial affair. Of course, the longer Senator Elkins remained the unquestioned ringmaster of the party, doling out patronage, the number of unhappy rejected applicants increased. They were left behind to plot strategy, necessitating a rear-guard action by those in power. As Judge John W. Mason remarked, "There were people in the world who always worship the rising sun,"[35] and for the anti-Elkins politicians the rising sun was Arnold Scherr. Efforts to reform also created animosities and took up much of the conservatives' time defending their interests. Following Governor A. B. White's tenure in office, the question of fair and equitable taxes continued into the administration of his Republican successor W. M. O. Dawson. During the gubernatorial election of 1904, opponents of

33 *Wheeling Intelligencer*, July 9, 1908.

34 As listed by the *Morgantown Post-Chronicle*, September 12, 1908, the members of the West Virginia Republican State Committee and the offices they held were Elliott Northcott, United States district attorney for the Southern District of West Virginia; Hugh Ike Shott, postmaster at Bluefield; S. C. Denham, postmaster at Clarksburg; Dr. S. M. Steele, superintendent of the Weston Insane Asylum; Charles D. Elliott, United States Marshal for the Northern District of West Virginia; Charles P. Light, member of the State Board of Agriculture; O. A. Petty, past postmaster at Charleston; Samuel Dixon, a Fayette County coal baron; J. E. Noel, also of Fayette County and the only African American on the committee, allegedly under Dixon's control; W. E. Glasscock, collector of Internal Revenue; W. W. Whyte, ex-sheriff of McDowell County; Amos Bright, member of the board of directors of the Weston Insane Asylum; and H. C. Woodyard, a member of Congress, chairman. Finally, Earl Martin, A. R. Stallings, and C. H. Watkins were listed as holding no state or federal offices. For various references to these members, see also the *Wheeling Intelligencer*, July 8 and 9, 1908 and an editorial on July 10, 1908.

35 Glasscock to John W. Mason, 1 October 1910, John W. Mason Papers, West Virginia University Library. Hereafter cited as Mason Papers, unless location is different.

tax reform in both parties caused Dawson to win by a narrow margin. Moreover, by 1908 the progressive element within the Republican Party felt confident enough to challenge the conservatives for party control in an effort to effect more reforms.[36] This could only be achieved, however, at the risk of further party disruption and possible defeat at the polls.

Even the lame duck president, Theodore Roosevelt, took note of the intra-party quarrel in West Virginia. One newspaper reported that President Roosevelt was quite concerned with party affairs in the state in 1908 and might try to settle the problem.[37] Rumors abounded that Republican presidential candidate William Howard Taft, although he avowed neutrality in the dispute, also favored the withdrawal of the two contenders in favor of a compromise candidate.

In August 1908, Taft, Frank Hitchcock (the national Republican Party committee chairman), Senator Elkins, Swisher, and Scherr met at Hot Springs, Virginia for several days. The vacationing Taft refused to become embroiled in state politics and was soon off to Cincinnati to continue his national campaign against the Democratic nominee William Jennings Bryan (now on his third run for the White House). In the meantime, his chief of staff, A. I. Vorys, and Chairman Hitchcock stayed behind to attempt a West Virginia settlement.[38] No firm compromise could be arranged at these meetings; hence, others were scheduled in New York City and conducted by a subcommittee of the national committee.

Speculation centered on Judge Nathan Goff, Senator Elkins's old party rival who had twice before lost the gubernatorial election. He refused to run, however, telling an interested party to "kindly advise that my name must not be used at this time in connection with political matters. Make it plain and positive."[39] Senators Elkins and Scott made it clear in public letters that they wholeheartedly supported C. W. Swisher. In a letter to S. V. Matthews, chairman of the Republican State Committee, Senator Elkins stated that he would "not support the opposition formed at Charleston, whatever name it may bear, especially when the leading plank in its platform is the condemnation of our

36   William E. Glasscock to Senator Nathan B. Scott, 22 April 1910, Glasscock Papers; Callahan, *Semi-Centennial History*, 246–47; Ambler and Summers, *West Virginia: The Mountain State*, 378–79.

37   *Wheeling Intelligencer*, August 11, 1908; September 3, 1908.

38   *Wheeling Register*, August 8–15, 1908.

39   Nicholas Clare Burckel, "Progressive Governors in the Border States: Reform Governors of Missouri, Kentucky, West Virginia and Maryland, 1900–1918" (PhD diss., University of Wisconsin, 1971), 337. Hereafter cited as Burckel, "Progressive Governors"; *Wheeling Intelligencer*, September 3, 1908; *Morgantown Post-Chronicle*, September 5, 1908.

Republican governor and the two Senators."[40] In a similar tone, Senator Scott wrote that he had voted straight Republican since he had cast his first vote for Abraham Lincoln while serving in the Union army, and was "too old to join a new political party."[41] The Republican conservatives had closed ranks, and they were prepared for a struggle to maintain party control.

To the delight of West Virginia Democrats, the GOP appeared entrapped in a political quagmire with no solution in sight. In an effort to resolve the difficulty, Senator Elkins had reportedly offered Scherr a federal appointment if he would withdraw from the race, but Scherr declined. To complicate the situation further, the Republican National Committee had hung out a "no funds" sign to the West Virginia Republicans until they settled their quarrel. It was a situation that they could ill afford since they were in need of financial assistance. Both Swisher and Scherr presented their cases before the subcommittee of the executive committee of the Republican National Committee, which met in New York City. These meetings accomplished little, since neither candidate would agree to a withdrawal without the other's resignation.[42]

After numerous trips between West Virginia and New York City and a number of encounters with top Republican officials, Republican leaders finally convinced Scherr and Swisher to withdraw for the good of the party. On September 21, Swisher submitted his resignation to the Republican State Committee, followed by Scherr on September 23. No doubt Senator Elkins had a hand in this action, although he made the decision sound unilateral when he wrote to presidential candidate Taft:

> I know you will be glad to know that Mr. Swisher, in the interest of the Republican party and not wishing to endanger its success in the coming election, on his own motion, without any conditions whatever, withdrew as candidate. This action has made him stronger in the State and insures our success without doubt.[43]

---

40   *Wheeling Intelligencer*, August 5, 1908; *Wheeling Register*, August 18, 1908.

41   *Wheeling Register*, August 20, 1908.

42   *Wheeling Intelligencer*, September 3, 1908; *Wheeling Register*, August 13, 1908; August 21, 1908; August 29, 1908.

43   Senator Stephen B. Elkins to William H. Taft, 23 September 1908, William H. Taft Papers, Manuscript Division, Library of Congress. Hereafter cited as Taft Papers, unless location is different.

In a compromise move, the Swisher people agreed to draw up a list of possible gubernatorial candidates from which the Scherr group would eliminate those people objectionable to them. From seventeen potential candidates, the Scherrites rejected seven, including William E. Glasscock. When, by a 9–6 vote, the state committee nominated Glasscock on September 23, the Scherrites felt betrayed,[44] yet they did not continue the fight. The Lincoln Republicans met that evening at Charleston where Arnold C. Scherr withdrew from the race and pledged his support to the new candidate, explaining "I have not taken this action from fear of the result, but simply because of the love I bear my party and my desire that in the presidential campaign now upon us it be not torn by differences and dissensions, but present an undivided front to our ancient enemy."[45] The Lincoln Republicans disbanded, however, without officially endorsing Glasscock, whom they resolved was "the direct personal selection of Senator Elkins, at his dictation, for his own benefit and for the propagation of his own machine."[46] On the other hand, Glasscock's ardently Progressive hometown newspaper, the *Morgantown Post-Chronicle*, took the view of the majority of the Scherrites:

> We admit that the nomination of W. E. Glasscock was the personal work of Stephen B. Elkins, but so far as the character and ability of the two men are concerned, that of Mr. Glasscock is vastly superior to Mr. Swisher, and he will be more acceptable to the voters. Under the circumstances, therefore, we did not feel justified in continuing the organized opposition to the state ticket.[47]

Making it easier for the Lincoln Republicans to accept Glasscock's candidacy, the state committee adopted new rules for the selection of delegates to the state convention. The new regulations recognized the magisterial district, not the county, as the key political unit and provided that delegates selected by the voters would represent each district in the state-nominating conventions. The *Morgantown Post-Chronicle* concluded, "The iniquitous county mass convention is relegated to the scrap heap, as are also all elegations chosen by county committees or named by candidates for office."[48] Perhaps, in typical candidate "modesty," Glasscock was as candid as the Lincoln Republicans when he wrote that he

---

44   *Wheeling Intelligencer*, September 23, 1908; *Wheeling Register*, September 19, 1908.
45   *Wheeling Register*, September 24, 1908.
46   *Wheeling Register*, September 24, 1908.
47   *Morgantown Post-Chronicle*, September 26, 1908.
48   *Morgantown Post-Chronicle*, September 26, 1908; *Wheeling Register*, September 24, 1908.

did not seek the nomination and "frankly I hoped some one else would be named but I have always tried to do my duty by my party and I am going to continue to do the same."[49] From the tone of his letter, Senator Elkins must have felt a sense of relief and satisfaction when he wrote to Taft "W. E. Glasscock, Internal Revenue Collector, and one of the best men, pure, clean, upright, and just, has been nominated by the State Committee to fill the vacancy."[50]

Senator Elkins claimed he had little to do with the Glasscock nomination. He stated that he had made no effort to control the outcome and, in fact, "hoped that either Judge Robinson or Judge Holt or Senator Blue would be the nominee." A report, however, indicated that he had visited Morgantown a few days before the withdrawal of Swisher and had talked over the situation with a number of friends there.[51] In the pages of the *Morgantown Republican*, Elkins was more explicit when he stated that he did not have anything to do with the nomination "more than a friendly interest that I might show in the candidacy of anyone who had been a true and faithful friend."[52] The extent and power of that "friendly interest" was open to conjecture. In a special report from Morgantown, the *Wheeling Register* stated its findings in the matter of the senator's involvement in the nomination:

> It is well known that a conference was held at the home of the Senator in Elkins on Sunday preceding the committee's meeting, attended by Sherman Denham and others, at which Mr. Glasscock was determined upon by the Senator as the candidate to succeed Mr. Swisher. That isn't all; neither the Senator or Mr. Glasscock will deny that during Sunday evening Mr. Elkins called Mr. Glasscock here by phone and informed him that he was slated for the place and urged him to accept, and that Mr. Glasscock asked for a little time in which to consult his wife, who was then absent from home. Senator Elkins and Mr. Glasscock may have concluded that their communications were private in every sense. Still in these days of 'political revelations and conversations' such things do get to the public.[53]

---

49   Glasscock to E. F. Ball, 1 October 1908, Glasscock Papers.
50   Senator Elkins to Taft, 23 September 1908, Taft Papers.
51   *Wheeling Intelligencer*, September 26, 1908; *Morgantown Post-Chronicle*, September 15, 1908.
52   Lambert, *Stephen Benton Elkins*, 294.
53   *Wheeling Register*, September 30, 1908.

To complicate matters even more, Senator Joseph H. McDermott of Morgantown, who had served in the state senate from 1905 to 1907, later wrote to Senator Scott, "I wish two others really named Glasscock for Governor."[54] From the evidence, one can only guess what persons were directly involved in the selection. McDermott was friendly with both United States Senators Scott and Elkins, especially with the latter. He was also on close terms with Davis Elkins, the senator's son, who was much involved in behind-the-scenes political maneuvers. Obviously, it would seem that the decision to nominate Glasscock emanated not from Charleston but from Morgantown or Elkins. Senator Elkins had earlier taken an interest in Glasscock's career, so it seems reasonable that he would continue.

Glasscock had six weeks to produce an effective campaign. In his letter of acceptance to the Republican State Committee, the nominee stated, "I have one promise, and but one, to make to the people of West Virginia. If elected, I will be governor in fact as well as in name."[55] This statement clearly indicated the mantra of the Republican candidate's political strategy: he had to convince the voters that he was not under the domination of Stephen B. Elkins. In a letter to Romeo Freer, Governor White's nomination opponent in 1899, Glasscock reiterated his independence, "I want to say to you that I was not Senator Elkins's choice for Governor and if elected will be dictated to by no one save and except Wm. E. Glasscock."[56]

Above all, Glasscock wanted to promote party unity by standing firmly on the Republican platform adopted in July 1908, which was attractive and "mildly progressive." It endorsed the administrations of President Roosevelt and Governor Dawson, along with the recently passed state tax laws. It also called for the passage of a local option law and the submission of a state prohibition amendment to the people. Planks were also declared in favor of an anti-injunction law "that would protect all persons alike and against boycotts and blacklists as being un-American" and a measure to limit "undesirable" immigration. It also called for the preservation of "the national resources" and the passage of a state primary election law "embodying some of the features of the Cooper bill," Senate Bill 114, which called for a statewide primary.[57]

---

54   Senator N. B. Scott to Glasscock, 1 March 1908; Joseph H. McDermott to Glasscock, 1 March 1910; Davis Elkins to Glasscock, 3 March 1910; all in Glasscock Papers.

55   *Wheeling Intelligencer*, September 28, 1908.

56   Glasscock to Romeo Freer, 29 September 1908, Glasscock Papers.

57   Burckel, "Progressive Governors," 338. See also Glasscock to Albert Plate, 30 September 1908, Glasscock Papers; *Wheeling Register*, July 9 , 1908.

As Glasscock strove to bring about a semblance of party unity, the Democrats proclaimed the virtues of their gubernatorial candidate, Louis Bennett of Lewis County. Born in Weston in 1849, Bennett's loyalties had been Southern during the Civil War. His father had been state auditor of Virginia, and Bennett served as a midshipman aboard the *Patrick Henry* stationed at Richmond, Virginia. After the conflict, Louis Bennett continued his education at the "old academy" at Morgantown, now West Virginia University, where he received his law degree. Following his graduation, he served as principal of the state normal school at Glenville for a three year period and one year as principal at Weston High School. In 1880 and again in 1884, Bennett served as prosecuting attorney of Lewis County and in 1890 was elected by the people of that county to the House of Delegates and selected as Speaker of the House in the ensuing session. After this brief excursion into state politics, he retired from active involvement until his nomination by the Democratic Party.[58]

In contrast to the Republicans, the Democrats enjoyed a higher degree of party unity, although they experienced dissension over the "Negro planks" in their party platform. By a vote of 712–411, the Democrats greatly weakened their chances of victory by committing the party to black disenfranchisement and "Jim Crow" cars.[59] Because many of the voters did not feel threatened by African-American enfranchisement, it became a false issue, playing into the hands of the Republicans. For political reasons, the GOP criticized disenfranchisement because most blacks in West Virginia belonged to that party. These African American voters were highly concentrated in the southern portion of the state, mostly in the Sixth Senatorial District. Of course, some Republicans opposed racism for moral reasons and had done so since Reconstruction. In a practical way, however, Glasscock attacked the plank by stating, "A law disfranchising the Negro at the same time disfranchises a large number of whites. The Republican Party herself cannot afford to sail under false colors and I myself will not do it."[60] In short, William Glasscock assailed the "Negro planks" because if the rights of one group of citizens could be taken away, then the rights of others could also. His argument was effective and well received, as he referred to it in nearly all of his addresses.

Early in October, the campaign began in earnest. It was a whirlwind contest with the Republican candidate scheduled to speak in twenty-nine counties. Prior to the

58 *Wheeling Register,* July 26, 1908.
59 Callahan, *Semi-Centennial History,* 247; Ambler and Summers, *West Virginia: The Mountain State,* 389.
60 West Virginia's Sixth Senatorial District was composed of McDowell, Mingo, Wayne, and Wyoming Counties. See *Wheeling Intelligencer,* October 20, 1908.

Loyal African Americans in southern West Virginia usually voted strongly for the Republican ticket. Courtesy of the *Wheeling Register*, Wheeling, WV, 1908.

beginning of the formal campaign, Glasscock spoke to a crowd of fellow townsmen at Morgantown and read to his audience a letter he had received from his Uncle John Millan of Rymer, who reaped much statewide publicity:

> Keep a cool head and a stiff upper lip; make a clean fight for all the people; steer
> clear of all factions; wear your own collar; don't forget your poor relations;
> fear God and keep His commandments and you will surely triumph.[61]

On October 5, Glasscock officially began his campaign with a speech delivered at Fairmont. The candidate gave three reasons for starting in that city. First, Fairmont was the home of former Governor Francis H. Pierpont, who had done more than anyone else to bring about West Virginia's admission to the Union. Secondly, Fairmont was a principal city in the First Congressional District, and thirdly, "when a boy of eighteen he left this city to fight the battle of life and he said that he wanted to start from this

61   *Morgantown Post-Chronicle*, October 4, 1908.

city on his way to Charleston."[62] The Republican aspirant might have added a fourth reason for beginning his campaign in Fairmont, a desire to appear in the hometown of the Fairmont Coal Company controlled by the powerful Watson family and to promote mine safety for workers.[63] Of course, mine safety would play well in the press and appease angry miners. In 1907, a mine explosion at Monongah, a mine owned by the Fairmont Coal Company, caused the greatest single loss of life, 361 deaths; the miners and owners gave contesting explanations for its cause.

In his opening speech, Glasscock called for a wide range of programs affecting nearly every area of society. He supported prohibition, county option, and a primary election law. He also advocated laws that would provide safety for the coal miner, an "intelligent" road building system, the encouragement of agriculture, and the betterment of schools and education. To the business community, Glasscock urged the equal treatment and protection of all corporations and shippers, so long as they "take no part in politics and confine themselves strictly to doing the things for which they were incorporated." It was, perhaps, a warning to former Governor Fleming, Clarence Watson, and the Fairmont Coal Company. Glasscock also called for provisions to increase the efficiency of the tax laws; the encouragement of capital entering the state; higher wages and good employment; the building of more railroads, factories, and manufacturing plants; the reduction of governmental expense; and the "employment of fewer attaches by the legislature."[64]

Democrats centered their attacks against Republican extravagance in office. In a speech at Elkins, the Democratic nominee stated that under his party's rule only $600,000 had been raised from taxation, while under Republican rule it had grown to over $3,000,000 and was used in an extravagant manner. Bennett explained that the Republicans had created unnecessary offices, pointing out that the senate attaches alone had grown in number from 28 in 1882 to 117 in 1908 when they averaged four per senator. He also charged that the cost of the attorney general's office had increased

---

62   *Fairmont West Virginian*, October 5, 1908.

63   The Fairmont Coal Company was the largest coal producing company in the state, which had been, since 1903, under the control of the Consolidation Coal Company, the largest in the world. The Fairmont Coal Company was closely allied with such Democrats as ex-Governor A. B. Fleming, director, and future U.S. Senator Clarence Watson, president, both important Marion County Democrats. See *Charleston Gazette*, May 13, 1909. See also William Graebner, *Coal-Mining Safety in the Progressive Period: The Political Economy of Reform* (Lexington: University Press of Kentucky, 1976), 73–74.

64   *Morgantown Post-Chronicle*, October 6, 1908.

The Republican point of view. Courtesy of the Wheeling *Intelligencer*, Wheeling, WV, 1908.

significantly since 1895, and the state now had a deficit of $300,000 or $400,000. Bennett then raised the familiar cry "that Glasscock had been selected by a coterie of the state ring and that it was futile for any Republican to aspire to be governor unless he belonged to the state ring."[65]

At Wheeling, Glasscock countered these accusations with the usual statement that he was not under the influence of any man. He also refuted the charge of Republican extravagance. The candidate pointed out that in 1904 under the old tax system "we paid into the state treasury on real and personal property $975,904 in round numbers," while under the new tax laws $464,970 was paid in 1907. He added that the Dawson administration would not have a deficit in the treasury "but has more than a million six hundred thousand dollars in it." Glasscock also reviewed other Republican accomplishments:

They now have a minimum school term of six months and more schools.
They pay 50 per cent more wages to school teachers and where they had

65   *Wheeling Register*, October 19, 1908.

U.S. Senator Elkins: the real heavy hitter. Courtesy of the *Wheeling Register*, Wheeling, WV, 1908.

fifteen state institutions we now have twenty-five. Now which of these would you abolish if the Democrats came to power?[66]

The ever-loyal *Wheeling Intelligencer*, a Republican newspaper, also extolled the new tax system in the best partisan manner:

> The Republicans have reduced the state tax from 35 cents to five cents; this reduced the volume of state taxes on real and personal property $520,000 a year. The grand aggregate of all taxes, state, county, district, and municipal, has been reduced from $5,712,000 to $5,086,000 on real and personal property. The taxes on railroad, pipelines, leaseholds and other pubic service corporations have been increased from $960,000 to $2,466,200.

66   *Wheeling Intelligencer*, October 20, 1908; October 22, 1908.

Fifty million dollars worth of leaseholds have been placed on the assessment books, which were never taxed before.[67]

Placing the Democrats on the defensive, the Republicans could prove that the burden of taxation had shifted from the individual to the different corporate bodies of the state, thanks to former Governors White and Dawson. Regardless of the fact that business could just as easily shift the burden of taxes to the consumer as a cost of doing business, the GOP felt confident with the results of the new tax reforms.

As the election neared, Glasscock received mixed reports from the Republicans around the state. E. M. Lewis, a former delegate from Monongalia County, wrote that since Glasscock's nomination, the political situation in Marshall County had undergone "a wonderful change and all Republicans are alive and working for their old time majority."[68] On the other hand, not all of his fellow members shared this view. Attorney George McClintic of Kanawha County wrote that he thought Glasscock should not have accepted the nomination because of the fear that he was an Elkins man. McClintic felt that two thirds of the opposition to Swisher had actually been against Senator Elkins, and since Glasscock was one "of his federal office holders and his personal attorney in Monongalia County," he would not be acceptable in Kanawha County.[69] Attorney G. W. Farr of West Union was not quite as pessimistic when he wrote, "I do however believe you will be elected by a small majority."[70]

By September 30, five weeks before the election, Glasscock could write that "As it looks now I think I shall be elected."[71] One Republican who was present at a speech made by Bennett in the southern part of the state reported that as a speaker he was a "fizzle," and Glasscock had nothing to fear. The Bennett speech seemed somewhat incoherent, "touching in a haphazard and desultory way a dozen things, saying nothing, for lack of time he said and because he probably would say more at night." Glasscock's informant further related that Bennett charged that the Democrats left a balanced budget whereas Governor Dawson would not, and that Glasscock would be Senator Elkins's "agent" if

---

67   *Wheeling Intelligencer*, October 23, 1908; Ambler and Summers, *West Virginia: The Mountain State*, 378–79.

68   E. M. Lewis to Glasscock, 26 September 1908, Glasscock Papers.

69   George McClintic to Glasscock, 23 September 1908, Glasscock Papers.

70   G. W. Farr to Glasscock, 7 October 1908, Glasscock Papers.

71   Glasscock to Charles M. Babb, 30 September 1908, Glasscock Papers.

W. E. Glasscock, fourth Elkins governor, 1909–1913 in a portrait by Alphonse Jongers. Glasscock was selected as a compromise candidate. A frail, religious man, he stood steadfast in the face of violence in West Virginia. Courtesy of the West Virginia Division of Culture and History.

elected governor. He added that the Democratic candidate said that he expected to be elected "by the votes of white men (cheers here)."[72] Staying on message, Bennett hammered away at the two main issues: bossism and African-American rights as clearly depicted in racist political cartoons in the Democratic press. Although reports seemed favorable to the Republicans, Glasscock was wary of overconfidence, especially in Kanawha County where Democrats had a powerful organization.[73] With expectations running high, the *Wheeling Register* predicted a win for Bennett.[74]

As he expected, Glasscock won the election, but by the modest majority of 12,133 votes.[75] Excepting the gubernatorial election of W. M. O. Dawson, the usual Republican

72   B. Randolph Bias to Glasscock, 16 October 1908, Glasscock Papers.

73   C. L. Topping to Glasscock, 28 September 1908, Glasscock Papers.

74   *Wheeling Register*, October 9, 1908.

75   Ambler and Summers, *West Virginia: The Mountain State*, 378–80; *Morgantown Post-Chronicle*, November 6, 1908; November 20, 1908; *Charleston Gazette*, November 6, 1908.

The Democratic point of view. Courtesy of the *Wheeling Register*, Wheeling, WV, 1908.

plurality had been about 20,000 votes. Of course, Glasscock did very well in the southern portion of the state, in the so-called "blackbelt" area. The governor-elect also overcame Bennett's popularity in the central and Eastern Panhandle counties,[76] with a solid majority in such counties as McDowell, Mingo, Fayette, Kanawha, Monongalia, and Preston. Some analysts believed there was some "cutting" (not voting for certain candidates) of the Republican ticket in areas where factionalism was still rampant.[77] Although state prohibition was not a major issue, many believed that the liquor interests had fought Glasscock, causing him to lose votes. The familiar refrain that the Republican candidate would be under the thumb of Senator Elkins also influenced some voters to either not vote or to support the Democratic candidate.[78] Of course, Republican support for African-American rights led others to vote for Bennett. The

76   Glasscock carried McDowell by a majority of about 3,600 votes, but Taft carried it by about a 4,500-vote margin, which was evidence of some dissatisfaction in that county. Dr. Henry D. Hatfield, a future governor and U.S. senator, had expected a victory for Glasscock of about 6,000-vote margin in his home county of McDowell, but it was still reliably Republican.
77   W. E. White to Glasscock, 5 November 1908, Glasscock Papers.
78   W. P. Hubbard to Glasscock, 6 November 1908, Glasscock Papers.

Democrats suffered a bitter defeat, one that brought back unpleasant memories for those who had struggled for lost causes in the past. Based on early returns the Democratic press had proclaimed Bennett the victor by a margin that would exceed 12,000 votes.[79] One Democrat later wrote to Bennett in disgust:

> 'Whom the Lord loveth He chasteneth.' It was so in the 'sixties,' it is true now. The negro [sic] and the 'home guards' and their descendants have won out and white men have lost.[80]

Since Glasscock's father had been a "home guard" during the Civil War, the correspondent was correct in his assessment. Another Democrat chastised the Democratic Party when he admonished that there "was not such a complete organization in the state as should have been."[81] In consolation, a Summersville Democrat concluded:

> . . . there is one place where we will be in a majority; a place where republicans and negroes [sic] cease from troubling, and weary, worn old rebels and democrats are at rest; that whilst they have fallen, they will be as 'the stars go down to rise upon a brighter shore.' We can thank God that we believe there are no republicans in heaven, and that we know there are no negroes [sic] there.[82]

In West Virginia, the Democratic Party weakened its chances at the polls when it adhered to that party's attempt to mollify southern Democrats in their desire to strengthen and spread "Jim Crow" laws. Other states, such as Maryland, went through similar situations, experiencing intra-party feuds between reformers and conservatives over African-American disenfranchisement, which often prevented the passage of reform legislation.[83] Segregation, with widespread separation in nearly all public facilities, spreading throughout the South and parts of the North, was not as

79 *Wheeling Register*, November 4, 1908.

80 Robert A. Kincaid to Louis Bennett, 6 November 1908, Bennett Papers.

81 D. W. Gall to Louis Bennett, 16 November 1908, Bennett Papers.

82 Robert A. Kincaid to Louis Bennett, 6 November 1908, Bennett Papers. See also C. Vann Woodward, *The Strange Career of Jim Crow* (New York: Oxford University Press, 1966), 97–102. Hereafter cited as Vann Woodward, *The Strange Career of Jim Crow*.

83 Burckel, "Progressive Governors," 525.

much an urgent issue in West Virginia. Perhaps, too, Booker T. Washington's famous dictum to give blacks a "man's chance" to prove themselves was more receptive in a state where thousands of workers toiled in coal mines where equality was much easier to accept than above the ground. In 1902, a migrant black worker from Alabama wrote to a friend back home that in the West Virginia coal camps a "collered [sic] man stands just as good as a white man here."[84] Moreover, Mountain State blacks had proven their loyalty and importance to the state's Republicans, and the GOP was not willing to change a winning formula. At this time, West Virginians were much more concerned with "bread and butter" issues and the prospect of lower taxes and a more efficient government.

William E. Glasscock's speaking ability (at least in comparison to Bennett's), his apparent sincerity before his audiences, and the proposed black disenfranchisement spelled defeat for the Democrats. Perhaps, too, the Democrats had become overconfident and paid too little attention to organization. Once West Virginia Republicans had fallen in line, aided by their good neighbor President-elect William Howard Taft and the lame-duck President Theodore Roosevelt, they exhibited determination reminiscent of their former vitality. Much credit went to Governor Dawson, who laid the groundwork for a well-organized party structure and for a well-oiled Elkins political machine.

Perhaps one of the most important moves Elkins made in his attempt to control the Mountain State GOP was to make Dawson the Republican state chairman in 1891. He was widely regarded as "the most astute politician in the state," a sentiment echoed by former Democratic Governor William MacCorkle.[85] In the end, the Mountain State GOP maintained control of the governorship and both houses of the legislature. This gave the new chief executive the chance to continue the reforms of his predecessors.

---

84   Corbin, *Life, Work, and Rebellion in the Coal Fields*, 62. Blacks experienced a higher degree of equality working in the mines than other industrial work places. Owners preferred a judicious mix of native whites, foreigners, and blacks in order to prevent union activity. Thus, operators would often play one group against another. Of course, this could lead to friction among the workers. Secondly, in union mines the UMW stressed equality among miners in order to maintain a united front. While there was segregation in most coal camps, that was not always the case in others. See Kenneth R. Bailey, "A Judicious Mixture: Negroes and migrants in the West Virginia Mines, 1880–1917," *West Virginia History* 34 (January 1973): 157–61. See also Ronald L. Lewis, "Black Presence in the Paint-Cabin Creek Strike, 1912–1913," *West Virginia History* 46(1985–1986): 59.

85   Williams, *West Virginia and the Captains of Industry*, 142. See also William A. MacCorkle, *The Recollections of Fifty Years of West Virginia*, (New York: G. P. Putnam's Sons, 1928), 451. Hereafter cited as MacCorkle, *Recollections*.

On the national level, Taft also defeated Bryan. It seemed to Glasscock and the state's politicians that West Virginia had a bright future with GOP dominance on the state level, plus two Republican U.S. senators in Washington. Although a tough election and a sweet victory for the frail Morgantown lawyer, it was nothing compared to the battles that lay ahead in his administration.

CHAPTER   THREE

THE EVOLUTION OF A
PROGRESSIVE GOVERNOR

" . . . while they asked for bread they have been given stone."[1]

SOON AFTER THE ELECTION, Governor-elect Glasscock went to Hot Springs, Virginia, for a vacation that lasted several weeks. While there, he had the opportunity to confer with President-elect Taft and try his hand at golf. After a month of intense campaigning, Glasscock felt it necessary to rest before going to Charleston to aid Governor Dawson's attempt to secure the passage of certain bills by the legislature. At that time, West Virginia had biennial sessions that were limited to forty-five days. The organization of state government was not always conducive to efficient continuity. While the governor was elected in November of an even numbered year and took office the next March, the legislature met biennially in odd numbered years, convening in January and adjourning before the new governor's inauguration. The newly elected governor would then have to wait two years before he could present his legislative program. However, this hardship was often alleviated when the incoming governor-elect could work with a cooperative chief executive, especially if the two were of the same party. Fortunately, this was the case with Glasscock and Dawson. Indeed, the latter had primarily written the Republican platform of 1908 on which the former ran. Proffering "a good room at the Governor's house, which we will be glad for you to occupy," Governor Dawson welcomed Glasscock's assistance in fulfilling party pledges.[2] Teamwork served the lame-duck Governor Dawson well. While he had grown weary because of many legislative battles, the newly-elected Glasscock applied his recently earned political influence with the legislators.

---

1   Glasscock to U.S. Senator Stephen B. Elkins, 21 February 1909, Glasscock Papers.
2   W. M. O. Dawson to Glasscock, 18 November 1908, Glasscock Papers. See also Burckel, "Progressive Governors," 302.

Although the Republicans held a majority in the legislature even after serious factional disputes during the 1900 and 1904 elections, Dawson's programs still faced formidable challenges because the party's strength was divided along progressive and "standpatter," i.e. conservative, lines. The House of Delegates, consisting of eighty-six members, was, as it had been in the past, more responsive to public opinion. On the other hand, the Senate, made up of thirty members, was criticized for being too conservative, too unresponsive, and too small to be democratic. For example, under the existing conditions, the more heavily populated, industrial counties usually dominated the senatorial race in their respective districts. Governor Dawson had previously noted this situation and urged for an increase in its membership. Later, he even suggested that each county have a representative in the upper house in order for it to be more in touch with the people.[3] Although the Senate had been uncooperative under Dawson, both he and Glasscock hoped that their joint effort would lead to positive results.

On January 13, 1909, Governor Dawson delivered a broad, reform-minded message to the legislature. His actions followed the philosophy of the progressive mayor of Cleveland, Ohio, Tom Johnson, who often said, "Don't rant at the individual. Get after the system."[4] Dawson's program, which would be familiar to most progressives around the country, contained legislation that would control or regulate social, political, and economic systems that had not kept in step with modern times. Reformers desired to instill orderliness and continuity by establishing methods, usually through administrative bureaucracies, that would standardize procedures. This was a difficult task, because powerful elites, usually corporate owners and their henchmen, such as Republican U.S. Senator S. B. Elkins and Democrat Henry G. Davis, usually benefited from maintaining the status quo.

In his message to the 1909 legislature, Governor Dawson asked for a local option bill and the submission of a state prohibition amendment to the people of West Virginia. Prohibition cut across party lines, pleasing supporters for obvious reasons, and even drawing support from many business leaders who desired a sober work force. In other areas of social concern, he called for further improvements in public education and an amendment to the constitution allowing women to serve on boards connected with public institutions. Dawson pointed out the deplorable condition of the state's jails and the need for laws limiting child labor. He also encouraged the conservation of

---

3   *Morgantown Post-Chronicle*, March 1, 1909.
4   Russel B. Nye, *Midwestern Progressive Politics*, 168.

the state's natural resources and asked for legislation to prevent the pollution of West Virginia's rivers.

In judicial and legislative reform, Governor Dawson stated that there was "an overwhelming public sentiment in this state which demands that the people be allowed to choose their political party nominees from United States Senator to constable by primary elections." He also urged the legislature to pass an indirect tax on the production of coal, oil, and gas in the form of a license fee based upon the gross earnings of corporations engaged in these industries. Attempting to tax West Virginia's extractive industries always opened the eyes of corporate moneymen in New York and Philadelphia, rushing their retainers and lobbyists to Charleston to inform the legislators of the deleterious effect of taxes upon their industries and the prospective development of a state badly in need of infrastructure.

Governor-elect Glasscock thought the time was ripe for a tax on gas production in the state. He pointed out, however, "The only danger that I can see is in the coal people joining forces with the gas people and liquor interests to defeat this."[5] His fear proved correct as many of the large corporations employed their heavy guns to prevent its passage. For example, A. B. Fleming of the Fairmont Coal Company actively lobbied for the coal and gas interests. In addition, political alliances of businessmen-politicians of both political parties united in their efforts to block legislation. Republican Joseph H. McDermott of Morgantown, speaking for the gas interests, urged former Democratic Governor Fleming to ask certain individuals from his county to write to key legislative members asking them not to vote for the coal, oil, and gas tax bills.[6] About a week later, a Wheeling manufacturer wrote to Fleming congratulating him on his successful opposition to the Dawson legislature for preventing "a lot of graft bills" such as the tax on coal, oil, and gas and the employers' liability bill. He went on to quote U.S. Senator Scott who allegedly said "there were two Thanksgiving days; the second on the 4th of March when we will be relieved of President Roosevelt and Governor Dawson."[7] Their action was successful. At the end of Dawson's tax reform session, Fleming sent comforting words to his fellow Philadelphia capitalists:

> ... I represent as General Counsel the Standard Oil interests in the state, and some of the largest coal interests, and generally appear before one or more of

5   Glasscock to M. L. Brown, 10 September 1909, Glasscock Papers.
6   Joseph H. McDermott to A. B. Fleming, 16 February 1909, in A. B. Fleming Papers, West Virginia University Library. Hereafter cited as Fleming Papers, unless location is different.
7   N. E. Whitaker to A. B. Fleming, 25 February 1909, Fleming Papers.

the committees every session of the legislature to discuss and object to some anti-corporation legislation proposed. We have always succeeded in defeating everything to which we objected, and that too without the use of money.[8]

Dawson further asked that the number of judges on the Supreme Court of Appeals be increased, the legislative sessions lengthened, and the lawmakers' salaries raised. Finally, he urgently requested a public service commission based on the belief that the government must play a leading role in order to solve economic problems:

> For more than thirty years there has been a struggle in this state for protection to the people and business interests from unjust discrimination and other injustices practiced by the railroads. So far in this contest the people have been defeated.
> Every railroad in these quasi-public corporations and companies is undoubted, both from a legal and from a moral point of view, and the duty of the legislature to protect the public is one of the highest put upon a representative body and the duty is urgently imperative.[9]

In tandem, both Glasscock and Dawson worked diligently for progressive legislation, and both appeared before the House Railroad Committee to urge the passage of a public service commission law similar to the one in New York. The bill was broad and comprehensive in scope. It provided for a three-man board, appointed by the governor, with the power to enforce the laws of the state and to modify unreasonable rates. The board obtained the means to prohibit rebates and other forms of unjust discrimination and provided more openness in business affairs (something not always desirable to corporate leaders), along with jurisdiction over all common carriers, pipelines, telephone, telegraph, and electric companies. This act also levied a tax on the regulated corporations to provide for the services of a well-paid commission,[10] which raised the ire of those who believed taxes hindered economic development.

Although Governor Dawson and Governor-elect Glasscock personally lobbied for the public service commission bill, it was defeated. Their efforts were successful in the House, which, as noted, was more in line with public sentiment, but failed in the Senate,

8   Williams, *West Virginia and the Captains of Industry*, 49–50.
9   *Morgantown Post-Chronicle*, January 13, 1909.
10 *Morgantown Post-Chronicle*, January 13, 1909; Burckel, "Progressive Governors," 341–42.

where the bill never progressed beyond the committee stage. Supporters of the status quo usually counted on the actions of key members in certain committees to hold up reform legislation, or in order to partially mollify the reformers, send the bill to the other house knowing there would either not be enough time for action or it would once again pigeon-hole the legislation in another committee. A study commission, often a delaying tactic, could also examine and debate the issue for years. The Republicans would see four planks of their platform fail to become law during Dawson's last legislative session: the prohibition amendment, the local option bill, the employer's liability bill, and a primary election law. Out of frustration, Glasscock intimated that he might call a special session after his inaugural.[11] He did not, and some observers felt that if he had, the time was ripe for enactment of a tax, at least, on natural gas. As was often the case, Senator Elkins evidently interceded. Elkins wrote to his close confidant and lieutenant Ira E. Robinson, "I want to talk with Governor Glasscock about an extra session of the legislature. I don't think we ought to have an extra session."[12]

While Governor-elect Glasscock worked diligently for the passage of those bills (Governor Dawson was ill during much of this time), it was the primary election act that placed him in a subtle tug-of-war with Senator Elkins, who was naturally conservative on the subject. In the United States, direct primaries had been in use locally since the 1840s. Reformers naturally believed that the direct participation of the voters in the political process was needed to break the hold of party bosses and their lobbyists, who often prevented the fruition of popular causes through the legislative process.

In 1903, under the influence of Governor Robert M. La Follette, Wisconsin became the first state to mandate a statewide primary. By 1917, all but four states followed this practice. In West Virginia, both parties were committed in their party platforms to this law, but there were divergent views, such as the GOP's qualified stance on the issue, as stated in their platform of 1908:

> We favor what is known as the direct primary election method of making nominations . . . whereby all candidates for all political parties for all elective offices shall be nominated. But as this will be a radical departure in this state, it may be wise to leave the nomination of county tickets optional,

---

11 *Wheeling Intelligencer*, January 17, 1909; February 2, 1909; *Wheeling Register*, February 21, 1909.

12 S. B. Elkins to Ira E. Robinson, 29 September 1909, Ira E. Robinson Papers, West Virginia University Library. Hereafter cited as Robinson Papers, unless location is different.

as to whether by primary or other method, as the proper party committee in the county may determine.[13]

While in Charleston, Glasscock received a number of letters from individuals with opinions on the primary law issue. Although, the prevailing sentiment seemed in favor of such a law, there was no consensus on its make-up. Former Governor A. B. White, for example, was skeptical of the use of the primary at the local level of government. He informed Glasscock that at the Republican convention he had actively supported the idea that county officials should use their discretion whether or not to hold a primary at their level of government. White advocated this provision in order to prevent any kind of "racial domination."[14] Another objection was that some of the primaries then in effect in other states made it possible for the minority party to come to power by manipulating the election. For example, Republican Representative Harry C. Woodyard of the Fourth Congressional District, wrote that Republicans in Oregon, Minnesota, Wisconsin and Illinois were having difficulties because the Democrats controlled the election by voting for a weak Republican in the open primary and then selecting the stronger Democrat in the general election.[15] Others felt that without careful regulation, a certain "class" of Democrats and Republicans could join forces in order to elect their candidate.[16] Senator Elkins wrote to Glasscock in a similar vein, stating that he favored "some sort of primary, but not a universal one." He pointed out that Secretary of State Elihu Root had come out strongly against the primary in his home state of New York. Elkins concluded, "it is a fundamental change in our government and laws and does nothing but mischief. The majority party always suffers."[17]

Despite the numerous expressions of opposition to a primary bill by leading West Virginia Republicans, Glasscock had made it clear that he favored such a law as long as it was drafted to prevent corrupt elections. If none could be passed in the present session, then he supported the creation of a bipartisan committee of the legislature to study the prerequisites of a strong bill.[18] During the campaign, Glasscock had supported

13 *Morgantown Post-Chronicle*, September 24, 1910.
14 A. B. White to Glasscock, 13 March 1911, Glasscock Papers. Large numbers of African Americans and immigrants coming into West Virginia to work in the coal regions most likely shaped former Governor White's opinion.
15 Harry Woodyard to Glasscock, 1 January 1909, Glasscock Papers.
16 Jno. L. Steele to Glasscock, 28 January 1909, Glasscock Papers.
17 Senator S. B. Elkins to Glasscock, 29 January 1909, Glasscock Papers.
18 Glasscock to Harry C. Woodyard, 4 January 1909, Glasscock Papers.

Senate Bill No. 114, the Cooper primary bill, drafted by Republican John T. Cooper, of Parkersburg, as presented in the legislature of 1907. Under this law, the primary would be used to nominate candidates for office by the direct vote of party members.

The Republican State Executive Committee would also inform the lawmakers of the voters' decision, instructing them to vote for the people's choice for the United States senatorial seats. This bill was commonly referred to as a statewide primary plan. In the legislature of 1909, Senate Bill No. 14, sponsored by Fred O. Blue of Barbour County, and House Bill No. 2, presented by E. R. Kingsley of Wood County, embodied many of the ideas of the Cooper primary bill. These measures left to the discretion of many local officials, i.e. small municipalities, whether or not to use a primary as a means of nominating candidates. House Bill No. 2, drafted by Republican C. W. Good of Kanawha County, went further. It stated that all county precincts should hold a primary for all candidates for congressional, senatorial, state, county, district officers, and for U.S. senators. Good's measure was broad and took "in the whole army of officials."

In addition to the above proposals, Senator Henry D. Hatfield of McDowell County submitted a primary bill that was more palatable to conservative taste. It was referred to as a kind of primary local option, which, in instances where primaries were required at all, were used only for selecting delegates to party conventions. It also provided no way of expressing an opinion for U.S. senatorial candidates. This measure did pass the Senate, but was rejected by House members.[19] Hatfield's draft, also called a district unit plan, created heated debate on the floor of the legislature. In his characteristic fashion, Hatfield later stated, "Cooper, the state wide primary man, was there, like a serpent in dog days, and was striking at most anything, which had a tendency toward the adoption of the District Unit plan . . ."[20]

When Senator Elkins learned that several House members had touted the Good primary bill, he was perturbed. He wrote to Glasscock cautioning that "a primary for the selection of Senators would be most disastrous."[21] He added that he did not believe in going "too far in the primary law, especially to the extent of the legislature surrendering its powers to elect United States Senators, which is a sacred right imposed

---

19   For the Hatfield and the Blue bills see *West Virginia Senate Journal*, 1909, 438–55 and 49, 319; for the Good and Kingsley measures see *West Virginia House Journal*, 1909, 87–104 and 98; see also *Morgantown Post-Chronicle*, February 12, 1909; *Wheeling Register*, February 10, 1909; and *Charleston Daily Mail*, January 19, 1909.

20   Henry D. Hatfield to H. C. Ogden, 14 October 1911, Glasscock Papers.

21   Senator S. B. Elkins to Glasscock, 30 January 1909, Glasscock Papers.

upon it by the Constitution of the United States."[22] Elkins found the Hatfield bill to be the least objectionable[23] because of its limited scope, which Congressman William P. Hubbard criticized.[24] Many observers considered that law a "gold brick,"[25] and Congressman George C. Sturgiss, acting with the unanimous support of the other West Virginia Representatives, opposed it. In the end, defeat ruled the day; the last Dawson Legislature passed no primary election law.[26] Senate resistance once again forestalled the passage of that bill. Toward the end of the legislative session, Glasscock, sick with bronchitis, disappointed with the legislative impasse, and assuredly prompted by Senator Elkins, left Charleston for Morgantown to recuperate for the inaugural. He wrote one last time to Elkins concerning the action of the lawmakers:

> I do not think it is necessary for us to enter into a discussion of the primary election law at this time because I believe the legislature will pass none at all. It has defeated the prohibition amendment and I am very much afraid the people of West Virginia will think that while they asked for bread they have been given stone.[27]

Nonetheless, some notable legislation did pass the legislature of 1909. One law created a State Commission of Public Roads, which provided for the upkeep of roads funded by a one-cent tax on every one hundred dollars valuation of all real and personal property. Governor-elect Glasscock was not very enthusiastic about this act, because he felt the counties were not ready to spend these funds in an "intelligent" manner, and as governor he planned to distribute the money cautiously.[28] Another bill that received some publicity called for the creation of a three-man committee, chaired as well as appointed by the governor, to investigate the pollution of the New and Kanawha Rivers.[29]

---

22   Elkins to Glasscock, 2 February 1909, Glasscock Papers.

23   Elkins to Glasscock, 16 February 1909, Glasscock Papers.

24   W. P. Hubbard to Glasscock, 19 February 1909, Glasscock Papers.

25   B. Randolph Bias to Glasscock, 13 February 1909, Glasscock Papers.

26   George C. Sturgiss to Glasscock, 8 February 1909; 19 February 1909, both Glasscock Papers; *Morgantown Post-Chronicle*, February 20, 1909; February 27, 1909.

27   Glasscock to Senator Elkins, 21 February 1909, Glasscock Papers.

28   *West Virginia Senate Journal*, 1909, 157–59, 258–66, and 266–67; see also Glasscock to Senator Elkins, 31 August, 1909, Glasscock Papers.

29   Subsequently, as governor, Glasscock appointed this commission, went to Washington for a conference with the Secretary of War, and held several conferences at the capitol with tannery and

A third reform law, and the one considered most significant by contemporaries, was the creation of a Board of Control, Senate Bill 165. During the legislative session, Glasscock had not only given the impression that he would be an active and independent governor, but also one determined to learn as much as he could about the workings of the state government. He set out on this mission shortly after a much needed three-week vacation at Hot Springs, Virginia.

When he returned to Charleston to aid Governor Dawson in the legislative battles, he worked long fourteen-hour days in the various departments in order to learn their functions.[30] Out of this experience, Glasscock suggested the composition of an act,[31] drafted by Senator Hatfield, creating a Board of Control to supervise all West Virginia public institutions. After all, the "gospel of efficiency" was another important theme of progressivism. His aims were to reorganize governmental agencies in order to eliminate redundancy and to establish clear lines of authority and accountability, as seen in other states such as Wisconsin under the direction of Governor La Follette. This was the way of the new century.[32]

The bill for the creation of a Board of Control had two main features. First, it established the Board of Control itself. Composed of three full time employees residing in Charleston, it had complete and direct charge of every institution except educational facilities.[33] Authorized to make all contracts, handle all money, and have full and unquestioned authority in management, the board provided for a centralized control of state finances. Secondly, this measure created a State Board of Regents, commissioned to supervise the curriculum of the state educational institutions, with four members appointed by the governor with the approval of the Senate, and the fifth filled by the State Superintendent of Schools. Most reformers, including progressive educators, supported this law, described by the state superintendent as "the crowning glory of the state educational system."[34]

....

mine operators concerning pollution. These sessions generated publicity, which, in reality, was its only power to influence, not to enforce, but resulted in the agreement of several of the tannery operators to limit the amount of pollutants let into the streams of the state. See the *Charleston Gazette*, November 23, 1909 and the *West Virginia Senate Journal*, 1909, 685–87, 828–29.

30   *Morgantown Post-Chronicle*, February 11, 1909; January 18, 1909.

31   *Morgantown Post-Chronicle*, February 11, 1909.

32   Nye, *Midwestern Progressive Politics*, 202.

33   *West Virginia Senate Journal*, 1909, 546–57.

34   Charles H. Ambler, *A History of Education in West Virginia* (Huntington, WV: Standard Printing and Publishing Co., 1951), 389–390. Hereafter cited as Ambler, *A History of Education*.

Overall, the results of the 1909 legislature disappointed the eager, newly-elected governor. However, he had gained important experience from the activity. Glasscock's actions also indicated that he would be an energetic chief executive, one interested in reform. Although Glasscock and the ailing Dawson had failed to achieve several important goals, it was largely through the efforts of the governor-elect and Senator Hatfield that the Board of Control was created. Working with Governor Dawson and providing yeomen service in the legislative hallways, proved to be valuable on-the-job training for the Morgantown lawyer who would soon be on his own. Governor Dawson, up to that time the most progressive of the Elkins governors, obviously influenced the political vision of the new governor, reinforcing his tendencies to seek reform.

CHAPTER FOUR

SETTLING INTO OFFICE

" . . . the fellow who has the longest pull and the biggest influence 'knocks the persimmon!'"[1]

AN AILING GLASSCOCK RETURNED TO MORGANTOWN for a short period of recuperation. While an exhausting experience for the delicate governor-elect, it was rewarding; he had participated in the state government from top to bottom, an activity on which he reflected at home.

The time to recoup his strength soon ended, however, as plans were made for his inauguration in Charleston. This led to a hectic period of preparations for the return journey to the state's capitol, an attractive city between the Great Kanawha and Elk Rivers, and the lavish reception site for the inauguration of West Virginia's thirteenth governor. Governor-elect Glasscock left Morgantown by train on March 2 in order to arrive early for his inaugural.

The State Geologist, Dr. I. C. White of West Virginia University, and M. L. Brown, a close friend and cashier of the Bank of Morgantown, accompanied him. Traveling on a later, special train which took them from Morgantown to Charleston, his wife and friends took the most practical form of transportation, minutely described by a local newspaper:

Every seat is reserved in the special chair car, chartered to convey a party of Morgantown and Fairmont people to Charleston for the inauguration. The special car which will arrive from Connellsville shops tonight will be attached to the regular train leaving here at six o'clock tomorrow morning. At Clarksburg the car will be transferred to the main line and attached to the morning express bound for Parkersburg. There the car will be switched to the river side of the city and continue to Point Pleasant over the Ohio River branch of the B. and O.

1   W. E. White to Glasscock, 16 November 1908, Glasscock Papers.

From Point Pleasant the car will be switched to the Kanawha and Michigan tracks, completing the run into Charleston on the K. and M. arriving at the state capitol [sic] soon after 5 o'clock.[2]

With the legislative session behind him, Glasscock prepared for his new duties. At the time of his inauguration on March 4, 1909, he was forty-six years of age. On that day the weather was seasonable and clear, with gusts of wind. Hundreds of Charlestonians and well-wishers lined the route of the inaugural parade. In addition to these spectators, Glasscock's wife, son, and aging father attended. The governor-elect's brother, Fuller, who was his law partner, was also present. Another brother, Stephen A. D. Glasscock of Bellingham, Washington, was unable to attend but wired his congratulations, "As with you in spirit remember these responsibilities are equal to the honors."[3] In a similar tone of seriousness, Glasscock replied:

> I have never in my heart rejoiced since my election because I realize the truth of what you said in your telegram that the responsibilities of the office are fully equal to the honors. However, I can only do the best I can and that I assure you I shall do at all times and under all circumstances.[4]

On that crisp March day a group of mounted police, the Second Regimental Band of the National Guard, and a battalion of state infantry led the inaugural procession. Situated between the infantry and a smart looking group of "Taft marchers," a horse-drawn carriage conveyed Governor Dawson, Governor-elect Glasscock and the state's four living former governors: A. B. Fleming, W. A. MacCorkle, George W. Atkinson, and A. B. White. Three other carriages followed carrying various newly-elected state officials to the inaugural ceremonies in the House of Delegates chamber.[5]

---

2 *Morgantown Post-Chronicle*, March 2, 1909; Malcomson, "William E. Glasscock," 12–14.

3 S. A. D. Glasscock to Glasscock, 4 March 1909, Glasscock Papers.

4 Glasscock to S. A. D. Glasscock, 6 March 1909, Glasscock Papers.

5 *Morgantown Post-Chronicle*, March 4, 1909; *Wheeling Intelligencer*, March 5, 1909; John G. Morgan, *West Virginia Governors* (Charleston, WV: Newspaper Agency Corp., 1960), 39–40. It is interesting to note that there were no automobiles present in Glasscock's inaugural parade. Henry D. Hatfield, his successor, would be the first Governor-elect to ride in one in his inaugural entourage. See Williams, *West Virginia and the Captains of Industry*, 248.

Judge Ira E. Robinson[6] of the State Supreme Court of Appeals, Senator Elkins's second choice for governor had Glasscock not accepted, administered the oath of office in an impressive but brief ceremony using the old, worn family Bible from which Glasscock's mother had read to him as a child. The opened Bible displayed the first Psalm, which began, "Blessed is the man that walketh not in the counsel of the ungodly . . ."[7]

As he took the oath of office, the underweight Glasscock (he carried only 130 pounds on his spare 5' 11" frame) was anything but a picture of health. Suffering from inflammatory rheumatism and lacking resistance to common ailments, his health would be an important factor in his administration.

Indeed, at his inaugural ceremony, bronchitis, a severe cough, and neuralgia plagued the ailing Glasscock.[8] According to the *Morgantown Post Chronicle*, "the conservation of his own physical resources will be one of the duties to which the new Governor will have to apply himself diligently."[9] Glasscock made it clear, however, that he intended to be an active, progressive chief executive. Parts of his inaugural address were reminiscent of earlier progressives who had sought reform through public agitation:

> I have believed for many years that publicity is the best correction for the wrongs known to man. You cannot by legislation make men honest. But there are few men who violate laws or commit crimes against society or mistrust their fellow man, who do not think at the time of the commission of the offense that the injured party will never know who caused the injury. We are taught that some men seek darkness rather than light because their

---

6   Judge Ira E. Robinson of Grafton, a former state senator and another Elkins lieutenant, was closely associated with the senator and was involved in legal affairs, obtaining loans from banks, and purchasing coal lands. Davis Elkins, the son, pushed hard to secure his father's support to back Robinson's desire to serve on the Supreme Court of Appeals. In 1907, Davis wrote Robinson that he "wired my father, and he phoned me he would do all that he could to secure you the position of judge," which he did. See Davis Elkins to Ira E. Robinson, 7 August 1907, Ira E. Robinson Papers, West Virginia University Library.

7   Fuller Glasscock to Glasscock, 6 March 1909, Glasscock Papers; Morgan, *West Virginia Governors*, 40.

8   Glasscock to Senator S. B. Elkins, 21 February 1909; Glasscock to C. D. Elliott, 15 March 1909; Glasscock to John L. Steele, 16 March 1909, all in Glasscock Papers.

9   *Morgantown Post-Chronicle*, February 4, 1909.

deeds are evil. If that be true, and it is true, why not turn on all the light possible in public as well as in private affairs.[10]

Governor Glasscock reminded the audience that both political parties were committed to a state primary law and the submission of the prohibition amendment to the people, and "the fight must go on, will go on until our platform pledges are redeemed and the demands of the people have been satisfied." He called on all state employees to adopt the motto of "An Honest Dollar for an Honest Day's work," and urged that the state constitution be brought up to date, because "it has outgrown the clothes given it by the Constitution of 1872."

In other areas, he advocated the further improvement and development of industry and education, the proper regulation of railroads, "pure" elections, and just taxation. He also declared that "the chief aim of good government should be to secure to the individual the largest measure of liberty and the enjoyment of the fruits of his labor."[11] As expected, the Republican press hailed Glasscock's address for its brevity and sincerity. As with the weather, the future was also uncertain, but few could question the goals that he propounded for himself and the state on that blustery March day.

Many observers, however, wondered if the new governor could endure the rigors of office. Often reported in the press, the public knew that Glasscock suffered poor health. From the beginning of his administration, the governor received medical advice from people who wanted to help him carry out his duties. He frequently heard from doctors, interested citizens, and especially from his associates in Morgantown. His friend and colleague George C. Baker wrote, "Don't let the little details of that office kill you. Life is too sweet and too short. Try to get out every day, and buy you a horse and go out horseback riding."[12] While Glasscock was recuperating at Hot Springs, Dr. T. H. Miller of Fairmont sent the governor-elect medical advice on how to maintain his health:

The cauliflour [sic] have cooked as I told you how to do. Don't be afraid of eating to [sic] little for supper, for it will give your nervous system a chance

10   Inaugural Address of Governor William E. Glasscock, March 4, 1909, State Papers and Public Addresses of William E. Glasscock, 1909–1913, West Virginia Division of Culture and History, Charleston, 1–8; B. Randolph Bias to Glasscock, 6 March 1909, Glasscock Papers; Burckel, "Progressive Governors," 343.

11   Inaugural Address of Governor William E. Glasscock, 1–8.

12   George C. Baker to Glasscock, 12 March 1909, Glasscock Papers.

to relax and will save you from taking anything to force rest, which will really not be natural rest.[13]

Dr. Miller also advised Glasscock not to fail to eat a lemon at night on retiring. He explained that he wanted to lighten the load on the liver, kidneys, stomach, "and get a natural action of the bowels, and to increase your nerve supply, which this will do and it will lesson [sic] the load on the nervous system in every part of the body, and will generate more energy, as what we eat should do."[14]

Miller wrote that he had heard some people express the opinion that Glasscock did not have the health that would permit him to maintain the functions of his office. In answer to this proposition the doctor advised the governor-elect that if he used half the energy "in trying to regain your health, that you did in the campaigne [sic], you will come out in good condition, and be the gainer all along the line."[15]

Soon after his arrival to Charleston, Glasscock acquired a grueling schedule, to aid Governor Dawson in his efforts to pass reform legislation and made his Morgantown friends speculate how long he could keep up with the frenzied activities in the governmental departments and legislative halls.[16] By early February 1909, what many people feared finally happened—Glasscock fell ill. The sickness occurred after he had stood in line for four hours shaking hands at a reception given by Governor Dawson, who was not a strong man himself and had recently suffered a "break-down." The editors of the *Morgantown Post-Chronicle* knew the governor-elect well and wrote the following in a personal article about him:

> The following morning found him [Glasscock] housed up with fatigue, a severe cold, and a lively assortment of chills and fevers. Glasscock is a delicate looking man, like Dawson, but he hasn't the physical strength of Dawson by a whole lot. He has the nervous temperament, the lack of which is doubtless a great help to the present governor in discharging both official and social responsibilities.[17]

13   Dr. T. H. Miller to Glasscock, 11 November 1909, Glasscock Papers.
14   Dr. T. H. Miller to Glasscock, 17 November 1908, Glasscock Papers.
15   Dr. T. H. Miller to Glasscock, 17 November 1908, Glasscock Papers.
16   *Morgantown Post-Chronicle*, November 6, 1908.
17   *Morgantown Post-Chronicle*, February 8, 1909.

Frequent bouts of debilitating illnesses bore heavily on Glasscock's mind, causing worry and periods of self-doubt. Another concern, however, less known to the public, caused the governor much anxiety: personal finances. Soon after taking office, Governor Glasscock wrote to a friend in Morgantown that he had lost track of his finances and was making an effort to consolidate his debts.

Like many politicians, taking care of the needs of the people of the state often conflicted with providing for his own family. The Governor struggled throughout his tenure in office to maintain the same standard of living that he and his family had enjoyed in Morgantown, thanks to a successful practice of law. Living in Charleston, however, limited the family's finances, causing Glasscock much anguish, often necessitating loans from various banks and friends in order to remain solvent. In an effort to supplement what he considered a meager salary of $5,000 a year, Governor Glasscock continued close contact with the "boys" in Morgantown, participating in business schemes that usually involved coal. Like most progressives, the governor accepted a well-regulated capitalist system, and he certainly had no problem with making a profit from his investments.

Although Glasscock's strong Methodist upbringing provided him much strength and tranquility in troubled times, he would frequently experience periods of doubt and insecurity. Excessive worry often sent the frail Governor to the "sick bed" in order to recuperate, which, in turn, affected his administration. In hard times, Glasscock most often turned to his small coterie of friends in Morgantown. They greatly influenced him and he had much respect for them. The "syndicate," in fact, served as an important reference group for the chief executive, who needed all the help he could muster to hold his finances together, as he explained to a church member who attempted to elicit a donation:

> This is the first time in my life since I was married that I have not been able to make enough to keep my family, and that being so it becomes necessary for me to deny myself many pleasures that I would otherwise enjoy. There is nothing I like more than to contribute to the building of churches but there is a limit to my financial ability to do so.[18]

18   Glasscock to Rev. S. M. Snider, 30 October 1909, Glasscock Papers. In 1909, Glasscock and state Senator Joseph McDermott, Davis Elkins, the son of the powerful U. S. Senator Stephen B. Elkins, and another party paid on a $2,000 note through the First National Bank of Parkersburg. He also owed on an $800 note to James T. Conn through the Bank of the Monongahela Valley.

Soon after his inauguration, Glasscock received word from M. L. Brown, cashier of the Bank of Morgantown, that his friends had included him in a proposal to purchase a 386-acre tract of coal located on Pumpkin Run, in Battelle District, Monongalia County, for $80.00 an acre. It had belonged to the Blaker estate.[19] Those purchasing the tract were Judge Frank Cox, Attorney George C. Baker, Professor Thomas E. Hodges, Attorney Fuller Glasscock, M. L. Brown, and William E. Glasscock. Baker also wrote to the governor explaining that he "suggested to the boys that when you left here you said you would go in with us on any deal and would trust our judgment very largely in the matter."[20] Glasscock acknowledged the purchase by the "syndicate," and added, "I certainly want to be in on the proposition because I know if you people will risk your money in it I am safe."[21]

Brown arranged with the Bank of Masontown in West Virginia to furnish them with $5,000 and secured the remainder of the down payment through the Bank of Morgantown. The group paid one-third on the delivery of the deeds and the remainder in one and two years at 5 percent interest.[22] Baker fully expected the coal to sell for $100 an acre by the next year and could not think of a better investment to leave his children. In fact, he felt that they would receive as much as $400 an acre in the next ten years.[23] These optimistic reports pleased the governor, because he knew he "was going to have a hard time in making a living here."[24] This deal typified the many financial arrangements he and the "boys" would make throughout the various banks in the state. They certainly were not as rich as John D. Rockefeller, but they, along with many of the professional middle class, were willing to bet on a growing industry-based economy in West Virginia. Compared to men such as Stephen B. Elkins, Henry G. Davis, and Johnson N. Camden, they were picking up the crumbs. On one occasion, Stephen Mason of Amos, asked the governor to help him sell 2,400 acres of the Kittanning and Freeport veins, offering Glasscock $10 for each acre he could sell. Governor Glasscock accepted the deal, using logic that might not be accepted today:

Now in regard to that coal proposition, if you have not sold it, I wish you would let me know at once just where the coal lies; under whose farms and

---

19   M. L. Brown to Glasscock, 30 March 1009, Glasscock Papers.
20   George C. Baker to Glasscock, 29 March 1909, Glasscock Papers.
21   Glasscock to George C. Baker, 31 March 1909, Glasscock Papers.
22   M. L. Brown to Glasscock, 29 March 1909, Glasscock Papers.
23   George C. Baker to Glasscock, 22 May 1909, Glasscock Papers.
24   Glasscock to S. F. Glasscock, 1 April 1909, Glasscock Papers.

all about it, and if I can do anything to assist you in making a sale of the same, I certainly would not hesitate to do so. There is no reason why any work I should do in that connection would be inconsistent with any of my duties as Governor, and I would have no more hesitation in recommending a good proposition now than at any other time.[25]

A review of the "Morgantown boys" who advised the governor in personal, financial, and political matters displays a network of friendship tied together with men who held highly responsible positions locally, nationally, and across the state. Politics, the economy, and making money occupied much of their time, not to mention helping each other's progression in society. Frank Cox, the apparent patriarch and former judge of the Supreme Court of Appeals of West Virginia, kept Glasscock abreast of local and state politics. During the election of 1910, Glasscock asked the judge to run for the state Senate, but he refused. In 1911, the governor also suggested to President Taft to name Cox to the United States Supreme Court, a plan that did not materialize.[26]

George C. Baker, Cox's law partner, former Lincoln Republican, and strong supporter of Arnold C. Scherr in 1908, also frequently advised the governor. Glasscock appointed him to his personal military staff, which pleased many of the reformers in the state. Fuller Glasscock, the governor's brother and law partner who was not directly involved in politics but was a keen observer and adviser to him, frequently corresponded with him, offering both personal and political advice. An unlikely member of the circle belonged to the Democratic Party, Professor Thomas E. Hodges of West Virginia University, president of the Bank of Morgantown, and a highly respected and loyal friend of Glasscock. The governor not only appointed him to a position on the Board of Control, but also, later, evidently supported his election as president of West Virginia University "as the proper 'Moses' to lead us out of the wilderness." Hodges had his "little crudities and mannerisms," but he also had "strong character."[27]

A particularly close friend, M. L. Brown, whom Glasscock mentored, provided a constant source of personal, political, and financial counseling, not to mention loans during hard times. Brown never hesitated to tell the governor the truth. For example,

25 Glasscock to Stephen Mason, 4 April 1910, Glasscock Papers. See also Stephen Mason to Glasscock, 30 January 1909, 10 March 1910, and 18 April 1910, all in Glasscock Papers.
26 Glasscock to President William H. Taft, 11 December 1911, Glasscock Papers.
27 M. L. Brown to Glasscock, 6 June 1910, Glasscock Papers.

Glasscock wrote to Brown, "Bring Mrs. Brown and come down and I will talk your right arm off because I am full of many subjects and want to turn myself lose [sic] on somebody and I know of no one to whom I would rather talk for about two days than yourself."[28] His career paralleled Glasscock's in several ways. A man in his early forties, he distinguished himself as a former schoolteacher and Monongalia County superintendent of Free Schools, succeeding Glasscock when the latter was elected circuit clerk. At one time, Glasscock suggested Brown run for the state Senate, but he refused. Governor Glasscock later appointed him warden of Moundsville Penitentiary in 1910.[29] The governor could be more open and frank with these hometown friends, whom he had known for years and with whom he had developed longstanding relationships. In formulating policy, making difficult decisions, and solving problems in general, they often carried more weight with Glasscock than most party leaders.

Other Morgantown correspondents who were not necessarily a part of the syndicate, but who received the close attention of the governor were Dr. Daniel B. Purinton, president of the university, and Frank Trotter of the law school, who mainly wrote educational news. Governor Glasscock also had an interesting relationship, usually cordial but sometimes strained, with Professor Henry S. Green, of the Department of Greek. Part owner of the *Morgantown Post-Chronicle*, a Progressive newspaper, Green did not always agree with Glasscock on political matters, and he never hesitated to voice his opinion in the local press, which often irritated many people and eventually led to his involuntary departure from the school. Finally, Frank L. Bowman, a young lawyer working in Glasscock's law office, was an acute observer of local political news. Bowman soon enjoyed a climb up the political ladder, no doubt aided by his association with the governor, to become postmaster of Morgantown from 1911 to 1915 and mayor of the same city from 1916 to 1917. In 1924, the voters of the Second Congressional District elected him as Representative to the Sixty-ninth Congress.[30]

One other correspondent from Morgantown should be mentioned. State Senator Joseph H. McDermott, president of the state Senate in 1907, mainly wrote in a political vein, particularly during the election of 1910. He was a staunch conservative, a standpatter in the Republican Party, and closely allied with Senator Elkins. McDermott and Glasscock did not always agree on party procedure, and there were times when the

28 Glasscock to M. L. Brown, 10 September 1909, Glasscock Papers.
29 *Wheeling Intelligencer*, November 17, 1910.
30 John T. Harris, ed., *West Virginia Legislative Hand Book and Manual and Official Register* (Charleston, West Virginia: Tribune Printing Company, 1926), 102–103.

senator actually worked against the governor's programs. On the surface, however, they remained cordial, and the governor always respectfully listened to his complaints.

It was not long after Governor Glasscock took office that he exclaimed, "Talk about work! I tell you I never knew what it was until within the last month."[31] Glasscock's reference was to the laborious task of filling positions in the various offices within state government. In this process, he actively sought and received advice from a number of people in the Mountain State; many were friends who had known him through political and business activities, and others were party members who deserved attention because of their influence. The identification of advisers, whom he consulted, the positions that he considered most vital, and the people whom he appointed, shed light on the thinking of the new governor. Intra-party feuds could erupt at any time, so it was necessary to assuage the party faithful.

Knowing the importance of maintaining party harmony and wishing to accommo-date certain regional bigwigs as much as possible, the governor attempted to ascertain the attitude and obtain the advice of party leaders. These Republicans represented a broad spectrum of the party, motivating Glasscock to attempt to make them as inclusive as possible. In the southern part of the state, Governor Glasscock often contacted Isaac T. Mann from Bramwell, a large investor in coal and a conservative leader in local politics. Also in that region, he turned to a physician, Henry D. Hatfield, whom he had known for several years. A moderate to conservative in politics, Hatfield was well respected and influential in McDowell County. In northern West Virginia, Glasscock often corre-sponded with his close friend Circuit Court Judge John W. Mason of Marion County. In the Northern Panhandle, the governor maintained contact with H. C. Ogden, editor of the powerful *Wheeling Intelligencer*. An active participant in party affairs, Ogden often vacillated from moderate to conservative politics. Since Glasscock was usually receptive to advice, many people corresponded with him, including A. B. White and the other former governors, but none could compare in frequency of their letters or the regard he held for them than the "boys" in Morgantown. Unlike Governor Robert M. La Follette of Wisconsin, who relied upon a trusted group of experts for guidance and advice, Governor Glasscock turned to his loyal group of Morgantown friends in times of need.

Following the inauguration, Governor Glasscock commenced to fill the various vacant offices, a time-consuming task. He had more than the usual number of people to place in his administration because of the creation of the new Board of Control and the

31   Glasscock to S. F. Glasscock, 1 April 1909, Glasscock Papers.

Board of Regents, and the office seekers were not long in knocking on the governor's door for handouts. For example, P. W. Morris of the *Parkersburg State Journal*, who had been a Scherr supporter and had not endorsed Glasscock's nomination, was among the first to seek a position and to eat a little "political crow." Morris informed the governor that it was through his action that he was now chief executive:

> . . . would it be worth while to come down and see you in regard to any position reasonably lucrative? You have the appointment to some places which have good salaries attached. I thus frankly speak because just now I need something which has pay rather than honor attached. I am in a position to leave the newspaper business at any time. If I could talk with you, I think that I could convince you that if it had not been for my course, you would not today be the chief executive officer of West Virginia. That you were not in sympathy with the course I pursued that operated in this way, I am fully aware, but the effect was the same.[32]

In reply, Glasscock sent Morris a summary of the appointments he would make in the near future: three members of the Board of Control with a salary of $5,000 each; four vacancies on the Board of Regents with a salary of $1,000 each; a commissioner of Public Roads with a salary of $3,000; a three-man committee to prepare a municipal code for West Virginia with a per diem of $10 and expenses; and a committee of five members to revise the printing laws of West Virginia with a per diem to be fixed by the governor. There were other committees, with expenses only, as well as a number of members to be named to the Board of Agriculture, Board of Examining Nurses, and the State Board of Health.[33]

In choosing a private secretary to deal with the various duties of the office, Governor Glasscock looked for continuity. Ultimately, Glasscock accepted the advice of former Governor A.B. White, who recommended the retention of E. L. Boggs. He had served with three governors and could act as a buffer against "the man with the foolish request, the time consumer and the cranks . . ."[34] The governor soon learned the truth of this advice and the value of having someone who could deflect obstacles in the road of

32   P. W. Morris to Glasscock, 12 March 1909, Glasscock Papers.
33   Morris was eventually selected as secretary of the Board of Regents. In all probability it was Glasscock who suggested his name to the Regents, since the Governor also wanted to please the Scherr group. See Glasscock to P. W. Morris, 7 April 1909, Glasscock Papers.
34   Malcomson, "William E. Glasscock," 17.

his administration from the continued services of Boggs. Glasscock next turned his attention to the newly created three-member bipartisan Board of Control, which was given supervision of the financial affairs of all state educational, charitable, penal, and correctional institutions. In effect, the board permitted a more efficient method of fiscal management of these state institutions and eliminated much waste and expense. For the first time, officials purchased large quantities of supplies and the let contracts on a competitive basis.[35] Although, some glitches appeared in the beginning of its operation, the board modernized the operation of the state's institutions.

Governor Glasscock had three important criteria for the selection of the Board of Control. First, he felt it was necessary to obtain individuals with some educational experience, because "one half of the institutions of our state are educational"; second, he wanted members with a background in business; and third, he thought the Board should be balanced as geographically effectively as possible.[36] Glasscock knew it would be impossible to satisfy everyone, perhaps taking to heart the comment of his friend and advisor ex-Judge Frank Cox, "If the Lord himself would come down and try to run the office of Governor of this State, he would be severely criticized."[37]

At one time or another, the governor offered a position on the Board of Control to former Governor Dawson, Isaac T. Mann of the southern part of the state, and to H. C. Ogden of the northern region, but they were all unable to comply for various reasons.[38] After perfunctory gestures to party leaders, Glasscock quickly secured the three appointees. From the northern part of the state, he selected James S. Lakin of Preston County. Lakin's success in business was well known and was an important factor in his appointment.[39] Learning that Attorney John A. Shepherd of Williamson was acceptable

35   Ambler and Summers, *West Virginia: The Mountain State*, 379.
36   Glasscock to John W. Mason, 15 March 1909; Senator S. B. Elkins to Glasscock, 20 March 1909, both in Glasscock Papers.
37   Frank Cox to Glasscock, 18 March 1909, Glasscock Papers.
38   It was mainly for lack of time that these individuals refused Glasscock's offer. See W. F. Hite to Glasscock, 31 December 1908, Glasscock Papers. Issac T. Mann headed a syndicate that ultimately owned over three hundred thousand acres of Pocahontas coal lands. See Joseph T. Lambie, *From Mine to Market: The History of Coal Transportation on the Norfolk and Western Railway* (Washington Square, New York: New York University Press, 1954), 137–243. Hereafter cited as Lambie, *From Mine to Market*. See also W. P. Tams, Jr., *The Smokeless Coal Fields of West Virginia: A Brief History* (Morgantown: West Virginia University Press/ West Virginia University Library, 1963), 93–94. Hereafter cited as Tams, *The Smokeless Coal Fields*.
39   Glasscock to Frank Cox, 15 March 1909, Glasscock Papers. See also Tams, *The Smokeless Coal Fields*. 89–90.

to Isaac T. Mann, whom the governor consulted, Glasscock also chose him, partially fulfilling the demands of southern West Virginia.[40] The final selection was to be a Democrat, the minority member, a selection that involved careful consideration.

As the Democratic member of the Board of Control, Governor Glasscock appointed Professor Thomas E. Hodges of West Virginia University and president of the Bank of Morgantown. With this appointment, Glasscock not only secured someone from Morgantown (he had decided to name an individual from his home community to either the Board of Control or the Board of Regents)[41] but also secured one with a degree of business acumen and experience in education. Judge Cox confided to the governor, "What he lacks in Jew qualifications he will make up in ability to grasp the needs of the State, both educational and otherwise."[42] More importantly, Hodges seemed to be a Democrat who would not play politics with him. Writing to his friend Judge Cox, the governor stated, "he is not only honest, but would be absolutely loyal and true to me."[43] Cox feared, however, that the governor could be placing Hodges in a position where he might try for Glasscock's office in the next election. Having already anticipated that possibility, Glasscock appointed Hodges to the four-year term, which would prevent him from being the Democratic gubernatorial candidate, since the law prohibited members of the board from running for elective office for one year following completion of their term.[44]

Next on the agenda of the governor was the appointment of the five-member Board of Regents, the fifth member being the state superintendent of Free Schools. This board was vested with the power to determine the general educational policies of the university and its preparatory branches at Keyser and Montgomery, the state normal schools, the West Virginia Colored Institute, and the Bluefield Colored Institute.[45] Governor Glasscock had a number of criteria for selecting these individuals, one being to endeavor to distribute the offices equally among the Congressional Districts of the state. He also wanted them to have special knowledge of educational work, to be residents of counties in which no educational institutions were located, and to represent a balance among the major religious denominations of the state. As he explained, "If

40   Isaac T. Mann to Glasscock, 29 March 1909, Glasscock Papers.

41   Glasscock to Frank Cox, 6 March 1909; Frank Cox to Glasscock, 11 March 1909, both in Glasscock Papers.

42   Frank Cox to Glasscock, 17 March 1909, Glasscock Papers.

43   Glasscock to Frank Cox, 15 March 1909, Glasscock Papers.

44   Glasscock to Frank Cox, 15 March 1909, Glasscock Papers.

45   Ambler, *A History of Education*, 390.

I do not do this and my selections would be all Methodists, or all Presbyterians or all Baptists it would be bad for me and for the schools, at least it might be so, and I do not care to take any chances of that kind."[46]

In making appointments to the Board of Regents, Glasscock corresponded closely with several members of the West Virginia University faculty. In particular, he did not want to choose anyone who might not be friendly to its interests. To this end, the governor corresponded with Professor Henry Green, soliciting his opinion of George S. Laidley of the Charleston school system. Glasscock related to Green that he had heard Laidley was "a strong school man" and a graduate of West Virginia University.[47] In reply, Professor Green was unenthusiastic. According to his sources, Laidley, a Democrat, "has manifested little or no interest in its [West Virginia University's] welfare, has been indifferent or worse to its interests." Professor Hodges, a Democrat, and I. C. White also opposed the appointment of Laidley.[48]

Disagreeing with his friends and showing a healthy streak of independence, Glasscock appointed Laidley, stating that he had investigated him carefully "and I do not think there is any one in Charleston who stands higher or who has more friends than Mr. Laidley." He also added that the "Normal School people are not very favorable to his appointment because they think he is friendly to the University."[49] In addition to Laidley, Glasscock's final selections included G. A. Northcott of Huntington; J. B. Finley of Parkersburg; M. C. Lough of Fairmont; M. P. Shawkey of Charleston as president; and P. W. Morris of Parkersburg as secretary.[50]

One would assume that the State Board of Agriculture, with its noble pursuit of agrarian simplicity and abundant productivity, would be the scene of relative calm, but that was not the case. There had been for some time a strained relationship between

46 Glasscock to Henry S. Green, 20 April 1909, Glasscock Papers.

47 Glasscock to Henry S. Green, 20 April 1909, Glasscock Papers.

48 There were a number of problems here. First, there was jealousy between the supporters of the university and those of the state normal schools. Second, there also existed tension between the "old school" educators and those of the "new school." The former believed teachers were born to their profession and emphasized aptitude and scholarship. The latter believed teachers were "made" and concentrated on methods and professional training. The "old school" was on the defensive during this period, hence their fear of "wrong" appointments. See Ambler and Summers, *West Virginia: The Mountain State*, 394; see also Henry S. Green to Glasscock, 24 April 1909; Thomas E. Hodges to Glasscock, 26 April 1909, both in Glasscock Papers.

49 Glasscock to Henry S. Green, 12 May 1909, Glasscock Papers.

50 Glasscock to Thomas E. Hodges, 20 May 1909; Septimius Hall to Glasscock, 22 May 1909, both in Glasscock Papers.

the College of Agriculture and the Experiment Station of West Virginia University and the State Board of Agriculture. The two institutions differed on whether the station, in cooperation with the college, should emphasize the teaching of agriculture on the secondary level and the promotion of farmers' institutes, or whether it should pursue the goals of scientific research and the publication of scientific bulletins.[51] Evidently, this problem, along with personality clashes among some members of the board, caused considerable friction.

According to University President Purinton, board members E. J. Humphrey of Wood County, Abram McCulloch of Ohio County, and W. D. Zinn of Barbour County "Cannot be depended upon to act in harmony with the college of agriculture and the experiment station."[52] R. E. Thrasher of Greenbrier County, also a member of the board, corroborated Purinton's view when he affirmed, "there are three members on the present board that will never cease to nag, and when the opportunity presents its self [sic], stab in the back, our Agricultural College and Experiment Station." Thrasher added that if these individuals were retained "I can much better spend my time at home."[53] H. E. Williams, state highway inspector, who had also been involved with the farmers' institutes, concluded that neither he nor Thrasher would have any desire "to agitate the cause of agricultural development through the Department of Agriculture" if certain members remained.[54]

In an attempt to bring about peace among the different agriculture organizations in the state, Governor Glasscock appointed J. S. Reger of Upshur County, to the State Board of Agriculture, because he had had "no part in past troubles."[55] He also recommended the selection of Reger as president of that body. Perhaps in order to mollify the university, Glasscock appointed T. C. Atkeson of Monongalia County, who had served as the first professor of agriculture at West Virginia University, as well as the first dean of the College of Agriculture.[56] With the placement of D. A. Arnold of Mineral County

51 William D. Barns, *The West Virginia State Grange: The First Century, 1873–1973* (Morgantown: Morgantown Printing and Binding Co., 1973), 109–136. Hereafter cited as Barns, *The West Virginia State Grange*. See also Ambler and Summers, *West Virginia: The Mountain State*, 356.
52 D. B. Purinton to Glasscock, 16 March 1909, Glasscock Papers.
53 R. E. Thrasher to Howard Sutherland, 27 March 1909, Glasscock Papers.
54 H.E. Williams to Glasscock, 31 March 1909, Glasscock Papers.
55 Glasscock to A. B. White, 17 June 1909, Glasscock Papers.
56 Glasscock to Thomas E. Hodges, 20 May, 1909, Glasscock Papers; Charles H. Ambler, *West Virginia Stories and Biographies* (New York: Rand McNally and Co., 1954), 346–47. In brief, the West Virginia Grange supported the teaching of agriculture on the secondary level and the promotion of farmers' institutes. They were often at odds with the scientific community at the

and Archibald Moore of Marion County to the State Board, with Moore serving as president from 1909 to 1913, the task was completed. Glasscock terminated Thrasher and Zinn from the board, but retained Humphrey and McCulloch.[57]

The besieged governor discovered that he not only had to make changes in the area of agriculture but that it was also necessary to clean house in the National Guard, and he was determined to face these unpleasant tasks as soon as possible. Early in his administration, dissension arose in the upper ranks of the National Guard between Adjutant General N. S. Burlew, the state's top military official, and his assistant, Colonel Carleton Pierce of Kingwood. Part of the problem involved the ambitions of Pierce who sought to secure the top post for himself.[58] In addition to his annoyance at the bickering between Burlew and Pierce, Governor Glasscock was displeased with the past performance of the West Virginia National Guard, writing, "the army officers who inspected our guard at the two encampments did not make very favorable reports."[59] The governor was perturbed by the army's report and shared a portion of it, writing that as of October 1, 1909, the guard "had exceeded appropriations up to that time to the amount of $19,000, leaving a balance due out of the 1910 appropriation of over $35,000."[60] With the state's military organization mismanaged, he felt changes were in order.

The governor took swift action. One of the first to go was retired army officer J. M. Burns, a Civil War veteran from Morgantown who had acted as an adviser to the guard. Appointed by Governor Dawson and given permission to remain in Morgantown, Colonel Burns performed his duties to the state militia from his hometown. Glasscock, however, believed that Burns was too old to assist him actively with military matters; he wanted someone who could reside in Charleston and be more accessible to the chief executive. Furthermore, the situation forced Glasscock to spend nearly twice the

---

West Virginia Agricultural Experiment Station. The appointment of Atkeson, a leader of the West Virginia Grange, ensured its influence at the university and on the state board. For this and further information on T. C. Atkeson see Barns, *The West Virginia State Grange*, 79–91.

57 *Messages and Documents, Session of 1913–1915, William E. Glasscock and Henry D. Hatfield,* vol. 1 (Charleston: Tribune Printers Co., 1913–14), 8–9.

58 Glasscock to A. B. White, 1 April 1909; Glasscock to George C. Baker, 31 August 1909; F. K. Bretz to Senator S. B. Elkins, 1 March 1909; Senator Elkins to Glasscock, 1 March 1909, all in Glasscock Papers.

59 Glasscock to George C. Baker, 10 September 1910, Glasscock Papers.

60 Glasscock felt that the state was not getting an adequate return on its money, pointing out that it was spending about $85,000 on the National Guard, of which $55,000 was appropriated by the state legislature and almost $30,000 came from the federal government. See Glasscock to Captain Eaton, 21 October 1910, Glasscock Papers.

amount of time on National Guard matters as on the Board of Control that managed twenty-one institutions.[61]

For political reasons, the firing of the old soldier caused some members of Glasscock's coterie to wonder anxiously if Burns would go peacefully. George Baker of Morgantown warned Glasscock to handle the veteran carefully lest he upset the "old soldiers," who still had "at least forty-five thousand representatives in West Virginia in the shape of sons and grandsons."[62] (Of course, women could not vote at this time.) As feared, Colonel Burns proved stubborn. Blaming Burlew for the trouble in the National Guard, Burns noted ominously, "I have thousands of influential men in the state at my back."[63] Ignoring his threat, Governor Glasscock asked for his resignation from active duty on October 30, 1909.[64] Fraught with political uncertainly, the determined governor had taken an important step toward reorganization of the state's military system. During the summer of 1909, Governor Glasscock concluded that only one man, Captain Harry A. Eaton, commandant at West Virginia University, could bring order to the guard. Eaton had a commendable record at that institution, and, as Glasscock informed Senator Elkins, "He is a West Virginia boy, being a native of Cabell County I believe, a graduate of the University, a good Republican and a very competent officer."[65] The governor wrote to Elkins that he had had nothing but trouble with the guard since his inauguration and that he wanted Captain Eaton of the 23rd Infantry assigned to permanent duty with the state militia. He asked Senator Elkins to do what he could in Washington, and he, as governor, would write to the president and secretary of war about the matter. Although Glasscock and Taft were then on congenial terms, the president would agree only to allow Eaton to serve during summer vacation at the university.[66] Glasscock's subsequent efforts to secure the services of Colonel D. T. E. Casteel also ran into opposition from the War Department and had to be shelved.[67]

61   Glasscock to George C. Baker, 10 September 1909, Glasscock Papers.

62   George C. Baker to Glasscock, 15 January 1910, Glasscock Papers.

63   J. M. Burns to Glasscock, 28 August 1909, Glasscock Papers.

64   Glasscock to Lt. Col. J. M. Burns, 30 October 1909, Glasscock Papers.

65   Glasscock to Senator S. B. Elkins, 13 July 1909, Stephen B. Elkins Papers.

66   Glasscock to Taft, 2 September 1909; Glasscock to Secretary of War O. M. Dickinson, 9 September 1909; Dickinson to Glasscock, 20 September 1909; Harry Eaton to Glasscock, 5 January 1910, all in Glasscock Papers.

67   D. T. E. Casteel to Glasscock, 1 August 1909; Glasscock to L. H. Landsittel, 11 September 1909, both in Glasscock Papers; see also Ambler and Summers West Virginia: The Mountain State, 523.

Relations between Burlew and Pierce worsened during the summer of 1909 while Glasscock was away visiting the Seattle Exposition. Apparently acting with the prior agreement of the traveling governor, Captain Eaton, on temporary assignment with the Guard,[68] issued general orders 25, 44, and 45, which in short were to say, "Pierce is out."[69] Pierce, however, was determined to remain, and according to Glasscock's private secretary, E. L. Boggs, made "vicious threats as to Burlew and myself," indicating that he would bring charges against the adjutant general. The situation was further complicated when General Burlew attempted to leak the news of Pierce's firing to the press before Pierce himself had been informed. According to Boggs:

> I told Burlew it was a grave mistake in his doing so but it seems Burlew doesn't know any better. He came mighty near getting a lot of stuff in Tuesday's paper and would have done so had we not cut it out just in time—He doesn't appear to have any sense or judgement and doesn't know what discretion is. I am working overtime in my endeavor to secure his resignation and hope to succeed.[70]

True to his word, Pierce attempted to bring charges against Burlew. He accused the Adjutant General "of incompetence, neglect of duty, disobedience of orders and probably of gross immorality." Ruling out a court martial, Pierce suggested, "that a commission be appointed to hear the charges and determine the matter, two of the commissioners to be selected by General Burlew, two by myself and they then select the fifth." He further informed Glasscock that he could not retain his "self respect and remain silent under the indignities that have been heaped on me as the result of this man's activities, although he was no doubt aided and abetted by others who have been advising you wrongly as you will later find out."[71]

Governor Glasscock's response was simply to acknowledge Pierce's charges and to state that he would "take such action in regard to the same as in my judgement shall seem best for the State of West Virginia and the National Guard."[72] The governor took

68   E. L. Boggs to Glasscock, 23 July 1909, Glasscock Papers.
69   This action was no surprise, since the Governor had previously stated to Senator Elkins that he was determined to let Pierce go, because he had "violated" his (Glasscock's) expressed orders. See Glasscock to Senator Elkins, 13 July 1909, Glasscock Papers.
70   E. L. Boggs to Glasscock, 29 July 1909, Glasscock Papers.
71   Carleton Pierce to Glasscock, 21 August 1909, Glasscock Papers.
72   Glasscock to Col. C. C. Pierce, 21 August 1909, Glasscock Papers.

no further action, and after tempers cooled, Pierce dropped the matter. Succumbing to administration pressure, Adjutant General Burlew resigned on December 23, 1909.[73] Avoiding a potential scandal for the National Guard and, perhaps, fodder for the state's newspapers, Glasscock and Boggs handled the situation discreetly and deftly.

It was not until January 1910 that Glasscock found an adjutant general. In selecting Major C. D. Elliott of Parkersburg, United States Marshall of the Northern District of West Virginia, the governor secured a West Virginian who could take control of the guard and make it a viable organization. Elliott was an experienced military man who had served as a major of the Third Battalion, Second West Virginia Volunteers in the Spanish-American War. He had also been a secret service operative, a special guard of Theodore Roosevelt at the White House, and a "political lieutenant under Senator Stephen B. Elkins."[74]

As it turned out, Adjutant General Elliott proved to be a man of initiative as well as one knowledgeable in military affairs. Elliott also had an eager assistant in the person of Captain J. I. Pratt. The governor turned to these men on numerous occasions, especially during the violent mine strikes of 1912–1913. Eventually, Elliott became not only an astute military adviser to the governor, but also a friend and political confidant.[75] Elliott, perhaps an opportunist, could just as easily work for the conservatives as with the reformers.[76]

Concluding the first round of stressful state appointments and dismissals, the chief executive enjoyed a short respite at Hot Springs, Virginia, suffering from what he described as something like "ptomaine poisoning."[77] Of course, not all political appointments led to mental anguish and worry. Indeed, whenever he could, Governor Glasscock was pleased to help a friend from his hometown of Morgantown. He was particularly interested in boosting the career of his close friend M. L. Brown, cashier of the Bank of Morgantown. During the 1910 mid-term elections, Glasscock considered Brown a good state senatorial candidate from his home district, the Eleventh, but Brown refused, speculating that it would be a close race and would possibly hurt his position at the bank. During the summer of 1910, perhaps while at Morgantown attending his

73 Glasscock to Gen. Burlew, 23 December 1909, Glasscock Papers.

74 George W. Summers, *Pages from the Past* (Charleston Journal, 1935), 41–42; Glasscock to Senator N. B. Scott, 13 January 1910, Glasscock Papers; *Wheeling Register*, January 3, 1910.

75 Glasscock to Senator Scott, 13 January 1910, Glasscock Papers.

76 Williams, *West Virginia and the Captains of Industry*, 129.

77 Glasscock to Henry S. Green, 23 November 1909, Glasscock Papers.

father's funeral in July, the governor proffered Brown the position of warden at the Moundsville Penitentiary. In August, Brown accepted.[78]

The operation of the penitentiary had been controversial for some time.[79] An investigation by a committee of the 1909 Legislature criticized the actions of acting-Warden C. G. Dawson and some of the directors for misuse of funds. Governor Dawson, in the meantime, appointed J. E. Matthews as the new warden. Little did he know that he had appointed a man who would provoke Glasscock. An informer from Marshall County wrote to the governor that his political opponents were "now endeavoring to control the politics of this county and it is not fair that the State Prison be run any longer by that element."[80] Glasscock had been aware of the problems for some time. Before his inauguration, the governor-elect had privately sought the opinion of "reliable" sources at Moundsville concerning the penitentiary. E. M. Lewis of Moundsville noted several questionable practices at that institution and made the following observations: too much secrecy in holding meetings of the board of directors, contractors given favors with "pen" labor, poor hiring practices of guards, patronage used to promote the financial and political interests of officials of the prison, and questionable procedures in the matter of paroles and pardons.[81] In addition, ex-Governor White had also written, "that pen crowd needs a thorough purging from all I can learn."[82]

During the early phase of his administration, Governor Glasscock watched the developments at the state jail closely,[83] particularly the actions of Warden Joseph Matthews, with whom he was displeased. Seeing no improvements by the summer of 1910, Glasscock approached Brown concerning the position. The political wheels were turning and the activist governor, as he had promised, was determined to open the various state institutions to public scrutiny.

As Glasscock developed the case of "misbehavior" against Warden Matthews, he brought into his confidence two employees of the penitentiary.[84] Upon learning that they had been informing against him, Matthews dismissed the two men. By September, the

---

78 M. L. Brown to Glasscock, 14 August 1910, Glasscock Papers.

79 *Morgantown Post-Chronicle*, January 22, 1909; February 19, 1909; *Wheeling Register*, February 21, 1909.

80 J. A. Sammons to Glasscock, 20 November 1909, Glasscock Papers.

81 E. M. Lewis to Glasscock, 17 December 1908, Glasscock Papers.

82 A. B. White to Glasscock, 18 January 1909, Glasscock Papers.

83 Glasscock to Albert S. Winter, 25 August 1910, Glasscock Papers.

84 Glasscock referred to these employees as March and Howard. See Glasscock to M. L. Brown, 21 November 1910, Glasscock Papers.

governor and the warden had reached an agreement that the latter would resign quietly. When Matthews did not announce his resignation on the appointed date, Governor Glasscock felt it necessary to take action.[85] While recuperating from an illness at Hot Springs, Virginia, the governor wrote to a friend that he could state "that the Warden will retire from his present position within the next month or so. The understanding was that he was to make this announcement last week, and if he has not done so I shall consider it incumbent on me to make it."[86] In November 1910, Brown became the Moundsville Penitentiary warden.[87]

Governor Glasscock lauded Brown's ability and predicted success for him in his new position; perhaps thinking of his own recent experiences, he warned him of the difficulty that lay ahead:

> I have great hopes my boy that you can make a record at Moundsville of which all the people of the State will be proud. I think you can not only be of great service to the State but you can be likewise very beneficial to the party. It may be that you will have to have a thorough cleaning out up there, and if so, I want you to do it early in your administration and have the fight over. It is going to take backbone and I think you have it. If you have not you had better decline the position even at this late date. Don't get discouraged when I talk about 'backbone' but I mean what I say and I have every confidence in the world that you will meet the situation.[88]

Glasscock later felt vindicated in replacing Matthews when the outgoing Warden admitted his mistakes to Brown, but contended it "was a mere difference in moral standards" between the governor and himself.[89] Glasscock wrote to Brown, "If I ever had any doubt about having done the right thing in dismissing Matthews that doubt has been dispelled by what he said to you."[90]

---

85 *Wheeling Intelligencer*, November 17, 1910.

86 Glasscock to Charley Ellison, 15 September 1910, Glasscock Papers.

87 Brown wrote his friend, the governor, of his warm gratitude, explaining that "your acts of helpfulness and expressions of confidence have been chief factors in whatever success that has come to me." See M. L. Brown to Glasscock, 17 November 1910, Glasscock Papers.

88 M. L. Brown to Glasscock, 21 November 1910, Glasscock Papers; see also Glasscock to M. L. Brown, 27 December 1910, Glasscock Papers.

89 M. L. Brown to Glasscock, 26 December 1910, Glasscock Papers.

90 Glssscock to M. L. Brown, 27 December 1910, Glasscock Papers.

It was not only the state offices that bedeviled Glasscock but also federal appointments, from which he attempted to remain aloof "because I have all I can do here in Charleston."[91] A rather interesting episode unfolded between Glasscock and former Governor White, who was very active in trying to secure Glasscock's former position of the Collectorship of the Internal Revenue Office for the State of West Virginia at Parkersburg for his brother William. William White wrote a revealing letter to Glasscock, explaining his urgent reasons for wanting the position:

> I do feel … that this is my last opportunity, and if I fail to get the Collectorship this time, there is nothing for me in politics in West Virginia, and I might just as well quit, because I realize that merit and qualification and attention to duties do not amount to a 'hill of beans'; that it is simply pull with the U.S. Senators, and the fellow who has the longest pull and the biggest influence 'knocks the persimmon!'[92]

In this instance, Senator Elkins made the final decision, choosing George Work of Sistersville, a popular selection with H. C. Ogden, editor of the *Wheeling Intelligencer* and a man of political force in that part of the state.[93] Former Governor White was unhappy with the outcome and wrote to Glasscock a final word on the subject:

> I think I can appreciate your position; but so far as Collector is concerned you are dead wrong. But we will not quarrel over it. I have no favors to ask; but I do expect to be in the political game from now on as a free American citizen, and will cheerfully aid, as far as practicable, when called upon.[94]

Not all appointments created tension. For example, when the governor learned that Dr. D. B. Purinton was on the verge of retirement as president of West Virginia University,[95] Glasscock began the careful and enjoyable process of selecting a replacement. After all, this appointment involved his beloved school, his hometown, and, of

---

91 Glasscock to S. F. Glasscock, 1 April 1909, Glasscock Papers.
92 W. E. White to Glasscock, 16 November 1908, Glasscock Papers.
93 Senator S. B. Elkins to Glasscock, 19 December 1908, Glasscock Papers.
94 A. B. White to Glasscock, 8 December 1908, Glasscock Papers.
95 On June 15, 1910, Purinton announced that he would retire on July 31, 1911, reportedly "owing largely to his wife's health." See M. L. Brown to Glasscock, 6 June 1910, Glasscock Papers; *Morgantown Post-Chronicle*, June 15, 1910.

course, the "boys" in Morgantown. The university had had its difficulties in becoming an institution of higher learning. There had been debates over curriculum, administration procedures, religion, and politics in general.[96] The period following the Civil War had been a time of change and growth, creating dissension over school affairs. Governor Glasscock was mindful of the difficulties that had beset the university, as he was an alumnus and a life-long resident of the area. Therefore, he was cautious in suggesting a successor to the Board of Regents.

State Senator Joseph McDermott was one of the first to suggest to the governor a possible replacement for the office. His choice was former Governor White, who should, he thought, be paid $6,000 a year. In the event that White was not acceptable "[Dr. Thomas E.] Hodges would be a great improvement on Purinton, in fact Hodges would be a first class man, but I favor getting a little further away from any one church, we have had too much religion mixed up with the University management." McDermott added, "the University belongs to all the churches and all the people," and he cautioned not to "act in haste and select some unknown carpetbager [sic], get a big man and pay a big salary."[97]

Since former Governor White had already informed the governor that he did not want the position, Glasscock could consider Hodges, who seemed the popular choice for the job.[98] Yet the selection of Hodges had its drawbacks too. Senator Elkins believed that the office belonged to the Republican Party, and Hodges was a Democrat. Still, the senator was willing to endorse him if the Republicans lacked a "suitable man."[99]

By August 1910, the governor was fully convinced that the Morgantown professor was the right person, as he explained to former Governor White, "Confidentially, I believe the Board of Regents will select Hodges for President of the University, and

96   At the university, following the Civil War, pro-Northerners and pro-Southerners could not agree on what direction the school should take. The former group favored co-education, retention of the Preparatory Department, rigid discipline, and a prescribed curriculum. In general, these were all opposed by the latter group. See Ambler and Summers, *West Virginia: The Mountain State*, 311–12.

97   In the beginning, some felt the Republican Party and the Methodist Episcopal Church were too well represented at the University. Under the presidency of Jerome Hall Raymond (1897–1901), dissension over his "appalling Puritanism" led to his forced retirement, thus McDermott's concern over alleged church affiliation. See Joseph H. McDermott to Glasscock, 3 June 1910, Glasscock Papers; Ambler and Summers, *West Virginia: The Mountain State*, 313–14.

98   Glasscock to Joseph H. McDermott, 6 June 1910, Glasscock Papers.

99   Senator S. B. Elkins to Glasscock, 20 September 1910; Glasscock to Elkins, 30 August 1910, both in Glasscock Papers.

as it now stands, I think he is the best man for the job."[100] Glasscock's friend, M. L. Brown, concurred, pointing to Hodges's "strong character, his great capacity for work and his tremendous enthusiasm."[101] Thus the Board of Regents, certainly acting under the influence of the governor, selected Thomas E. Hodges, a Democrat, as president of West Virginia University in September 1910. After the announcement, a small banquet attended by his close friends was given in his honor at Morgantown. At the banquet, Hodges stated that the position would be a full time job and he would never resign it "to accept any political office, if any such should be offered him." He would find that promise difficult to keep, especially after conflicts with the State Board of Regents over entrance requirements. Honored with a brief appearance by President Taft, Hodges was installed as president in November 1911.[102] Glasscock must have felt a sense of pride as he later conducted the installation, since he was a former student. He must have also been pleased because he had been in a position to help one of the "Morgantown boys."[103]

Relieved of the tedious but necessary duty of making official appointments, Governor Glasscock could concentrate on the process of obtaining his goals and those of his successors to create a more smoothly run government. The governor was open-minded and made his selections carefully and deliberately, seeking the advice of those interested in state affairs. He attempted to distribute the offices geographically, always seeking the advice and consent of the party leaders in those areas. Glasscock was also very cautious in selecting candidates for positions concerning education,

---

100 Glasscock to A. B. White, 15 August 1910, Glasscock Papers.

101 M. L. Brown to Glasscock, 6 June 1910; M. L. Brown to Glasscock, 25 September 1910, both in Glasscock Papers.

102 Student activities would move smoothly under President Hodges, and policy-determining powers were restored to the faculty. There would be difficulty, however, between Hodges and Superintendent Shawkey, president of the State Board of Regents, and the so-called "new school educators" over entrance requirements at the University, which President Hodges would refuse to lower. Perhaps because of this fact, Hodges would resign his position in 1914, as he said he would not do, to accept the nomination of the Democratic Party as its candidate-at-large from West Virginia. Hodges would be unsuccessful in his bid for the congressional seat. Dean Frank B. Trotter of the College of Arts and Sciences would be appointed acting president; later he would be installed as president. See Ambler, *A History of Education*, 507 and 510; Ambler and Summers, *West Virginia: The Mountain State*, 416; *Wheeling Intelligencer*, November 2, 1911.

103 While President Taft was present at Hodges' installation ceremonies, Governor Glasscock suggested to him the possible appointment of Judge Frank Cox of Morgantown to the Supreme Court of the United States. See Glasscock to Taft, 11 December 1911, Glasscock Papers; see also *Wheeling Intelligencer*, November 4, 1911.

making sure none would harm the welfare of his alma mater, West Virginia University. Overall, however, his Morgantown friends carried much weight with the governor and he sought to aid them, whenever practical, by his favors and actions. Although, Glasscock thought it the best system of securing proven talent, the exigencies of the moment often called for highly partisan considerations, sometimes sacrificing ability for personal and political considerations. The governor was independent-minded, but he was also careful not to agitate the powerful United States Senator Elkins, who kept a watchful eye on Glasscock's actions. In an attempt to assuage the concerns of Elkins, the governor explained, "In making appointments I must use my best judgement and I do not believe you can find a single appointee who is unfriendly to you."[104] The problem was not only finding good men but also selecting individuals who were acceptable to the party leaders in order to prevent further discord.

104 Glasscock to Senator Elkins, 27 April 1909, Elkins Papers.

THE 1910 CRASH OF THE
REPUBLICAN PARTY

" . . . truth crushed to earth will rise again."[1]

F OLLOWING THE ADJOURNMENT of the Dawson legislature, Governor Glasscock
toyed with the idea of calling an extra session and considered suggesting to
the lawmakers a county local option law, a gas production tax, and a public
service commission. After much deliberation, however, he concluded that it would be
better to wait for the regular session, as the mood of the people was not conducive to
additional legislative action at that time. He further reasoned that failure to pass the
above laws would "stand out as a monument to our weakness and put us in a worse
position than we are now."[2]

Deciding to wait until 1911, when the legislators would meet again, the governor
laid plans for the election of 1910. He had two goals: to educate the public about the
need for reform legislation and to secure the nominations of those candidates who
would represent his views in Charleston. With the first goal in mind, Glasscock spoke
out strongly in support of a production tax on gas during the summer of 1909.

In his attempt to stimulate interest in the proposal, Governor Glasscock relied
upon the expertise of West Virginia State Geologist, Dr. I. C. White, who had informed
the public in 1908 that as much as two hundred fifty million cubic feet of natural gas
within the state was escaping daily into the air, wasted. This was the equivalent of ten
thousand tons of coal.[3] At a Board of Trade meeting in Huntington during the fall
of 1909, the governor also presented an elaborate compilation of data to support his
view that West Virginians were not receiving a fair return on this valuable natural

1 Glasscock to J. O. Henson, 14 November 1910, Glasscock Papers.
2 Glasscock to W. P. Hawley, 17 December 1909, Glasscock Papers.
3 Ambler and Summers, *West Virginia: The Mountain State*, 466.

resource, used mainly outside the state. The figures to which he referred showed the value of the state's total production of natural gas consumed within the state, the value of the production used outside its borders, and the relative percentage of each to the total production:[4]

Year	Value of Gas Consumed Within State	Value of Gas Consumed Outside State	Percent of Gas Consumed Within State	Percent of Gas Consumed Outside State
1897	$791,192	$121,336	87	13
1898	914,969	419,054	69	31
1899	1,310,675	1,025,189	56	44
1900	1,530,378	1,428,664	52	48
1901	2,244,758	1,709,714	57	43
1902	2,473,174	2,917,007	46	54
1903	3,125,061	3,757,298	45	55
1904	3,383,515	4,730,734	42	58
1905	3,586,608	6,489,196	36	64
1906	3,720,440	10,014,903	27	73
1907	3,757,977	12,913,185	23	77

Earlier, many West Virginians had hoped that the abundance of the state's natural resources would provide employment for its people. Governor Glasscock himself firmly believed that the state's leaders should push the Mountain State to go into the manufacturing business and to "work up its raw material."[5] Senator Elkins was in accord with this line of thought and felt that it was unfortunate that nothing could keep the owner of the natural gas from sending it out of the state. As Elkins observed to Glasscock, "This deprives us of a great source of wealth, because natural gas is the finest fuel in the world."[6] The senator concluded that the best alternative was to impose a production tax.

4   *Charleston Daily Mail*, October 13, 1909; William E. Glasscock, *Speech Delivered by Governor Glasscock, before the State Board of Trade, Huntington, West Virginia, October 12, 1909* (Charleston: Union Typographical Label, n. d.), 7–8.
5   *Charleston Daily Mail*, October 9, 1909.
6   Senator S. B. Elkins to Glasscock, 28 August 1909, Elkins Papers.

In calculating the advantages of such a levy, Governor Glasscock estimated that a tax of half a cent on a thousand cubic feet would produce annual revenue of $600,000, and a tax of one cent would net the state more than $1,000,000. He concluded that the price of the fuel would increase, "but we must not forget that probably three-fourths of the gas produced is piped out of the State so that the people of West Virginia would have to pay only a small part of it."[7] Another benefit would be the possible reduction of other state taxes.

Although the governor and the senator agreed upon the need for such legislation, Elkins was more cautious in his views on taxation lest the state frighten off prospective investors, "I know there are millions of dollars waiting for investment in the state if the parties can have assurance against over taxation." He added, "I know further that there are five hundred miles of railroads ready to be built, depending upon the question of taxation and the attitude of your administration and the Republican party towards railroads and capital seeking investment."[8] The senator, taking the businessman-politician attitude, figured that a *moderate* tax should bring the state $300,000 to $400,000 in revenues.[9]

After hearing the public and private debates concerning the gas question, Glasscock decided to act affirmatively, if necessary, "by making a gentleman's agreement" with the gas producers not to increase the levy in the future.[10] In the legislatures of 1911 and 1913, the governor would call for a half-cent tax (as Elkins had suggested) on a thousand cubic feet of gas produced. Although this figure was more in line with the conservative-minded business interests within the state, Glasscock failed in both attempts to obtain its passage, but he did use the support of a gas tax as a type of litmus test for prospective Republican candidates for the election of 1910.

In the early part of 1910, the governor had occasion to agitate for another piece of legislation: a public service commission. A number of West Virginia shippers, headed by the Fairmont Coal Company, charged that the B&O Railroad had deliberately allowed its track and equipment to deteriorate in the Mountain State because the Pennsylvania Railroad, together with the Harriman interests, owned forty percent of its stock.[11] The shippers stated that the Pennsylvania Railroad served Pennsylvania coal interests and in some places competed with the B&O for coal shipments. They alleged that the two

7   Glasscock to Senator S. B. Elkins, 31 August 1909, Elkins Papers.
8   Senator S. B. Elkins to Glasscock, 29 September 1909, Elkins Papers.
9   Senator S. B. Elkins to Glasscock, 28 August 1909, Elkins Papers.
10 Glasscock to Senator S. B. Elkins, 31 August 1909, Elkins Papers.
11 *Wheeling Register*, January 10, 1910; January 11, 1910.

railroads had made an agreement to let the B&O fall into disrepair. The shippers called for an investigation, to which the governor agreed.

Glasscock turned the matter over to his attorney general, William G. Conley, along with information that the B&O's "motive power, rolling stock, and possibly its roadbed" had been allowed to deteriorate so badly that the railroad could handle less than half the freight offered by its customers along its line. In addition, the governor pointed out that by October 1909 the B&O's tidewater shipments of coal had decreased 30.9% in comparison with shipments in 1908. On the other hand, the C&O Railroad had increased its tidewater business by 41.1% during the same period. Using another comparison, Glasscock also informed Conley that the Western Maryland Railroad, recently in the hands of receivers and with little roadbed or trackage, was better equipped for handling traffic than the Baltimore and Ohio Railroad.[12]

In the end, publicity resulting from the investigation led top officials of the B&O to admit that there was some cause for complaint. The railroad promised the addition of more locomotives and other improvements to handle 50% more business. The management stated that the problem was twofold: (1) the builders of locomotives failed to deliver the machinery when agreed upon; and (2) the coal companies failed to make contracts for delivery when the coal could be transported.[13] Nevertheless, the mere fact that the governor was willing to bring the problem to the attention of the public elicited a favorable response from the railroad.

Convinced that conditions on the railroad would improve and pleased that his administration had not overreacted,[14] Glasscock, in a typical progressive manner, used the episode to educate the people about the need for a public service commission. In an interview with the Wheeling Register, he pointed out the merits of House Bill 312, which had failed to become law in the previous session of the legislature. The bill would have created a public service commission with the power to compel any person, firm, or corporation engaged in public business in the state "to establish and maintain adequate and suitable facilities for performing such service."[15] The exigencies of the twentieth century demanded more than just promises from corporation officials to improve their operations. Reformers sought to eliminate chaos and cutthroat competition through legislative law and the creation of regulatory agencies.

12   Glasscock to Senator S. B. Elkins, 31 August 1909, Elkins Papers.
13   Charleston Gazette, January 12, 1910; Malcomson, "William E. Glasscock," 29.
14   Glasscock to John W. Mason, 3 February 1910, Glasscock Papers.
15   Wheeling Register, January 10, 1910.

With the election of 1910 in mind, Glasscock's attention turned to state politics in preparation of the laborious process of making nominations to the legislature. He anticipated that old party wounds had still not healed and that the former factions were active. Acknowledging these differences, the governor carefully divided appointments to various state positions among the factions in order to please as many party members as possible. In the case of his military staff, which performed ceremonial duties without recompense, he was reminded of the lingering factional tensions. For example, State Senator Joseph McDermott, a party "regular," refused the appointment because he would have to associate with George C. Baker, an "insurgent" who had supported Arnold C. Scherr in the 1908 gubernatorial campaign.[16]

Bitter feelings also ran deep among West Virginia's Congressional delegation. On one occasion in March 1909, Glasscock, along with the Mountain State's senators and congressmen, had an interview with President Taft to discuss appointments and local politics. Representatives George C. Sturgiss of Morgantown and William P. Hubbard of Wheeling, both progressives, later expressed to Governor Glasscock their desire to meet again with the governor and the president, but without the conservative Senators Elkins and Scott. Sturgiss told Glasscock that he had approached Taft concerning such a meeting, and the president stated that the governor did not need the assistance of "Smoothe Steve" or "Blustering Scotty" to make an appointment with him. Congressman Sturgiss added, however, that Taft could not break with the senators at that point in his administration "as he needs their help in the confirmation of his nominees."[17]

Maneuvering for political power clearly signaled that there was a definite lack of party harmony among the Republicans at state and national levels. To add fuel to the volatile situation, many conservatives suspected Governor Glasscock of encouraging the progressives in their efforts to weaken the influence of the party "regulars." It appeared likely that the 1908 gubernatorial compromise had solved nothing, and the behind-the-scenes machinations of the factions indicated trouble ahead, particularly for the 1910 election.

The year 1910 would prove to be a difficult time for Governor Glasscock and the Republican Party, starting with troubles within his administration, political factions within the party, and ill health. During the winter, newspapers alleged that T. C. Townsend, the state tax commissioner, had taken a legal case outside his official duties and had accepted a bribe. There was a clamor in the press and many Republicans,

---

16   Joseph H. McDermott to Glasscock, 20 May 1909, Glasscock Papers.
17   Congressman George Sturgiss to Glasscock, 27 March 1909, Glasscock Papers.

including Senator Nathan B. Scott, urged the governor to release Townsend.[18] After all, it was an election year. Nevertheless, the report of a committee appointed by the Kanawha County Bar Association concluded that while the tax commissioner had not been very prudent in his actions, he could not be charged with gross unprofessional behavior. The committee recommended no further action.[19] Glasscock struggled with the Townsend matter because the commissioner was a young man with a wife and two children, and he had made his own way in the world. The governor explained, "When he [Townsend] was a boy, only four years old, his father and mother parted, and he never knew what it was to have a home until he married and had a home of his own. He deserves a very great deal of credit for what he has made of himself."[20]

Governor Glasscock decided to let Townsend serve the remainder of his term, later appointing Fred O. Blue to that office in November 1910. Before making the decision to retain Townsend, Glasscock, by his own admission, worried himself sick over the affair. By March 9, 1910, the governor's private secretary was handling the mail, explaining that the chief executive was ill and had "not been able to leave his room for a week past."[21] At the invitation of his friend Dr. L. V. Guthrie of the West Virginia Asylum in Huntington, who had also treated Glasscock medically, the governor vacationed in Roseland, Florida for an extended period. While in Florida recuperating from his attack of rheumatism, Glasscock fell in love with the water. He wrote:

> The fishing there is fine, and I spent every day on the water boating and fishing, and never had such an appetite in my life—at least not since I was a boy. I am going to make a great effort now to take care of myself and not get into that condition any more—in fact I would be afraid to ever allow myself to get run down as I was before I left.[22]

---

18   U.S. Senator Nathan B. Scott to Glasscock, 14 February 1910; M. L. Brown to Glasscock, 5 April 1910, both in Glasscock Papers. See also *Charleston Gazette*, March 3, 1910 and *Wheeling Intelligencer*, March 3, 1910.

19   Glasscock to Messrs. Craig & Wolverton, 5 April 1910, Glasscock Papers.

20   Glasscock to John W. Mason, 9 April 1910, Glasscock Papers. Townsend eventually served as Prosecuting attorney for Kanawha County, issuing many of the John Doe warrants during the 1912–1913 labor conflict on Paint and Cabin Creeks. He became a strong supporter of labor and in 1932 Townsend ran unsuccessfully as the Republican gubernatorial candidate defeated by Herman Guy Kump. See C. Belmont Keeney, "A Republican for Labor: T. C. Townsend and the West Virginia Labor Movement, 1921–1932," *West Virginia History* 60 (2002–2006): 1–18.

21   E. L. Boggs to J. W. Dawson, 9 March 1910, Glasscock Papers.

22   Glasscock to M. L. Brown, 2 April 1910, Glasscock Papers.

The governor spent most of March 1909 in Florida, where he expressed the desire that if he were out of office he would "take a vacation for a year and do nothing but fish and boat ride."[23] In reviewing his period of illness, Glasscock stated that he had never been more discouraged in his life, "but I feel first rate now, and I am going to try my best to keep in my present condition." Concerned over the governor's health, M. L. Brown wrote Glasscock's private secretary that a man of the governor's temperament "should not use tobacco at all, and yet he seems to be using it excessively."[24] Glasscock, though, admitted his worst problem when he wrote to former state Senator Joseph McDermott, who had also been seriously ill:

> You want to cheer up now and not allow things to worry you as I do. In fact it was worry that made me sick and I am afraid you are taking things too seriously. As Swisher and Matthews say you must observe 'Rule Seven,' that is, not to take yourself too serious. I think of that often and am trying my best to observe the rule, and I want to recommend its observance to you.[25]

After Glasscock's return from Florida, his friend, Attorney George C. Baker, commented that the governor's handwriting indicated that his health had improved. He also informed Glasscock "your friends here are all anxious that you hold your holts physically, but you can not do this by constant worry and anxiety over details of state affairs when your subordinates must make good or get off the 'perch.'"[26] Nearly all who knew him agreed that Governor Glasscock carried his worries too far, which affected him physically; but after his latest illness, the governor resolved to do all in his power to maintain his quality of life. In order to function as the head of government in Charleston, Glasscock relied even more heavily on the support of his family, his religion, and acknowledgement that periodic respites from official duties were necessary to maintain his delicate health. The recognition of his physical disabilities and the necessity to compensate for them carried the governor through the end of his administration.

On January 10, 1910, Congressman William P. Hubbard announced that he would challenge U.S. Senator Scott's reelection in the legislature of 1911. Declaring that

23 Glasscock to M. L. Brown, 2 April 1910, Glasscock Papers.
24 M. L. Brown to E. L. Boggs, 12 April 1910, Glasscock Papers.
25 Glasscock to Joseph H. McDermott, 2 April 1910, Glasscock Papers.
26 George C. Baker to Glasscock, 8 April 1910, Elkins Papers.

prominent state Republicans had urged his candidacy, Hubbard called for members of the GOP to support him while denying any intention of rupturing the party, "Any one having the constitutional qualifications may aspire to it, without becoming factional, and may obtain it, if the people so will, even though some persons may not approve."[27] The senatorial aspirant also called for a practical primary system by which the voice of the people could be heard:

> A primary held in a county will give every voter equal right and power, and a primary held throughout a senatorial district will do the like, and will also prevent the smothering of Republican votes in the smaller counties of the district in selecting a nominee.[28]

While Hubbard and Scott were both wealthy Civil War veterans who resided in Wheeling, they were completely different in political philosophy. Hubbard received support from politicians such as former Governor Dawson and many individuals from the old Scherr faction. The congressman had aligned himself with the "insurgents" in the 1908 gubernatorial campaign in support of Arnold C. Scherr, and in general, he was progressive in political philosophy.

For a number of years, Hubbard had called for party reforms including the removal of federal and state officeholders from the Republican State Committee, an action that did not endear him to his conservative cohorts.[29] As it stood, Congressman Hubbard agreed with many of his fellow reformers that Senator Nathan Scott was "a back number and of little use to our party, as he has served his time and like everything else he had to go."[30]

On the other hand, Scott was a conservative, or "regular," Republican. He had close ties to Senator Elkins and was a supporter of the party machinery and the strong tariff policies of traditional Republicanism. The senator believed that the industrial growth of the nation and of West Virginia depended on protective tariff, and he planned to continue such programs if elected to a third term in the U.S. Senate.[31]

----

27 *Charleston Gazette*, January 19, 1910.
28 *Charleston Gazette*, January 19, 1910.
29 W. P. Hubbard to Glasscock, 5 May 1910, Glasscock Papers; *Morgantown Post-Chronicle*, May 9, 1910.
30 George C. Baker to Glasscock, 19 January 1910, Glasscock Papers.
31 Senator Nathan B. Scott to Glasscock, 17 September 1910, Glasscock Papers.

Actually, neither of the two senators desired a break from the traditional Republican Party stand on a protective tariff for personal business reasons and national economic policies. Scott, however, was a "stand-patter" and had no desire to see big changes in the status quo.

Fearing further divisions among the state's Republicans, the governor refused to endorse publicly either Congressman Hubbard or Senator Scott. It was difficult, however, not to offend one candidate or the other as the campaign progressed. The first and probably the most important election took place in Ohio County. As the home county of both contenders, the results were sure to influence other elections. The outcome was also significant since it was the first time that West Virginia voters had been able to choose a nominee for the U.S. Senate in a primary election by instructing their legislators on the senatorial vote.[32]

On May 20, 1910, the Republicans of Ohio County selected Senator Scott by a large majority.[33] On the following day, Kanawha County Republicans strongly voted for Congressman Hubbard, causing Scott's supporters to allege that former Governor Dawson was in control of the county committee through Sheriff Press Smith, a member of that body. When the committee decided not to place the names of the two United States senatorial candidates on the ballot, avoiding instruction of the legislators, Senator Scott was angry, having "failed to nominate a single man for office."[34]

An embittered Senator Scott blamed his Kanawha County defeat partially on Governor Glasscock's inaction and partially on former Governor Dawson's control of the election officials. Scott sent a heated letter to Glasscock in which he complained that a word from the governor would have discouraged the committee from setting up "the contemptible job" that they did. Scott closed with the following threat:

> . . . I do know this, Governor, that a great many of you are much younger men than I am and will want to remain in politics after I have been defeated or elected or have quit politics; but never, as long as I have life in me or a dollar in the world, will I hesitate to punish those who are trying to disrupt the party for purely personal and selfish motives.[35]

32 *Charleston Gazette*, May 21, 1910; *Morgantown Post-Chronicle*, May 20, 1910; May 21, 1910.
33 *Charleston Gazette*, May 21, 1910; Senator Scott won by over 1,000 votes, which was considered a substantial victory.
34 *Charleston Gazette*, May 22, 1910.
35 Senator Scott to Glasscock, 20 April 1910, Glasscock Papers.

Glasscock quickly replied to Scott's charges, informing the senator that he was not afraid of him or his money and that he should get his facts straight before making threats. While admitting that he had indeed become involved, the governor insisted that he had pleaded with those members in control of the Kanawha County Committee to add the names of the U.S. senatorial candidates to the ballot, but to no avail. Despite his urgings, "these people" had ignored his pleas for an open and complete primary. In conclusion, Governor Glasscock reminded Senator Scott:

> . . . it might be well for you to remember that in 1904 and 1908, when the party was having as serious troubles as it is now going through, some of us were here standing at our post of duty and doing all we could to prevent disruption when you were not within the borders of the State. I do not like to say these things, and neither do I like to be accused of trying to disrupt the party that I love just as well as you do.[36]

By the end of May, Blustering Scotty's temper mellowed, as he could count on the pledge of twenty-five legislators to Hubbard's seven.[37] As the nomination again appeared to be his, a jubilant Senator Scott was particularly pleased that he had won in Monongalia County, where he had expected difficulty. In a more congenial letter to the governor, but perhaps still unable to resist having the last word, he reminded Glasscock, "You told me once I could not carry your good old county. I fear you will have to correct your 'thinker,' governor."[38]

Although Glasscock generally attempted to maintain a low profile during the nominations, he discreetly encouraged the candidacy of certain men who supported his legislative proposals and the Republican state platform of 1908.[39] He especially watched the political situation in his home county, Monongalia. The governor tried to persuade Henry S. Green, a member of the university faculty and editor of the *Morgantown Post-Chronicle*, to run for the House of Delegates. Glasscock reasoned that the editor could be a service to the state not only as a teacher but also as a lawmaker.[40] Green was receptive to the idea, but since there were other Republicans who desired the same

36 Glasscock to Senator Scott, 22 April 1910, Glasscock Papers,
37 *Morgantown Post-Chronicle*, May 25, 1910.
38 Senator Scott to Glasscock, 4 June 1910, Glasscock Papers.
39 Glasscock to Frank Bowman, 19 April 1910, Glasscock Papers.
40 Glasscock to Henry S. Green, 23 November 1909, Glasscock Papers.

position, he thought it best not to become a candidate. He chose to work for the party by advocating reforms in his newspaper.[41]

Governor Glasscock mainly supported Professor Green because they both sought such reforms as a production tax on gas and a primary election law. By the summer of 1910, however, the governor and his old Morgantown friend found it difficult to agree on a campaign strategy because Green continued to offend party regulars even after they had won primary victories. Because of the "divisive attacks" in his newspaper, the governor informed Senator Elkins that "Professors of the University should not engage in any outside work, and if Hodges is elected President [of West Virginia University] I am going to take the matter up with him."[42] Davis, the son of Senator Elkins, had earlier written to his father that "Glasscock promised me time and time again that he would make changes in the University. Also that the professors should not engage in other business than what they were employed to do."[43] After Hodges became president, Green was discharged from the school "for alleged political activities" in February 1911.[44]

The nomination of a state senator from his home senatorial district, the eleventh, also concerned Glasscock. He particularly supported the selection of Judge Frank Cox of Morgantown, who had served on the West Virginia Supreme Court of Appeals. In a letter to Circuit Court Judge John W. Mason of Fairmont, Glasscock indicated that his second choice would be M. L. Brown, "a good, safe and honest senator."[45] As both individuals expected a close race in that district, they decided not to seek office, opening the field to former state Senator Joseph H. McDermott of Morgantown, and Ellis Yost, a delegate from Monongalia County.

Since Yost had the reputation of being an extreme prohibitionist, which would limit his appeal to voters, Glasscock gave a lukewarm endorsement to McDermott. The governor's reservations stemmed from McDermott's refusal to campaign for a gas production tax until he knew what the people of his district wanted. This area,

----

41   Henry S. Green to Glasscock, 3 March 1910, Glasscock Papers. Dr. David Courtney of Morgantown eventually received the Republican nomination to the House of Delegates from Monongalia County. He also won the election.

42   Glasscock to Senator S. B. Elkins, 22 September 1910, Glasscock Papers.

43   Davis Elkins to U.S. Senator S. B. Elkins, 7 April, 1910, Elkins Papers.

44   Ambler, *A History of Education in West Virginia*, 528. Green's release from the university is a disturbing feature that came as a result of his continued attacks on Republican nominees in his newspaper. This incident might even qualify as a "purge" by the governor, who, of course, was hard-pressed at that time.

45   Glasscock to John W. Mason, 11 November 1909, Glasscock Papers.

he noted in a letter to Glasscock, was "almost, if not, the largest gas producing and consuming District in the State."[46] Governor Glasscock probably agreed with his friend M. L. Brown who wrote to the governor, "But don't you be deceived. He [McDermott] has been against you from the time you were inaugurated . . . He is not for you or a single one of the vital matters that you want to see carried out."[47]

In the end, after the campaign was thrown into question, at one point because of McDermott's poor health,[48] the former state senator won the nomination. During his strenuous campaign, however, McDermott concluded that Glasscock was not aiding him and that, in fact, he was fighting alone in Morgantown.[49] Davis Elkins corroborated McDermott's complaints to his father, Senator Elkins, stating that Governor Glasscock was a good friend, "but he is influenced a great deal by a set of men that are not such good friends."[50] Senators Scott and Elkins decided to help McDermott in Monongalia County "no matter what we may have to do."[51] Along with Senator McDermott's victory in the primary, McDermott won the right to name the delegates from his home county to the Eleventh Senatorial District Convention, held in Fairmont.[52]

In March of 1910, Glasscock, bothered by a painful bout of rheumatism, traveled to Florida to rest. Party dissension, however, once again greeted the governor upon his return home toward the end of the month. Many observers viewed the political scene as complex and the problems intractable, involving many issues, interests, and personalities. In the first place, the reformers continued to seek organizational control of the party. In addition, federal appointments, which officially were not the concern of Glasscock, continued to plague his administration. Different groups within the party vied for these positions for political sustenance, especially for control of the local post offices. Knowing that it was impossible not to become actively involved, Glasscock resorted to the role of referee and arbitrator, using his influence with the U.S. senators, who controlled federal patronage.

---

46   Joseph McDermott to Glasscock, 20 January 1910, Glasscock Papers.

47   M. L. Brown to Glasscock, 23 January 1910, Glasscock Papers.

48   Davis Elkins to Glasscock, 23 April 1910, Glasscock Papers.

49   McDermott pleaded for Glasscock's assistance. The senator viewed Morgantown as the "headquarters of the Insurgents" and the *Morgantown Post-Chronicle* as their "mouthpiece"; see Joseph McDermott to Glasscock, 22 January 1910, Glasscock Papers.

50   Davis Elkins to S. B. Elkins, 7 April 1910, Elkins Papers.

51   Senator Scott to Glasscock, 1 March 1910, Glasscock Papers.

52   Joseph McDermott to Glasscock, 16 June 1910, Glasscock Papers; *Morgantown Post-Chronicle*, May 10, 1910.

Especially intense bickering between the two factions occurred for post office appointments in Marion County in McDermott's Eleventh Senatorial District. George Jacobs, an insurgent, headed the "Jacobs-Lehman faction." Howard Fleming, a conservative friend of Senator McDermott, led the other faction. The Jacobs people disliked McDermott. In addition, they wanted control of the post offices at Fairmont and Mannington. Governor Glasscock attempted to ease the situation when he tried to persuade Senator Elkins to secure a position for Fleming in Washington, D. C.[53] McDermott, in an effort to save his election, offered each faction an equal number of votes at the district convention, but the Jacobs-Lehman people refused to compromise.

Since the Jacobs people felt they had not received their fair share of federal appointments, and because of their intense dislike of Senator McDermott, they formed their own party, calling themselves the Regular Progressive Republican Party. Eliminating McDermott's name, they drew up their own list of candidates and petitioned the ballot commissioners for their inclusion on the official ballot. In turn, McDermott and his following secured an injunction to prevent the Regular Progressives from going on the ticket, but the State Supreme Court overruled it. Special Judge M. M. Neely dissolved the injunction, taking the position "that the candidates on the Progressive ticket had a legal right to go on the official ballot under their position and emblem."[54] Mason and Wetzel Counties also experienced similar difficulties, causing further tensions on the seams of the Republican Party.

To make matters worse, the prohibition issue divided Republicans between the "Wets," who were anti-prohibition, and the "Drys," who were in favor of restrictions on alcohol. Adjutant General Charlie Elliott, an acute political observer, kept the governor posted, especially on conditions in Clay and Mason Counties. The problem centered on the "whiskey interests," who sought control of politics in Point Pleasant. Arguments over the appointment of ballot commissioners caused dissension in Mason County. Elliott informed Glasscock that "Wet" Democrats and Republicans had joined in an effort to prevent the election of "Dry" Democrats and Republicans. Prohibitionists also united in support of the Democratic candidate for Congress, Rankin Wiley, because of his stand against alcohol. Elliott further related that he "failed to discover a bit of the old time loyalty among the leaders in Mason County."[55] Of course, Elliott had the reputation of

53   Glasscock to George Sturgiss, 16 February 1910, Glasscock to Senator S. B. Elkins, 27 July 1910, both in Glasscock Papers.
54   Joseph McDermott to Glasscock, 13 July 1910, Glasscock Papers; *Morgantown Post-Chronicle*, November 3, 1910; November 5, 1910.
55   Adjutant General C. D. Elliott to Glasscock, 27 September 1910, Glasscock Papers.

sometimes creating a sense of panic in order to enlist more money from the party to buy votes or influence lobbyists. This election tactic often led some members of the party to suspect that it meant more money for him. Nevertheless, he knew the political game and he played it effectively; at an earlier time Senator Scott commented, "I would not for the world hurt Charlie's feelings, for nobody appreciates his worth to the party more than I do."[56] Nevertheless, Elliott had made a career of moving from one faction to the other and somehow always landing on his feet. For example, in 1895 he was Senator Elkins's man "on the ground" in the legislative session that successfully beat off anti-corporation and railroad legislation. During that session, a Democrat attempted to enlist the aid of Senator Camden to obtain an annual railroad pass on the Ohio Railroad for Elliott's good services. He further explained, "the railroads and other corporations and parties who have anything owe [Elliott] a lasting debt of gratitude."[57] The 1910 mid-term election, however, presented a daunting task for the skillful political opportunist.

Governor Glasscock also took a personal interest in the election in Wood County by asking Sheriff W. H. Carfer to run for the House of Delegates.[58] In the Third Senatorial District, which included Wood County, R. L. Gregory of Tyler County opposed E. R. Kingsley, a progressive from Wood County whom Glasscock supported. Elliott stated that Gregory had spoken out against Senator Elkins and the state administration and advised the voters that prohibition would cause an increase in their taxes. Apparently the ploy worked, as Gregory won the nomination with the votes "of these good people," the property owners.[59] The adjutant general further explained:

> Sheriff Carfer did all he could do, but moral suasion and appeals to party loyalty fell flat. Scores of the Democratic ward heelers were out in the open for Gregory; many of them, in spite of all we could do, were allowed to vote, as the election machinery was weak in many places. I am of the opinion, however, that we would have been defeated even if we had had as much money as they had.[60]

Adjutant General Elliott spared no effort in his desire to execute the governor's plans. While enlisting the aid of former Governor A. B. White in preventing the nomination of

56 Williams, *West Virginia and the Captains of Industry*, 129.
57 Wesley Mollohan to J. N. Camden, 19 February 1895, Camden Papers.
58 Glasscock to Mrs. W. H. Carfer of Parkersburg, 2 April 1910, Glasscock Papers.
59 Adjutant General Elliott to Glasscock, 13 July 1910, Glasscock Papers.
60 Adjutant General Elliott to Glasscock, 13 July 1910, Glasscock Papers.

R. L. Gregory, Elliott complained that Congressman Harry C. Woodyard of the Fourth Congressional District and Senator Scott did nothing to stop Gregory. The prohibition issue brought about strange bedfellows, but was typical of the myriad of complex problems facing the politicians. Furthermore, Elliott learned that the senator, in an attempt to straddle the fence, would have been as happy with Gregory as with Kingsley and "did as much for the other fellows as he did for us."[61] Glasscock, who attempted to remain behind the scenes, was perturbed with these reports. Furthermore, it appeared that party unrest was not just a local and state affair, but was also rampant on Capitol Hill. Indeed, many Republicans feared defeat in the fall. Glasscock's confidant, M. L. Brown, had written to the governor before the nominations commenced that he was uneasy over the intense fighting at the nation's capitol because of reformers' attempts to strip the near-dictatorial powers from the conservative reactionary Speaker of the House "Uncle Joe" Cannon, whom Taft supported. Conservative U. S. Senator Nelson Aldrich of Rhode Island was also successful in passing the Payne-Aldrich Tariff Act of 1909, a protective tariff that aided the trusts and angered the progressives. Brown wrote, "This anti Aldrich and anti Cannon cry is too long and too persistent not to mean something. If Mr. Taft does not show himself able to hold the plow and drive the team too, I am fearful of the results of next fall."[62]

In fact, at that time, President Taft not only found it difficult to unify his administration but also to placate his wife. In a letter to former President Roosevelt, Taft remarked about his wife's ill health, saying she "is not an easy patient and an attempt to control her only increased the nervous strain."[63] In September, Glasscock's brother, Fuller, was philosophical when he learned that Maine had gone Democratic in that state's election. He explained that he "was not surprised at all at the returns, and I hope the people will get what they seem to want."[64] A woeful Senator Elihu Root of New York also wrote to a friend saying, "The country has made up its mind to change parties. It is like a man in bed. He wants to roll over. He doesn't know why . . . but he just does; and he'll do it."[65] In quick succession, Vermont also fell to the Democrats,

61   Adjutant General Elliott to Glasscock, 13 July 1910, Glasscock Papers.

62   M. L. Brown to Glasscock, 21 December 1910, Glasscock Papers.

63   William Henry Harbaugh, *Power and Responsibility: The Life and Times of Theodore Roosevelt* (New York: Farrar, Straus and Cudahy, 1961), 388–89.

64   Fuller Glasscock to Glasscock, 13 September 1910, Glasscock Papers.

65   Richard W. Leopold, *Elihu Root and the Conservative Tradition* (Boston: Little, Brown and Co., 1954), 82. Hereafter cited as Leopold, *Elihu Root and the Conservative Tradition*.

sending a shudder through West Virginia Republicans. Governor Glasscock viewed the returns from those states as a warning to his party "that we should get together if we hope to win this fall."[66] He also reminded his fellow Republicans of the necessity of securing a majority in the next legislature, because that session would redistrict the state. Glasscock, along with many Republicans, feared that the Democrats would gerrymander the "Blackbelt" counties of southern West Virginia, which had always been loyal to the "Grand Old Party."

By the end of summer, Governor Glasscock's health fared no better than the deteriorating condition of his party on both national and state levels. An early illness in June of 1910 portended a bad period for the governor. Glasscock's health seemed to worsen with the news that his father had fallen ill. In June he wrote to Senator McDermott that he had "a very hard week ahead" as he had "to deliver about three commencement addresses this week and I feel more like going to bed this morning than trying to do any work."[67]

Adjutant General Elliott feared the governor's health was slipping when Glasscock's father died in July. The concerned adjutant general wrote to his friend the governor, "I hope, however, that you will not allow the trouble to affect your nervous system, which I felt was impaired when I last saw you."[68] This was sound advice, and again, during his incapacity the governor admitted, "the greatest trouble with myself is that I worry about things more than I should,"[69] which evidently led to or coincided with an acute attack of rheumatism. Whatever the origin of the illness, Governor Glasscock experienced severe pain that he described to Dr. M. H. Brown of Morgantown:

> I was glad to hear from you. I have been having the most severe attack of rheumatism I have had for many years. It commenced in my hands and feet principally and then extended to nearly all the joints of my body, and finally this week I have been suffering from lumbago. Thursday and Friday mornings I would hardly get out of bed, and in fact was not able to get to the office until noon of each day. In the afternoon it got better and I am feeling fairly well today. I think my general condition is very much improved and

66 Glasscock to J. S. Darst, 14 September 1910, Glasscock Papers.
67 Glasscock to Joseph McDermott, 6 June 1910, Glasscock Papers.
68 C. D. Elliott to Glasscock, 13 July 1910, Glasscock Papers.
69 Glasscock to John W. Mason, 13 July 1910, Glasscock Papers.

hope I shall now be able to get along all right, but I have suffered enough pain in the last two or three weeks to kill a man.

I am not certain that I shall go to Hot Springs because I am taking baths and massage treatment here practically every day and I believe I am getting along as well as I would at Hot Springs or any other place.

I was getting along mighty well until we had this trouble over the attempted lynching of the negro [sic] at Hinton and that kept me on the go nearly all the time, day and night for two or three days, and I felt much worse after it was over.[70]

Frustration over the severity of his recent illness led Glasscock to speculate on its origin, especially since he had taken "pretty good care" and did not know how to account for this attack except that "I have been eating a good deal more meat than formerly. I am going to cut it down again and see if I do not get better." He also determined to stop smoking and "expect to quit chewing within the next few days."[71] Glasscock was always receptive to medical advice; at one time he had even thought of becoming a physician. When he heard that the removal of the tonsils could possibly improve his painful malady, he checked into the matter further. The governor communicated with Dr. Cooper of Hinton, "a very celebrated surgeon in that part of the state," who informed Glasscock that many physicians considered the tonsils as a source of infection for the disease "articular rheumatism"; a tonsillectomy, Cooper asserted, would be a wise preventive measure.

Although time was near for the mid-term elections, many of the governor's friends advised him to go to Hot Springs to recuperate; but he felt that he had "been away from home so much that I am ashamed to leave my office any more."[72] Former Governor Dawson could sympathize with Glasscock, and he, too, suggested a long vacation:

Now if you will pardon me, you are trying to do too much work. I know how distasteful it is to hear people say this, but there are a great many details you can throw off and you ought to do it. The trouble with Governor White was that he insisted on answering every letter himself and would not let General Boggs or myself relieve him; the result was that he broke down and had to go to Atlantic City for three months. I had to learn to let other people look

70   Glasscock to Dr. M. H. Brown, 20 August 1910, Glasscock Papers.
71   Glasscock to M. L. Brown, 20 August 1910, Glasscock Papers.
72   Glasscock to S. J. Snyder, 10 August 1910, Glasscock Papers; see also Fuller Glasscock to Glasscock, 3 August 1910, Glasscock Papers.

after details. I found things went on all right while I was away and that nothing had suffered.[73]

By the end of August 1910, Governor Glasscock decided to go to Hot Springs, Virginia, for an extended vacation. He then moved to White Sulphur Springs, West Virginia, where he set up headquarters and fully intended to stay until January, the beginning of the next legislative session, if it took that long for him to regain his health.[74] The "White" was famous not only as a resort for vacationers who wished to socialize during the "heated season," but also as a curative spa for those seeking mental and physical recuperation. Robert E. Lee spent the last three summers of his life there and it played host to a number of presidents;[75] now the governor of West Virginia prayed the famous spa would work its wonders on him so that he could attend to government and party affairs. At this time in his administration, Glasscock had some profound thoughts about his office and his ability to do the work, as he reflected to a friend:

> My health is fairly good now and I hope I shall be able to get through the winter all right. But, Judge, I made a great mistake in accepting the nomination for Governor, and if I had it to do over nothing in the world could induce me to take it. Of course I appreciate the confidence of my fellow citizens of West Virginia, and while I have done many things I should not have done and left undone things that I ought to have done and wish I had done, nevertheless, I feel that the administration has not been wholly bad, and I am not ashamed of my record, but the work is too much for a man of my physical condition.[76]

At White Sulphur Springs, Governor Glasscock and Adjutant General Elliott devised a strategy for the fall campaign. Together they planned a meeting of top Republican leaders to join the governor at the "White" on September 20.[77] At the appointed date congressmen, former governors, and two United States senators, as well as Glasscock and members of his administration, met in order to resolve problems in their party. The leaders decided to leave the question of local disputes virtually in the governor's

73   W. M. O. Dawson to Glasscock, 8 September 1910, Glasscock Papers.
74   Glasscock to S. A. D. Glasscock, 15 September 1910, Glasscock Papers.
75   Ambler and Summers, *West Virginia: The Mountain State*, 560.
76   Glasscock to John W. Mason, 1 October 1910, Glasscock Papers.
77   C. D. Elliott to Glasscock, 14 September 1910, Glasscock Papers.

hands, which, in effect, placed him at the head of the state Republican Party, and, unfortunately, possibly captain of a sinking ship. They also concluded that Glasscock should issue a public call for unity to his fellow party members.[78]

On September 24, Governor Glasscock released a lengthy public message, reviewing the goals and accomplishments of the GOP, asking his fellow Republicans to unite and remain loyal, "I do not ask you to vote for dishonest candidates but I earnestly plead for the triumph of Republican principles."[79] After reading his plea, M. L. Brown wrote to his friend, the governor:

> I have read your public letter with much interest and think you have struck the proper note. If they will only let you lead and the other leaders give you proper support we will win out. This state is not Democratic. All this discontent and dissatisfaction is a protest against improper methods and bad leadership.[80]

As the campaign progressed, the Democrats used the road law, which had increased taxes; the game law, which required state residents to purchase hunting licenses; and the "wasteful" Board of Control as ammunition against the Republicans.[81] Glasscock was pleased that they were attacking the board, because, at the appropriate time, he planned to announce that it would have a surplus of a quarter of a million dollars at the end of the fiscal year.[82]

While hopeful that the election could still be won with a slim majority, Glasscock fretted about the factional disputes. Following the advice that "the way to disregard the factions in the Republican party was by regarding them,"[83] he met with the different leaders of the "warring" groups in Charleston, where he pleaded for unity.

By the middle of October, he reported that problems were fairly well worked out in Clay and Mason Counties, but there were still two tickets in the Fifth Senatorial District, comprised of Cabell, Lincoln, and Putnam Counties.[84] A frustrated Governor

---

78 *Parkersburg Sentinel*, September 20, 1910; *Morgantown Post-Chronicle*, September 24, 1910; C. D. Elliott to Glasscock, 22 September 1910, Glasscock Papers.

79 *Morgantown Post-Chronicle*, September 24, 1910.

80 M. L. Brown to Glasscock, 25 September 1910, Glasscock Papers.

81 H. Roy Waugh to Glasscock, 6 September 1910, Glasscock Papers.

82 Glasscock to H. Roy Waugh, 9 September 1910, Glasscock Papers.

83 Glasscock to J. W. Mason, 1 October 1910, John W. Mason Papers, West Virginia University.

84 Glasscock to C. F. Snyder, 11 October 1910, Glasscock Papers.

Glasscock lamented that "each faction will tell you that it is going to elect its ticket when they don't have any more snow than a snow ball."[85] In his view, the splinter groups had very little real power to effect change within the political landscape.

Marion County proved to be the most troublesome. Senator McDermott, who wrote that he was "ready to jump in the river and get away from everything political,"[86] was caught between the two factions in that county in his attempt to win the state senatorial election. In this local dispute over post office patronage, he had sided with the "regulars." In retribution, the insurgents, or "Progressive Republicans" refused to put his name on their ticket. In a word, McDermott claimed the Progressives were willing to send the entire Republican ballot to certain defeat, because they thought they had been unfairly treated. Senator Scott, perturbed at the turn of events, wrote to Glasscock that he was "fed up" with politics and would gladly quit if he advised him to do so.[87]

In an attempt to ameliorate the situation, Glasscock again pleaded with the Progressives of Marion County. He had previously met with George and J. M. Jacobs, who led that faction, but his entreaties had gone unheeded. Senator Scott had even advised the governor to withdraw state funds from the Peoples National Bank of Fairmont, where several of the insurgents were officers, "if they did not get their rump ticket out of the road."[88] Glasscock did not follow the advice of "Blustering Scotty," but he was happy to receive Senator Scott's promise to "get another position for Fleming so that the Post Office matter there may be settled before election" in order to appease the Jacobs' people (in other words, to remove him from local politics).[89] Receiving no help from Senator Elkins, the governor went to Fairmont for a meeting with the Jacobs faction. It was a failure, as he explained to a friend:

> As you probably know the Lehman-Jacobs faction, of Marion County, refused to put McDermott's name on their ticket after I had made every proposition. I came to them to effect a compromise. They finally notified me that they would not only not put his name on the ticket but that they would fight him at the polls.[90]

85 Glasscock to J. W. Mason, 1 October 1910, Mason Papers.

86 Joseph McDermott to Glasscock, 10 October 1910, Glasscock Papers.

87 Senator N. B. Scott to Glasscock, 10 October 1910, Glasscock Papers.

88 Senator N. B. Scott to Glasscock, 10 October 1910, Glasscock Papers.

89 Glasscock to C. F. Snyder, 11 October 1910, Glasscock Papers. See also Glasscock to J. W. Mason, 1 October 1910, Mason Papers. In July, Senator Elkins wrote Glasscock that he was doing all he could to aid McDermott in Marion County, which was evidently not enough.

90 Glasscock to George C. Baker, 21 October 1910, Glasscock Papers.

As the difficult task of maintaining Republican unity appeared bleak, the governor asked the Greens of the *Morgantown Post-Chronicle* not only to advocate the election of Senator McDermott but also to renounce the action of the insurgents of Marion County. Green replied that he had advised the inclusion of McDermott's name on their local ballot, but he mused that it was no wonder that the senator was having trouble since some of his "fool friends" had treated the Lehman-Jacobs faction improperly at the senatorial convention.[91] In reality, McDermott received little aid from the *Post-Chronicle*, which in most cases followed a progressive course.

In desperation, Glasscock also turned to Senator McDermott's primary opponent, Ellis Yost. He asked Yost to go to Marion County to help McDermott, because "It would be very humiliating to me to have the candidate in my own district defeated, and especially when the normal Republican majority in the district is practically 2000."[92] Yost, however, refused, stating that he did not like Senator McDermott, who he claimed had used "underhanded" methods in the past and was suspected of being involved with the "whiskey interests."[93]

With Glasscock's unsuccessful attempts to mediate the dispute, avenues to peace and harmony were exhausted. One of the last reports from M. L. Brown in Morgantown sounded a note of frustration, "We are ready to give up the senatorial fight in disgust." Brown's words rang true. In the Eleventh Senatorial District, the Democratic candidate beat Joseph McDermott by a wide margin. McDermott lost in Marion County, which was no surprise, and in Taylor County. He did manage to carry his home county, Monongalia, by 684 votes.[94]

The ailing governor and his close advisers feared that statewide voter apathy would doom the party in West Virginia.[95] This fear, along with party disunity caused by factional disputes and emotional issues prompted many voters either to stay home or to vote the issue and not the party. No one, however, expected the severe drubbing the Republicans received on Election Day. The only Republican congressman elected was James A. Hughes of the Fifth Congressional District, and even that reliable district

91 Glasscock to Robert R. Green, 22 October 1910; Robert R. Green to Glasscock, 24 October 1910, both in Glasscock Papers.
92 Glasscock to Ellis Yost, 24 October 1910, Glasscock Papers.
93 Ellis Yost to Glasscock, 31 October 1910, Glasscock Papers.
94 M. L. Brown to Glasscock, 2 November 1910, Glasscock Papers; *Wheeling Register*, November 10, 1910.
95 M. L. Brown to Glasscock, 29 September 1910; George C. Sturgiss to Glasscock, 2 October 1910, both in Glasscock Papers.

kept political veterans watching the voting results very closely. The Fifth, comprised of McDowell, Cabell, Lincoln, Mason, and Putnam Counties, experienced factional dissension, leading to more votes than usual for the Democratic candidate, Rankin Wiley. Only the "Blackbelt" McDowell County secured Hughes's victory, which provided him with a handsome plurality of 3700.[96]

In all, the Republicans won only four state senatorial seats. Yet there was still reason to be thankful, because that body remained evenly matched with 15 members from each party, which would give the GOP a voice in organizing the upper chamber and in redistricting the state. Again, the "Blackbelt" counties proved their importance, as the Republican candidate, M. Z. White, ran unopposed in the Sixth Senatorial District.[97]

The disunity displayed by the Republican Party largely explained its defeat. In contrast to 1908 when Democrats had won state Senate seats in only the First, Tenth, and Fifteenth Senatorial Districts, they fared much better in 1910 when the Democrats won the senatorial races in the Second, Third, Fifth, Seventh, Eighth, Ninth, Tenth, Eleventh, Twelfth, Thirteenth, and Fifteenth Districts. Republicans won only in those districts that experienced little dissension, such as the First, Fourth, Sixth, and Fourteenth. Searching for a ray of hope, Glasscock wrote, "the combined vote of the Democratic candidates for Congress in this State at this last election was only 103,293, whereas Mr. Bennett, my opponent, received over 118,000 two years ago. This state is not Democratic."[98]

The outcome of the 1910 mid-term election proved just as disastrous for the national Republican Party and the Taft Administration. The Democrats gained control of the House, with the Republicans holding the Senate by a slim margin, giving the insurgents the balance of power.[99] News that the voters of New Jersey had elected the former president of Princeton University as their governor had little impact on West

---

96   *Wheeling Register*, November 9, 1910; November 10, 1910.

97   The four winning GOP senatorial candidates were J. G. Hearne, of the First; B. A. Smith, of the Fourth; M. Z. White, of the Sixth; and O. A. Hood, of the Fourteenth. See the *Wheeling Register*, November 9 and 10, 1910.

98   In contrast to 1908, when the Republicans had elected all five congressional candidates, they succeeded in only one contest in 1910. The fact was many Republicans had stayed home, and some that voted chose Democrats. The Democrats also won a majority of the races for the House of Delegates. In 1908, the House had been composed of 32 Democrats and 54 Republicans; after the election of 1910, the new composition was 62 to 24, respectively. See Glasscock to George C. Sturgiss, 19 December 1910, Glasscock Papers; The *Wheeling Register*, November 5, 6, 7, and 8, 1908 and November 10, 1910.

99   Richard W. Leopold, *Elihu Root and the Conservative Tradition* , 82.

Virginians at that time. Woodrow Wilson, however, would be a well-known name by 1912.

When the dust settled, Republicans could only reminisce about happier days. Distraught with the results, Judge John W. Mason, a party member since 1861, admitted that he had experienced defeats in the past, "but none quite so severe as this." In resignation, he concluded, "The Democrats did not do it. We did it to ourselves. Not many Republicans voted the Democratic ticket; some few did; many did not vote at all, and others threw away their votes on 'independent' & 'insurgents.' It is a good lesson but learned at great expense."[100]

Conversely, Governor Glasscock tried to remain positive, perhaps overly optimistic, when he gave a younger friend the following advice, "Don't be blue, my boy, because all is well that ends well and the Republican party has simply been chastised for some things it has done and others that it has left undone. We belong to the best party on earth and truth crushed to earth will rise again."[101]

It is difficult to know how well Senator Elkins took the defeat; he was seriously ill at that time, reportedly with stomach cancer, and his family thought it best to break "the news to the Senator piecemeal."[102] Most likely, if Elkins had remained well and active on the political scene, there would have been little difference. It seemed that the state and the nation simply wanted to "roll over in bed," for no obvious reason according to some politicos.

On the other hand, Senator Scott was philosophical, although he admitted that his forty years on "the firing line" had ended. By letter he expressed his warm sentiments to the governor (they were friends again), explaining that "the first two or three days the sting was a little sharp, but now that is all passed."[103]

In concluding his thoughts, he advised Glasscock not to hesitate to call upon him for assistance:

> Now, Governor, I leave for Washington this afternoon and will be glad to hear from you and see you at any time and I want you to rest assured that the road is never too long or the night too dark for me to do you or any other friend of mine a favor. *The old man will be around when the party bugle blows and don't you forget it.*[104]

---

100 John W. Mason to Glasscock, 14 November 1910, Glasscock Papers.
101 Glasscock to J. O. Henson, 14 November 1910, Glasscock Papers.
102 C. F. Snyder to Glasscock, 23 November 1910, Glasscock Papers.
103 Senator N. B. Scott to Glasscock, 14 November 1910, Glasscock Papers.
104 Senator N. B. Scott to Glasscock, 14 November 1910, Glasscock Papers. Emphasis Scott.

Obviously, intra-party divisions contributed directly to Republican losses. Although the prohibition question affected both parties, it weakened the GOP more because the reform wing challenged conservative control of party machinery from the national to the local level, an act that affected party loyalty and participation. On the other hand, the better-organized Democrats were in a position to take advantage of their opponent's disunity.

During the state campaign, the Democrats had played upon the alleged extravagance of the Republicans and a number of unpopular laws, such as the road and the game laws. The governor conceded that the legislation had hurt the party, along with the "stay at home" vote and the high cost of living.[105] More importantly, though, he was convinced that the Republican State Committee needed a complete reorganization in order to obtain the loyalty of party members.[106] Glasscock, of course, also directed much of the blame to the unfair tactics of the county committees, and, in a proactive, progressive way, explained, "I think the crying need of the hour is a good primary election law. We must get rid of this committee business and permit the people to have some say in the nominations."[107] Because of the chaotic conditions that existed in the 1910 election, the governor resolved, more than ever, to create an orderly process under state law with which the voice of the people could be heard.

Clearly, Glasscock had been unable to hold his party together on the state level. His own administration had begun in dissension and old wounds were yet to heal. Perhaps if the governor had had better health he would have been more persuasive in his effort to arbitrate differences. Yet Glasscock had received little aid from the Republican higher echelon. Personal problems and an unruly congress had rendered President Taft useless to West Virginia Republicans. When asked to campaign for the party nationally, even former President Roosevelt refused stating that congressional leaders had gone back on their promises too many times. In a disparaging remark about the Republican conservatives, the colonel wrote, "Our party leaders did not realize that I was able to hold the Republican Party in power only because I insisted on a steady advance, and dragged them along with me. Now the advance has been stopped."[108]

---

105 Glasscock to C. N. Finnell, 14 November 1910; Glasscock to Senator Scott, 15 November 1910, both in Glasscock Papers.
106 Glasscock to H. C. Ogden, 21 November 1910, Glasscock Papers.
107 Glasscock to J. W. Mason, 1 October 1910, Mason Papers.
108 Harbaugh, *Power and Responsibility*, 388.

On the state level, Senator Scott's position had been precarious, and he had to fight for his own political existence. Senator Elkins had been ill during most of the difficulties; when he did attempt to use his influence, it was too little and too late. The Elkins machine, still a viable political force with its ties to industrialists living in distant places and its legions of devotees, showed signs of age, like its leader, and stumbled in the 1910 election. The longer his organization held power, the more political debts Elkins incurred until it was no longer possible to satisfy all who wanted to feed at the public's expense; in addition, the number of unhappy rejected applicants accumulated. The mood of the state and the country had also changed with the *zeitgeist* of the time demanding reforms and a reordering of priorities for the "new order." The voice of the people grew in strength and intensity, demanding change. Everyone's change or reform was not necessarily the same, but it seemed that a clear majority wanted a differnt form of leadership from the state to the federal level. While the Republican Party had come under attack both nationally and locally, the Herculean job to mend party fences fell to the governor, a task that he faced directly but failed to achieve to any meaningful degree.

THE RUNAWAY LEGISLATURE OF 1911

"Our Senators are standing like a stone wall."[1]

O N NOVEMBER 18, 1910, Governor Glasscock, Republican members of the legislature, and other influential party members convened in the governor's office to discuss strategies for the coming session of the legislature. After this conference, Glasscock expressed confidence that the Republican lawmakers would work together in harmony,[2] "even though they may not be successful in getting any thing done."[3] It was too early to predict what the Democratic plans for the session might be, but the governor felt certain that the Democrats, "as friends of the corporations,"[4] would fight the creation of a public service commission.

By painting the Democrats as darlings of the corporations, Governor Glasscock hoped to generate enthusiasm. Actually, both parties had close ties with big business, making it a flawed claim. His sentiments, however, could have indicated that he had become more ardently associated with the reform elements in his party, especially after the 1910 Republican debacle. The governor further opined that the gas and oil interests in this struggle would aid them saying, "I think the corporations are going to be as well represented in the next legislature as they have been for the past twenty years." Furthermore, in conversation with some of the leading Democrats, Glasscock learned that they planned to oppose a primary election law. He queried, "Just why they are going to do this I cannot understand, but you can rest assured they are going to make mistakes just as we have done."[5]

----

1   Glasscock to A. B. White, Parkersburg, Western Union telegram, 14 January 1911, Glasscock Papers.

2   Glasscock to Judge Frank Cox, 22 November 1910; Glasscock to H. C. Ogden, 21 November 1910; both in Glasscock Papers.

3   Glasscock to Judge Cox, 22 November 1910, Glasscock Papers.

4   Glasscock to Judge Cox, 22 November 1910, Glasscock Papers.

5   Glasscock to Judge Cox, 22 November 1910, Glasscock Papers.

Going into the legislative session, the Republicans had only one opportunity of gaining a position of power: the state senate was deadlocked between the two parties. The Republican goal was to elect a GOP president of that body, since the president was in effect a lieutenant governor, who would succeed the chief executive in case he died. As Glasscock explained to Senator Scott, "You know life is uncertain and if anything should happen to me I want to know that I am to be succeeded by a Republican." With this maneuver, they also hoped to prevent "unfair gerrymandering," especially of the "colored voters" in the so-called "Blackbelt" counties of southern West Virginia.[6]

In early December, the Democrats held a planning session at Parkersburg. Reports reaching Glasscock indicated that his partisan opponents hoped to challenge the election of two Republican state senators in order to gain control of the upper house.[7] The governor recognized that the Republicans would have to fight for everything they wanted, as the Democrats seemed determined to capture the presidency of the state senate. Yet the Governor had "no fear of the result," if his fellow party members stood together.[8]

Before the governor's strategy could be tested, however, tragedy struck West Virginia Republicans when, on January 4, 1911, Senator Elkins died. This numbing news sent shockwaves throughout the Republican rank and file because in this moment of loss the Democrats saw a gain. Since the mid-term election of 1910, even the casual observer expected the Democrats would win Senator Scott's seat in the United States Senate since his term of office was up, but now, with fate on their side because of the untimely demise, the Democrats aimed for two seats in the nation's capitol.[9]

Soon after Elkins's death, Glasscock appointed the Senator's son, Davis, to complete his father's short-lived term until the West Virginia legislature could meet in regular session and elect a successor. It appears that Senator Elkins had made a last-minute plea with Governor Glasscock for his son to succeed him. After the death, Colonel Snyder, the senator's personal secretary, wrote to thank Glasscock for Davis's appointment. Snyder stated that was what Senator Elkins had desired.[10] The *Wheeling Intelligencer* also reported that Colonel Snyder had visited the governor shortly before Elkins's death, "bearing a personal message from the Senator."[11] Evidently, it was a wish that was hard

---

6   Glasscock to N. B. Scott, 21 November 1910; Glasscock to Judge Cox, 14 November 1910, both in Glasscock Papers.
7   Glasscock to C. P. Craig, 10 December 1910, Glasscock Papers.
8   Glasscock to Howard Sutherland, 10 December 1910, Glasscock Papers.
9   *Wheeling Intelligencer*, January 5, 1910.
10   C. F. Snyder to Glasscock, 3 January 1911; January 24, 1911, both in Glasscock Papers.
11   *Wheeling Intelligencer*, January 9, 1911.

to refuse and seemed appropriate at the time, but Glasscock would later regret the day that he continued the Elkins machine.

During the election of 1910, many Republicans had not realized the seriousness of Senator Elkins's illness as Glasscock had. As the governor explained to Judge Mason shortly after the senator's death:

> I am very much hurt over the death of Senator Elkins. It is not only a loss to the State, but coming at this time it was most unfortunate for our party. I am sorry the Republicans of the State did not appreciate the gravity of the situation more during the campaign. When I was in Fairmont trying to get the factions together there I told some of our mutual friends in a confidential way that the probabilities were that this Legislature would have to elect two United States Senators. I have been fearful of this all the time, but I did not know until Monday of this week that the family had given up all hope of the Senator's recovery.[12]

The death of Senator Elkins made the presidency of the state Senate even more urgent to the Republicans. Since they conceded the loss of both U.S. senatorial seats because of the deadlock in the state's upper house, they felt they at least deserved the top post in that chamber. Many Republicans also recognized the fact that their governor was a frail man, who should be succeeded in case of death, they thought, by a member of his own party.

As the politicians pondered their respective positions, the legislature convened, and Governor Glasscock delivered the traditional message. While Glasscock presented an ambitious program, many of his proposals were familiar to his audience. He asked for a referendum on the liquor question, the ratification of the federal income tax amendment, the creation of a public service commission similar to one in Wisconsin, and the passage of an employer's liability law similar to the Pennsylvania statute of 1907. The governor also desired a stronger anti-trust law and the imposition of a tax on natural gas. The revenues created by the tax would be used to upgrade schools and to improve state highways. Finally, he called on the lawmakers to pass an anti-lobby law requiring lobbyists to register with the Secretary of State and the abolition of the state tax of 4.5 cents on general property, or its reduction to one cent.[13]

12   Glasscock to Judge John W. Mason, 6 January 1911, Glasscock Papers.
13   Regular Biennial Message of Governor Glasscock to the Legislature of 1911, January 11, 1911, State Papers and Public Addresses of Wm. E. Glasscock, 1909–1913, 1–71, West Virginia Division of Culture and History.

In the area of education, Governor Glasscock urged the addition of agricultural courses at the state normal schools and called for the erection of a new agricultural building at the university. Glasscock then asked the lawmakers to provide free textbooks for the children of the state.[14] He also promised to fulfill party pledges and carry out the platform of 1908, especially after the debacle of 1910. In this effort, he reminded the legislators that both parties were pledged to a primary election law and quoted relevant portions of both platforms.[15]

While most state politicians agreed on the need for reform legislation, they were slow to act. The difficulty lay in organizing the state Senate. When the Republicans learned that the Democrats planned to contest the election of Senators Hearne and White, the fifteen GOP senators secluded themselves in the governor's reception room, preventing a senatorial quorum and the organization of the upper chamber.[16] The Democrats needed the addition of one Republican senator in order to organize so that they could elect two United States senators. Frustrated, they even threatened to arrest one or more of the delinquent senators if they refused to present themselves. In turn, the governor stated he would protect his colleagues if he had to declare martial law around the capitol building.[17]

Adjutant General Elliott, to whom the job of protecting the Republican senators had fallen, was a veteran of many political feuds, and he played a key role in the developing situation. The Democrats nominated James E. Mehen of Parkersburg as Sergeant of Arms of the Senate, ordering him to arrest and produce a GOP senator for the upper chamber. Mehen, who was a former Parkersburg police chief and a former Confederate soldier, was a good match for Elliott. Fearing a confrontation, the Republican senators decided to remove themselves from the state.

---

14 *Wheeling Intelligencer*, January 31, 1911. Perhaps as a result of his visit to Midwestern universities in January 1910, Glasscock's interest in education and agriculture was stimulated. Upon his return, the governor actively participated in a revival of the "back to the farm" movement in West Virginia. There were no immediate results other than acknowledgement of the importance of the state's farms and the inclusion of agricultural legislation in the governor's message to the legislature.

15 West Virginia Senate Journal, 30th sess., January 11, 1911, 41. Both parties had made it clear in their platforms that they favored all nominations for public office, state and local, by a general primary election.

16 *Wheeling Intelligencer*, January 9, 1910.

17 *Charleston Gazette*, January 13, 1911; January 14, 1911; *Wheeling Intelligencer*, January 13, 1911; January 14, 1911.

During the cold, wintry night of January 17, the fifteen runaways, along with Elliott and the approval of the governor, fled to Cincinnati, Ohio, in order to avoid conflict.[18] An unprecedented action, the "united" Republican senators composed quite a list of distinguished individuals.[19] In the meantime, Governor Glasscock sought the support of Republicans from around the state and sent urgent telegrams requesting their presence in Charleston. He explained, "The fate of the party is at stake. We are only asking a square deal and that we intend to have. Our Senators are standing like a stone wall. Bring any friends who will come."[20]

The governor also sent similar telegrams to West Virginia's representatives in Congress, appealing for their support. He stated that he feared Democratic control of the state Senate and the possible redistricting of the state. On a positive note that was perhaps somewhat exaggerated, the governor concluded, "Our people are united as they have not been since nineteen hundred and four."[21]

Except for Congressman Hubbard, who did not approve of such tactics, most prominent members of the party supported Glasscock. At first, Senator Scott wired the governor to "stand-pat"; later he reiterated the opinions of a number of United States senators who believed the Republican state senators had weakened their case by leaving the state. Scott added, "several of them thought that we ought to get them back into the state, if not at Charleston certainly somewhere within the borders of the state."[22]

After a week of seclusion, the worried leaders finally made a compromise. The fifteen Republicans would return to the state Senate and the Democrats would elect

18 *Wheeling Intelligencer*, January 18, 1911; see also George W. Summers, *Pages from the Past* (Charleston Journal, 1935), 42.

19 Summers, *Pages from the Past*, 43. The fifteen senators were Henry D. Hatfield, who later became president of the state Senate, governor of West Virginia, and a U.S. senator; Howard Sutherland, who later became a U.S. Senator and then Alien Property custodian of the federal government; E. T. England, who later became a U.S. Congressman; William S. Johnson, who later became state treasurer; Charles G. Coffman of Clarksburg, C. P. Craig of St. Marys, J. W. Flinn of Kingwood, W. C. Grimes of Moundsville, Julian G. Hearne of Wheeling, W. S. Meredith of Fairmont, H. P. Shinn of Point Pleasant, D. B. Smith of Huntington, B. A. Smith of Spencer, M. Z. White of Williamson, and Harry Zilliken of Wellsburg.

20 Glasscock to Albert B. White, S. C. Denham, R. A. Hall, Amos Bright, Joe Williams, William P. Hawley, and U. G. Young, telegrams, 14 January 1911, Glasscock Papers.

21 Glasscock to the Honorables George C. Sturgiss, N. B. Scott, Harry C. Woodyard, J. A. Hughes, Joseph H. Gaines, and W. P. Hubbard, telegrams, 14 January 1911, Glasscock Papers.

22 William P. Hubbard to Glasscock, 28 February 1911; N. B. Scott to Glasscock, 21 January 1911, both in Glasscock Papers.

their two U.S. Senators, duly recognized and commissioned by Governor Glasscock. In return, the GOP would elect a Republican president of the Senate as long as he was agreeable to the Democrats. Although the tactics were unusual to say the least, they were effective. The governor successfully maneuvered his "united" Republicans, while he negotiated with the Democratic leadership. In the end, the determination of Glasscock and the unity of the Republican legislators averted what could have been a "clean-sweep" to power by the opposition party.

On January 29, the upper chamber finally organized with Senator Henry D. Hatfield of McDowell County as president. This was evidently thanks to his promise of support of several Democratic favored pieces of legislation, such as the elimination of the State Road Commissioner because of its patronage possibilities.[23] The Democrats, however, had difficulty within their ranks in Charleston over the senatorial selections. A Democratic caucus nominated C. W. Watson, president of the Fairmont Coal Company, for the short term to the U.S. Senate and William E. Chilton, publisher of the *Charleston Gazette*, for the long term. Critics called the two nominees the "gold dust twins" because of the money at their disposal and their alleged support of "giant corporations."[24] Irate lawmakers, including some Democrats, alleged that the position had cost Watson more than $100,000 and he "had come to Charleston with nothing in the world but a fountain pen and a checkbook."

After Democratic leader Senator Robert F. Kidd suddenly changed his vote during the fifth ballot from Joseph McGraw to William Chilton, whom Watson desired, people wondered if the allegations were true. Kidd's vote gave Chilton the required forty for nomination.[25] In addition, powerful coal operators such as John C. C. Mayo of Kentucky were often present at the legislature to lobby for the selection of Clarence Watson. Several days after the caucus chose Watson and Chilton, eleven Democrats bolted over the nominations, charging that the two men had resorted to bribery and

23　*Wheeling Intelligencer*, January 21, 1911; January 28, 1911; January 30, 1911; *Charleston Gazette*, January 29, 1911; January 30, 1911. See also Carolyn Karr, "A Political Biography of Henry Hatfield," *West Virginia History*, 28 (October, 1966): 46–47.

24　For example, it was well known that C. W. Watson, president of the Fairmont Coal Company, was closely allied with the Standard Oil Company, operated by John D. Rockefeller. See John Alexander Williams, *West Virginia and the Captains of Industry*, 139. See also Charles E. Beachley, comp., *History of the Consolidation Coal Company, 1864–1934* (New York: Consolidation Coal Company), 1934, for an overview.

25　William P. Turner, "John T. McGraw: A study in Democratic Politics in the Age of Enterprise," *West Virginia History*, 45 (1984): 36.

corruption. N. C. Hubbard of Ohio County and James W. Robinson of Harrison County led the dissidents.

The allegations seemed to make little difference, however, and Watson and Chilton, recognized and commissioned by Governor Glasscock, became United States senators. One irate citizen stated, "It beats hell that a coal miner from Kentucky can come over here in West Virginia and elect a Maryland citizen." (Watson spent much of his time in Baltimore, Maryland.)[26] To the consternation of Democrats, such as the reform-minded Joseph T. McGraw who supported progressive legislation, the Watson-Chilton faction acting with the "Kanawha ring" proved a formidable combination, especially with the influence of former Governor William MacCorkle behind them. Moreover, with the acquisition of the *Charleston Gazette* on May 4, 1906, by the Charleston Publishing Company, owned by Chilton, the alliance now controlled much of the Mountain State Democratic Party. Glasscock, however, believed "that Governor MacCorkle is the real leader of the Democracy of West Virginia."[27]

To the dismay of the Democrats, the so-called scandal would not go away. Members of both parties were unhappy with the outcome and demanded an investigation of the charges made by the dissident Democrats. Former Governor G. W. Atkinson and Senator Scott asked the governor to call an inquiry. Atkinson stated:

> . . . Since a large number of Democratic newspapers and practically all Republican papers of the State are charging the corrupt use of money in said election, it would be wise and proper for you to send a special message to both houses urging them to take hold of the matter.[28]

Governor Glasscock gathered information on his own through private sources, but chose not to act. Instead, he devoted his attention to the more important matter of legislation. Much time had been lost in organizing the solons and electing the two U.S. senators and the governor was eager for the lawmakers to act on his legislative proposals. In the remaining period, however, important bills lingered in debate or were pigeonholed in committees. Glasscock was especially angry at the state Senate for

---

26 Carol Crowe-Carraco, *The Big Sandy* (Lexington: University Press of Kentucky, 1979), 88.

27 Turner, "John T. McGraw," 34. See also Glasscock to C. D. Elliott, 23 August 1911, Glasscock Papers.

28 G. W. Atkinson to Glasscock, 8 February 1911; N. B. Scott to Glasscock, 11 February 1911, both in Glasscock Papers.

once again not acting on the primary election law, and he was particularly perturbed with the Senate Judiciary Committee. The governor believed a primary election bill would have passed the full Senate if that "unfriendly" committee had reported it out.[29] Glasscock was further discouraged when the legislature eliminated the office of State Road Commissioner, repealed the road funds act, and failed to act on the federal income tax provision.[30]

On the positive side, the legislators passed some important educational legislation. The Johnson-Edwards bill stipulated that if three-fifths of the voters of a district consented, bonds could be issued for the building of new school buildings. The law also permitted the State Superintendent to classify high schools by size, allowing the state to aid in funding and expenses. This bill aided the growth of high schools in West Virginia, which increased to 115 by 1912. In other areas, the legislature created the office of State Agriculture Commissioner and provided for the submission of the state prohibition amendment to the people of the state in the general election of 1912.[31] Governor Glasscock was especially elated over the latter action, perhaps preparing the way by "greasing the skids" early in the session. According to tradition, at the beginning of each new biennial session, legislators expected a reception that combined business, plenty of libation, food, and conviviality. The governor's office was charged $47.95 for liquor and $61.00 for cigars, a fitting way of saying goodbye to legalized drinking in the state.[32]

The fear of Democratic redistricting efforts continued to haunt the governor and his fellow Republicans, causing many party members to watch the legislative session closely to the final minute. One worried Republican wrote to Glasscock in confidence concerning such action, warning the governor of "11th hour" activity in the Senate, because he had been at many closing sessions himself:

....

29   Glasscock to John W. Mason, 4 April 1911, Glasscock Papers.

30   Acts of West Virginia Legislature, 30th sess., 1911, 150, 43–46, 94–97. See also *West Virginia House Journal*, 1911, 285, 325–26, 383–84.

31   *Journal of the West Virginia Senate Journal*, 1911, 69–71, for the Johnson-Edwards bill; see also *West Virginia House Journal*, 1911, 265–67, for the creation of the office of State Agricultural Commissioner; and *West Virginia House Journal*, 1911, 101, 123, 154, 184, 188, 307, for action concerning the prohibition amendment. See also James M. Callahan, *Semi-Centennial History of West Virginia* (Charleston: Semi-Centennial Commission of West Virginia, 1913), 561.

32   Statement from Jos. R. Peebles' and Sons Co. to Glasscock, 12 January 1911; statement from L. J. Falone, Imported Key West and Domestic Cigars to Glasscock, for the period 11 January 1911 to 30 January 1911, both in Glasscock Papers.

There are at least two hold over Republican senators who are very likely to get drunk on the closing night and either be 'non compis [sic] mentis' on voting, or absent. You may not know who they are but a little guarded inquiry will easily disclose their names.

Anything short of murder would be justified in keeping them sober and at their seats.[33]

The fear of redistricting did not materialize, and Republicans drew a sigh of relief. In all, it turned out to be a rather calm session, with surprisingly little animosity. Governor Glasscock reviewed the sparse results of the lawmakers with resignation, since the Democrats were in the majority and, in his opinion, it could have been worse. Later, he reminisced:

We had a great time here last winter. Sometimes we were a little like the fellow who went to war and said that he thought every minute was going to be the last. That is what I thought many times during the excitement in the early days of the session. After the Legislature was regularly organized things moved rather smoothly and pleasantly. Strange to say there was not much bad feeling, everybody seemed to be in a fairly good humor. Of course there was not a great deal of legislation enacted and probably it is best that that was the case.[34]

Soon after the arduous legislative session, Governor Glasscock felt the need to recuperate and contemplate the need of an extra session with a rest at White Sulphur Springs, followed by a vacation in Roseland, Florida, during the latter part of March and April. Finances, always a problem, followed the governor to the land of sunshine. While in Florida, Glasscock's private secretary wrote to his brother, Fuller, in Morgantown, to send money. Whether in jest or not, Fuller sent this reply to the Governor's emissary, perhaps as a way of chiding his brother for his careless spending habits:

You say the Governor needs this money very much but it seems to me that if he would not be so extravigant [sic] with his salary during the sessions

33 M. S. Hodges to Glasscock, 21 February 1911, Glasscock Papers.
34 Glasscock to Stephen Mason, 8 April 1911, Glasscock Papers; *Wheeling Intelligencer*, February 25, 1911.

of the legislature, and not spend too much money playing poker and while he is fishing and hunting in Florida, that he could get along without any money other than his salary, and thereby relieve the stringency in the money market here.[35]

Perhaps Fuller Glasscock's comments were not far from the truth. By November 1911, U.S. Senator Nathan B. Scott urged Glasscock and some other "good" Republicans to buy stock in the *Charleston Daily Mail*, which was in receivership and in danger of falling into Democratic hands. Unable to comply, the governor explained, "So far as I am concerned I am pretty nearly bankrupt. I have to borrow money to pay interest on the notes I have already given and also to meet running expenses."[36]

While vacationing, Governor Glasscock learned that the United States Supreme Court had rendered a decision in the Virginia Debt Case that was adverse to West Virginia. Since the separation of West Virginia from Virginia during the Civil War, the Mountain State's share of Virginia's public debt had remained a question. Concerning this problem, there had been much controversy in selecting a method to compute the debt, and the case had moved slowly through the courts.[37]

Since 1871, Virginia had figured West Virginia's liability based on the population and territory of the two sections, and allotted about one-third of its public debt to its former citizens. The Mother State funded that portion in the form of certificates of indebtedness to be collected by their holders when West Virginia paid its part. The Mountain State, on the other hand, wanted to determine its debt based on benefits derived from the sale of Virginia bonds with proceeds applied to internal improvements in both sections. This total figure would have been much smaller. The Supreme Court, however, used its own method of computation, based upon the estimated value of the real and personal property of the two states, slaves not included, at the time of separation, June 20, 1863.[38]

---

35 S. F. Glasscock to H. P. Brightwell, 2 April 1911, Glasscock Papers.

36 Glasscock to Senator N. B. Scott, 25 November 1911, Glasscock Papers.

37 For a concise account of the debt question, see Elizabeth Cometti and Festus P. Summers, eds., *The Thirty-Fifth State* (Morgantown: West Virginia University Library, 1966), 516–18. For an excellent study of the Virginia Debt question see Elizabeth J. Goodall, "The Virginia Debt Controversy and Settlement," Part I, *West Virginia History*, 24 (October 1962): 42–74; Part II, 24 (April 1963): 296–311; Part III, 24 (July 1963): 332–351; and Part IV, 25 (October 1963): 42–68. Hereafter cited as Goodall, "The Virginia Debt Controversy."

38 Goodall, "The Virginia Debt Controversy," Part III, 340–47.

In March 1911, Justice Oliver Wendell Holmes stated that West Virginia owed Virginia $7,182,507.48. This sum amounted to 23.5 percent of Virginia's contested public debt. The court also determined that the Mountain State owed interest on this amount, but left the question open to compromise between the two states.[39] This was simply another step in trying to work out the unique legal and constitutional problems of one state separating from another, without its consent, during a period of war. Abraham Lincoln and other statehood supporters knew that it would be a long legal process, one that many contemporaries never lived to see solved.[40]

After the court's decision in 1911, former Governor Dawson wrote to Glasscock in Florida that the justices had been hasty in their decision, ignoring legal questions raised by the West Virginia lawyers.[41] He advised the governor, who was on record as promising to fight the debt question to the "bitter end," to move slowly and to make "an elaborate statement for publication in the *Intelligencer* and other newspapers."[42] Adjutant General Elliott also advised that the West Virginia lawyers should proceed cautiously in the case. He informed the governor that it was a good time for diplomacy

39 *Richmond Dispatch*, September 21, 1911, clipping in the Glasscock Papers; John W. Mason, "The Virginia Debt," in *West Virginia Legislative Hand Book and Manual and Official Register, 1916*, ed. John T. Harris, (Charleston: The Tribune Printing Co., 1916), 810-825

40 The news of West Virginia's indebtedness to the mother state was certainly not a surprise to West Virginians. The debt had previously been acknowledged in the "Wheeling Ordinance," which called for the creation of a new state, and the West Virginia Constitution of 1862. In retrospect, settlement of the debt matter had moved slowly until February 26, 1906, when Virginia sued West Virginia in the United States Supreme Court. Virginia acted in the capacity of trustee for the "West Virginia certificate" holders, who were a variety of people of different political persuasions. The Court decided to appoint a Special Master to gather data from both states from which it would later act on the question. This occurred during the administration of Governor William M. O. Dawson, who wrote confidentially to Senator Elkins in 1907 to lobby the Court subtly in an effort to secure a western man, not an individual from the big money centers. The Justices chose Charles E. Littlefield of Vermont as Special Master. See the *Charleston Gazette*, November 6, 1911, clipping in Glasscock Papers; W. M. O. Dawson to Senator S. B. Elkins, 16 December 1907, S. B. Elkins Papers.

41 In 1911, the West Virginia lawyers were W. M. O. Dawson; former United States Senator John C. Spooner of Wisconsin; ex-Secretary of the Treasury John G. Carlisle of New York; West Virginia Attorney General William G. Conley; Professor Charles E. Hogg, Dean of the College of Law of WVU; and the law firm of McClintic, Mollohan and Mathews of Charleston. See *Wheeling Register*, May 4, 1909; *Morgantown Post-Chronicle*, October 6, 1908; and *Charleston Gazette*, March 18, 1910.

42 Former Governor Dawson to Glasscock, 7 March 1911, Glasscock Papers.

and added, "Legally, I am sure not a cent of this money can be collected, yet we must not be placed in the position of refusing to settle the points of the controversy in some diplomatic manner."[43] Fuller Glasscock viewed the debt as one of "deep seated equity," and when it "fully matured" the Supreme Court would enter a final decree in favor of Virginia for about seven million dollars, "but not much interest."[44]

In contrast, former Governor Atkinson had already devised a way for West Virginia to pay the debt. He felt that West Virginia's attorneys should meet with their Virginia counterparts and work on a line of compromise suggested in the closing paragraph of Justice Holmes' opinion. He added, "The amount of the judgment is much larger than any of us expected but it is not so great if we can get rid of the forty odd years' of interest." Atkinson stated that the present constitution permitted the legislature to issue twenty-year bonds sold at 4% interest "and create a sinking fund to meet the bonds at maturity, which can be done without greatly increasing the taxes of our people." The former governor concluded that the lawyers should meet during the summer to reach a compromise, and then Glasscock should call an extra session of the legislature to deal with the controversy.[45]

Upon his return from Florida in late March, Glasscock carefully studied the possible avenues of action and contemplated the possibility of adding the debt case to a special call of the legislature. He felt somewhat embarrassed about the whole matter, as it had arisen at a most inopportune time. He feared that it might detract from issues like a primary election law to which he assigned higher priority. There were those who advised him not to add the Virginia Debt Case to a special call, if indeed he issued one, because "the primary law is more important."[46]

As it appeared at that time, the governor had three alternatives: (1) make arrangements to pay; (2) repudiate the debt; or (3) appoint a commission to confer with a like commission from Virginia. In any event, it would not be unwise, Glasscock surmised, to leave the matter in the hands of the lawyers, "and let Virginia get anxious."[47] In concluding the episode, Governor Glasscock agreed with his friend, Judge John W. Mason of Fairmont, that the case could not be constitutionally added to a special call to the legislature, since it had not been dealt with during the regular

---

43 C. D. Elliott to Glasscock, 11 March 1911, Glasscock Papers.
44 S. F. Glasscock to Glasscock, 12 April 1911, Glasscock Papers.
45 G. W. Atkinson to Glasscock, 27 March 1911, Glasscock Papers.
46 W. C. Grimes to Glasscock, 10 April 1911, Glasscock Papers.
47 W. C. Grimes to Glasscock, 10 April 1911, Glasscock Papers.

session. As it had so many times in the past, the debt question would be carried over to the next regular session.[48]

Following the debt decision, Glasscock quickly turned his attention to the legislature. By early April, he had determined to call a special session despite the fact that most Republican leaders advised against it. Yet as Glasscock told one correspondent in April, "The only thing I have serious doubt about is as to the time when it should be called."[49] The governor concluded that the legislature would only pass a primary election law during a special session where they could devote their undivided attention to it.[50] He also believed that if the law were submitted to the people, seventy-five percent of them would vote for it. Glasscock further reasoned:

> Ever since 1890 our party in Convention assembled has declared in favor of a primary election law, and the Democrats have been doing likewise. Since that time we have had six regular sessions of the legislature and nothing had been done, except that the House of Delegates at three different sessions has passed a fairly good bill, but in each instance it has failed in consideration in the Senate. It would, therefore, seem that we have no hope for such a law at a regular session and the only means left to secure it is through a special session.[51]

Glasscock recognized that he had to force the primary bill out of the Senate Judiciary Committee that had prevented its passage. He knew of at least eight Republican Senators who would vote affirmatively and was sure of enough Democrats to secure its passage.[52]

---

48   Glasscock to John W. Mason, 7 April 1911, Glasscock Papers; William G. Conley, Commonwealth of Virginia v. State of West Virginia 220 U.S. 17 (1911). Virginia was perturbed at West Virginia's inaction. It appealed to the Supreme Court to decide the case in full. The Court had previously stated that it would settle the matter of interest if the two sides could not get together, but agreed with West Virginia Attorney General Conley's request for a delay of time.

49   Glasscock to W. C. Grimes, 5 April 1911, Glasscock Papers.

50   H. C. Ogden to Glasscock, 3 April 1911, Glasscock Papers. Prominent Republicans against the special session included H. C. Ogden, editor of the *Wheeling Intelligencer*; Circuit Court Judge John W. Mason; former Governors White and Atkinson; and former Senator N. B. Scott. On the other hand, former Congressman William P. Hubbard led the sentiment for it. See also Glasscock to State Senator Jake Fisher, 5 April 1911, Glasscock Papers.

51   Glasscock to W. C. Grimes, 5 April 1911; Glasscock to J. W. McIntire, 5 April 1911, both in Glasscock Papers.

52   Glasscock to John W. Mason, 4 April 1911, Glasscock Papers.

As a matter of record, the Governor had received encouragement from a number of "primary" Democrats. Democratic Senator Jake Fisher favored the bill and pledged the support of Senator Phillips as well. Senators Bland and Preston were also expected to add their support.[53] In addition, Democratic Committeeman John T. McGraw had also written in favor of the measure.[54] The time seemed ripe for its passage,[55] and the governor, with his prestige on the line, prepared for battle.

On April 18, Governor Glasscock issued a call for the legislature to meet in a special session on May 16 to consider the passage of a primary election law and to amend or re-enact the Corrupt Practices Act of 1891, which, according to the governor, contained too many loopholes.[56] When the legislature convened, it was evident that there would be difficulty in enacting the desired legislation.[57] As the session proceeded, Glasscock perceived that there would be trouble in the House, where the Democrats held a majority. It was also clear that some "stand-patters" in his party on the state and national levels were determined to prevent the passage of a primary law. In at least one instance, Glasscock appealed for the intervention of President Taft when he learned that two West Virginia postmasters were lobbying for the defeat of the measure.[58]

Governor Glasscock and most Republican legislators supported the Coffman primary bill, as introduced in the Senate. The bill provided for the nomination by the electorate of all candidates of both parties on the local, county, and state levels, including those for the United States Senate.[59] Also under consideration and similar in scope was the Democratic-endorsed French bill,[60] which called for a referendum before

---

53 Glasscock to Jake Fisher, 5 April 1911, Glasscock Papers; *Wheeling Intelligencer*, May 29, 1911.

54 Glasscock to John T. McGraw, 20 April 1911, Glasscock Papers.

55 Glasscock to F. A. MacDonald, 29 April 1911; Glasscock to S. A. D. Glasscock, 5 May 1911, both in Glasscock Papers; *Parkersburg Dispatch-News*, April 14, 1911 and *Parkersburg Sentinel*, April 19, 1911, both clippings in Glasscock Papers. The Republican press, such as the *Parkersburg Dispatch-News*, took the view that the two United States Senators, Watson and Chilton, opposed a primary election law because they were not willing to risk defeat at the hands of party members. The Democratic newspapers, however, had a different opinion. The *Charleston Gazette*, the *Fairmont Times*, and *Parkersburg Sentinel* believed that it was due to the folly of the fifteen Republican senators that there was a need for a special meeting of the legislature.

56 Glasscock to John W. Mason, 7 April 1911, Glasscock Papers.

57 *Fairmont Times*, May 19, 1911, clipping in Glasscock Papers.

58 Glasscock to President Taft, 22 May 1911, Glasscock Papers.

59 *West Virginia Senate Journal*, Extraordinary Session, 1911, 1–7.

60 *West Virginia Senate Journal*, Extraordinary Session, 1911, 30–35.

enactment. If a majority of voters accepted the proposal, it would become effective on July 1, 1913. Many Republicans pointed out that the date would exclude the election of Senator Watson, who would have been already chosen by the legislature of 1913. According to the progressives, it would also give the conservatives an opportunity to manipulate the vote to their favor during the referendum. Governor La Follette had the same fears when faced with a referendum in Wisconsin; the voters of that state, however, passed a direct primary bill by a majority of over 50,000.[61] The GOP also stated that the French bill was unconstitutional because there was no provision in the West Virginia Constitution giving the right to the voters to enact legislation; therefore, the measure could not be submitted to the people in the form of a referendum.[62] A deadlock ensued, centering on a primary election law, allowing little time for passage of a new or revised corrupt practices act.

The fight moved to the House, where the governor hoped that the members would be more receptive to reform legislation as they had in the past. To his consternation, the anti-primary Democrats and Republicans and allegedly the "Chilton-Watson" Democrats combined to prevent any compromise.[63] The crux of the matter was that the referendum clause was unacceptable to the GOP, and the Democrats refused to eliminate it. With time running out, the Democratic majority voted to refer the question of a direct primary law to a bipartisan commission that would report its findings to the next legislature. The solons adjourned without accomplishing anything. Among others, John T. McGraw expressed frustration when he commented, "I think the Democratic House made a grave mistake in adjourning without the enactment of a primary election law."[64]

H. C. Ogden, editor of the *Wheeling Intelligencer*, who had been against the special session, expressed the sentiment of many Republicans when he wrote that the Democrats had hurt themselves and were now in a weakened condition.[65] Glasscock was confident that the legislature of 1913 would pass a primary election law, because of the failure of the extra session to do so. He believed the Democratic bosses, the same ones who had secured the election of Chilton and Watson, got control of the House and prevented its passage into law. The governor also had "reliable information" that some members of the Republican State Committee were under the domination of Senator Watson and

61   Robert M. La Follette, *La Follette's Autobiography* (Madison, Wisconsin: The University of Wisconsin Press, 1968), 127.

62   *Wheeling Intelligencer*, May 29 1911; May 31, 1911.

63   *Huntington Herald-Dispatch*, May 26, 1911, clipping in Glasscock Papers.

64   *Clarksburg Telegram*, June 1, 1911, clipping in Glasscock Papers.

65   H. C. Ogden to Glasscock, 2 June 1911, Glasscock Papers.

the Fairmont Coal Company. Moreover, Glasscock felt that the problems existing in the GOP would not be solved until there was a reorganization of the State Committee.[66]

In calling an extra session, Governor Glasscock had gambled and lost, but he firmly believed the sake of his party depended on passage of progressive legislation. Other leaders, such as his Kentucky neighbor Democratic Governor James B. McCreary, had achieved the elusive goal of obtaining a direct primary, using logic that was familiar to Glasscock, "The government should be brought close to the people, and there can be no bosses or rings in connection with a primary election legally and honestly held."[67] The governor had good intentions, but good intentions do not always make a strong leader. The fact remains that Glasscock had entered the battle for reform legislation against the advice of leading Republicans and was unable to maneuver the bills through the legislature. He had pushed aside the investigation of the Watson-Chilton election and the problem of the Virginia Debt matter to deal with later. In hindsight, perhaps, he should have attacked those problems sooner and, as a result, weakened the opposition. But, for the present, Glasscock looked ahead to the 1913 legislature in hopes of vindication.

66   Glasscock to H. C. Ogden, 25 November 1910, Glasscock Papers.
67   Burckel, "Progressive Governors," 229.

DIVIDED REPUBLICANS PREPARE
FOR THE WAR OF 1912

"We could all get together, call each other names, 'cuss' a little . . ."[1]

S INCE THE 1908 ELECTION, Governor Glasscock and other top Republicans concluded that the Republican State Committee needed a complete reorganization
because they had lost confidence in its ability to lead the party to victory and
to do its duties fairly. After all, the governor knew firsthand the inner workings of that
group and, in fact, was a member when they selected a compromise gubernatorial candidate in 1908. The severe defeat in the 1910 election convinced Governor Glasscock
that a complete overhaul of the central body was necessary in order to prevent defeat
in 1912.[2] While many people at that time sang a new popular refrain "Cuddle Up Little
Closer, Lovey Mine," others were also singing, "You're In The Right Church, But The
Wrong Pew." Glasscock, for one, felt that some members of the State Committee were
also in the wrong pew. In his opinion, they had been too biased and too conservative in
the past; he believed it had been too easy for some party members to influence committeemen because most of them were federal and state officeholders.[3] This usually meant
they owed their jobs to a higher political figure who could later call in debts. Glasscock
wanted to put an end to that practice.

---

1   U.S. Senator Nathan B. Scott to Glasscock, 28 March 1911, Glasscock Papers.

2   H.C. Ogden to Glasscock, 18 February 1911, Glasscock Papers.

3   The State Committee was composed of sixteen members. In 1908, at least nine of these men
had been officeholders. In 1911, the committeemen were O. A. Petty of Charleston; W. W. Whyte
of McDowell County; S. V. Matthews of Charleston; Sherman Denham of Clarksburg; Howard
Fleming of Fairmont; James E. Doyle of McMechen; W. R. Messervie of Ritchie; Sam Dixon of
Fayette County; J. E. Noel of Fayette County, the one African-American member; Robert Hazlett of
Wheeling; Harry Woodyard of Parkersburg; L. G. Forman of Parkersburg; Amos Bright of Weston;
Virgil Highland of Clarksburg; J. M. Sanders of Bluefield; and E. K. Martin of Buckhannon.

Following the election of 1910, Governor Glasscock sought the aid of President Taft in an attempt to secure the resignations of the federal officeholders on the State Committee. Taft agreed with Glasscock and delegated the responsibility of obtaining the resignations to Senator Scott. For his part, the governor planned to persuade the state officials to vacate their posts.[4]

Governor Glasscock knew it would be no easy task to remove some members, fearing they would rather disrupt the party than retire. Yet, some were also ready to resign for a price. Sherman Denham of Clarksburg and Howard Fleming of Fairmont indicated their willingness to retire if reappointed postmasters in their respective cities.[5] After all, President Taft's Postmaster General, Frank Hitchcock, considered the prime dispenser of federal patronage in the administration, could easily make that a reality. Bringing peace to the Republican Party in West Virginia in exchange for job security did not seem a bad deal in order to satisfy the factions.[6] In addition, insiders informed the governor that Democratic Senator Clarence W. Watson of the Fairmont Coal Company had influence over other committee members. Glasscock wrote to Judge John W. Mason of Marion County, "I want to suggest that one of the greatest troubles in your county is that the Republican party, as well as the Democratic party, is dictated to by the Fairmont Coal Company and its officials."[7] With his own party divided, and with alleged Democratic influence on the State Committee, the reform governor faced difficult times.[8]

Many Republicans advised Glasscock to bring party members together in some type of meeting. Some, including Senator Scott, supported the idea of a general convention, where they could meet and work out their problems. As Scott told Glasscock, "We could all get together, call each other names, 'cuss' a little, if it helps anybody, but thresh out all our differences before we have a Convention or primary, so that when we meet to nominate candidates we will all be together."[9]

Governor Glasscock, however, preferred to have the State Committee convene first and then issue a call for a state convention. The committee would authorize

4   Glasscock to President Taft, 9 December 1910; Senator N. B. Scott to Glasscock, 28 March 1911, both in Glasscock Papers.
5   Glasscock to H. C. Ogden, 25 November 1910; Glasscock to C. F. Snyder, 29 November 1910, both in Glasscock Papers.
6   Harbaugh, *Power and Responsibility*, 385.
7   Glasscock to J. W. Mason, 17 June 1911, Mason Papers.
8   Glasscock to H. C. Ogden, 25 November 1910, Glasscock Papers.
9   *Wheeling Intelligencer*, March 20, 1911; Senator Scott to Glasscock, 28 March 1911, Glasscock Papers.

the convention to select new committee members and adopt guidelines for all committees in the state, county, and congressional districts. This was a logical first step, since much of the factionalism in the party existed in these local bodies. In brief, along with new faces, Glasscock also wanted different rules and regulations.[10] Glasscock and his fellow reformers concluded that the organizational operation of the Republican Party had to become transparent in order to eliminate the abusive power of certain elites from the county to the state level. The old system of handpicking certain candidates to run for office for the benefit of a clique or machine was no longer acceptable to the majority of the people or compatible with the spirit of the times. The "new order" demanded regularity and orderliness to maintain a sense of fairness, efficiency, and continuity in step with other professional and industrial structures of the new century.

During the spring of 1911, the governor met with State Committee Chairman S. V. Matthews, a Charleston attorney, to commence plans.[11] He and Matthews agreed upon the necessity of reorganization and the need for all officeholders to resign. Soon after this conference, it was announced that Republicans would meet in a state convention at Charleston on October 11 to hear plans for the restructuring of the State Committee. Action appeared probable.

In the meantime, the weary governor set up headquarters at White Sulphur Springs to endure the "heated season" better.[12] In a letter to a fellow Republican, Glasscock wrote "I play golf twice a day and have plenty of time between times to do all the work that I care to do during the heated season, in fact I am able to do more than I would in Charleston because I am not bothered so much."[13] At that peaceful setting, he and others, such as H. C. Ogden, drafted plans for the gathering in Charleston. The governor supported a plan to lessen the power of the county committees in an effort to eliminate dissension on the local level. His proposal provided for district primaries, which would choose representatives to a state-nominating convention. During these primaries, the electorate would also vote for candidates who were running for state office, using the results to guide the delegates in their convention deliberations. The reformers also intended to ask for the resignation of all federal and state officeholders

---

10   Glasscock to H. C. Ogden, 20 February 1911, Glasscock Papers.
11   Glasscock to H. C. Ogden, 5 April 1911, Glasscock Papers.
12   Glasscock to C. D. Elliott, 17 July 1911; Glasscock to M. L. Brown, 17 July 1911, both in Glasscock Papers.
13   Glasscock to S. M. Smith, 9 August 1911, Glasscock Papers.

on the Republican State Committee.[14] If all went well, the GOP would regain the confidence of the people.

Once party affairs seemed to be moving in a desirable direction, the governor turned his attention to old business, the alleged fraudulent election of the Democratic U.S. Senators Chilton and Watson. Glasscock felt the time ripe for action against the "gold dust twins." He wanted the members of the State Committee to prepare a petition to be filed with the United States Senate asking for an investigation of the charges preferred by the Democratic members of the state legislature against the two senators.[15] In a speech at Pineville, Wyoming County, Senator Chilton had challenged the Republican Party to investigate him and Watson. Governor Glasscock had responded that the challenge would be accepted at the proper time "and before the proper tribunal, an investigation of these charges will be made and it will not be in Pineville."[16] Glasscock had two motives in going after the Democratic politicians:

> I am not willing that the Republican party should be placed on the defensive, we must be the aggressor, and we must go after them from every angle and in every legitimate way. I am not only in favor of this investigation from a political standpoint, but I believe the primary and first consideration is to defend the fair name of our State. If these senators were elected by the methods charged by Democratic members of the Legislature it was a disgrace to the State.[17]

Although Glasscock acted with the encouragement of disgruntled Democrats, fellow Republicans, former governors, and the Republican press, the investigation led to no convictions. In August 1912, Governor Glasscock personally took the evidence that he, William S. Edwards, and his hired investigators had gathered to Washington D. C., placing it with New York Senator Elihu Root, hoping for a Senate

---

14   Glasscock to John W. Mason, 8 August 1911; H. C. Ogden to Glasscock, 12 August 1911; Glasscock to the subcommittee appointed by the Republican State Committee, 27 October 1911, all in Glasscock Papers.

15   Glasscock to John W. Graham, 4 October 1911, Glasscock Papers.

16   *Wheeling Intelligencer*, January 17, 1911; September 25, 1911; *Charleston Daily Mail*, September 19, 1911; September 25, 1911.

17   Glasscock to H. Roy Waugh, 31 July 1911, Glasscock Papers. Senators Watson and Chilton were later cleared of these charges for lack of evidence. See the *Charleston Gazette*, February 9, 1913.

resolution for investigation. Root, slow to act, perhaps because there had been so many other investigations in recent months, eventually turned the papers over to the Senate Committee on Privileges and Elections. In February 1913, the committee completely exonerated Senators Watson and Chilton. Chairman Dillingham of the same committee stated, "The only charge was traceable to the assertion by Delegate Shock of the West Virginia legislature that he had been paid $1,000 and promised more if he would vote for the two senators. He has retracted that statement and with that retraction the entire accusation falls to the ground."[18]

The plans for reform were laid, but difficulty, as expected, came in the person of Committeeman Sherman Denham. Denham, allegedly supported by Davis Elkins, was doing all he could to prevent a reorganization of the State Committee. Glasscock learned that the former postmaster had sent letters asking certain members of that body not to retire.[19] Adjutant General Elliott, not a novice when it came to political battles, reviewed the situation with the governor and informed him that he had "conclusive evidence" that Davis Elkins and the postmasters on the committee were doing everything they could to disrupt party reforms. Elliott added that he had "information that would convict in court," and he could come to no other conclusion than "somebody at Washington is of the opinion that you are easy and do not know which way the wind blows."[20] The lines were drawn, and Glasscock prepared for trouble.

On October 10, 1911, West Virginia Republicans gathered in Charleston to discuss plans for the reorganization of their party. It was an enthusiastic meeting that left many optimistic that those reforms would eventually occur; however, Glasscock was not entirely pleased with the results. Instead of adopting a statewide primary with the magisterial district as the unit, the State Committee proposed a statewide primary with the state as the unit. H. C. Ogden and Henry D. Hatfield attempted to convince the committeemen of the advantages of a district primary, but the mood of the convention seemed to favor a broader plan.[21] Ogden was also of the opinion "that our friend Denham and probably some other gentleman from the extreme lower end

---

18   Malsomson, "William E. Glasscock, Governor of the People," 37. See also Richard Randolph McMahon to Governor Glasscock, 20 January 1912; 24 January 1912, Glasscock Papers, and the *Parkersburg Sentinel*, February 8, 1913.

19   H. C. Ogden to Glasscock, 4 August 1911, Glasscock Papers.

20   C. D. Elliott to Glasscock, 11 August 1911, Glasscock Papers. Elliott and Glasscock believed the federal officeholders were receiving support from Postmaster General Frank Hitchcock in Washington, D. C.

21   Henry D. Hatfield to H. C. Ogden, 14 October 1911, Glasscock Papers.

pulled the wool over the eyes of some members of the State Committee,"[22] because several men thought they were voting for a magisterial plan when they supported the resolution.

Governor Glasscock experienced another disappointment when the committee failed to act on his suggestion to appoint a group of Republicans "to go into each of the counties in which there are two committees and try to harmonize the differences between the factions."[23] yet, the office-holding members did offer their resignations. In the meantime, the same people were in command of the situation,[24] and they appointed a subcommittee to meet in Clarksburg on November 6 to devise rules and regulations for a statewide Republican primary to be held June 4, 1912.

The subcommittee began its work almost immediately and asked leading Republicans to present in writing their ideas on the proposed statewide primary. Governor Glasscock seized this opportunity to publicize the assets of a district plan. In an interview, the governor confirmed that he was a believer in direct primaries, but he made an important distinction. He stated that he would support a state primary if the legislature passed such a bill;[25] a state law with penalties for misconduct would at least ensure, to a larger degree, a fair election. Yet he also feared that a mere plurality of votes for state candidates would discriminate against West Virginia's lesser populated counties;[26] a district plan would be more equitable. Moreover, it would be much more difficult to "fix" an election by using a primary along with a delegate convention. In short, the governor supported the Lilly primary bill, devised by A. A. Lilly of Raleigh County, which expressed these sentiments.[27]

---

22   H. C. Ogden to Glasscock, 17 October 1911; Glasscock to J. W. McIntire, 13 October 1911, both in Glasscock Papers; *Wheeling Intelligencer*, October 10, 1911; October 11, 1911; October 12, 1911.

23   Glasscock to Thomas P. Jacobs, 13 October 1911; Glasscock to J. W. McIntire, 13 October 1911, both in Glasscock Papers.

24   *Wheeling Intelligencer*, October 11, 1911; October 12, 1911; *Charleston Daily Mail*, October 11, 1911.

25   *Wheeling Intelligencer*, October 30, 1911.

26   Glasscock to Henry D. Hatfield, 23 October 1911; Glasscock to Colonel S. Dixon, 7 November 1911, Glasscock Papers.

27   Glasscock to the subcommittee appointed by the Republican State Committee, 27 October 1911, Glasscock Papers. In brief, the Lilly plan provided for the holding of district primary elections for the selection of delegates to a Republican state-nominating convention. In addition to voting for delegates, Republicans were also to choose candidates for office, instructing the delegates of their choice.

On November 6, Glasscock attended the subcommittee meeting in Clarksburg. Unfortunately, the situation did not go well for the governor. The five members, as selected by the full committee, felt they had no other choice than to recommend a statewide primary with the state as the unit, as called for by the Charleston resolution. Glasscock continued to believe that some of the members still failed to distinguish between the state and the magisterial district units. In concluding its activity in Clarksburg, at which the governor had made his plea, the subcommittee met in a closed session on November 8 to complete formulation of the rules and regulations for a statewide primary. They decided to present their results to the full committee in Parkersburg on November 13, which allowed the governor one last chance to speak for his plan.[28]

As so often happened, Governor Glasscock fell ill with bronchitis and was unable to attend the meeting. His Charleston physician, Dr. Moore, placed him on a special diet to gain weight, because Glasscock did not eat enough.[29] He had, however, been in touch with certain members of the State Committee and thought that at least three would vote for the district plan. The governor needed nine votes to make the change.[30] H. C. Ogden felt that Glasscock could count on the votes of five members of that body, but he was discouraged and thought, "the whole situation is developing into a worse condition of affairs than existed before the Charleston meeting."[31]

In addition to poor health, Governor Glasscock once again struggled with his personal finances. By 1911, money preyed heavily on his mind as debts accumulated; he attempted to pay on two notes of $1,250 each owned by George C. Baker and the Oak Grove Cemetery, plus his share of the investment in the Battelle District coal deal. The Bank of Morgantown held a note for $6,000, on which Glasscock owed an interest of $82.50, and the Bank of Masontown held one for $5,000, on which he owed $37.50. In November 1911, he found it impossible to pay the interest on these debts and asked his friend M. L. Brown to pay them for him.

The governor was disheartened, but Brown reasoned that although it was a financial drain on him now, there would be plenty of opportunities to make money

---

28   The subcommittee was composed of S. V. Matthews of Charleston; Virgil L. Highland of Clarksburg; J. M. Sanders of Bluefield; E. K. Martin of Buckhannon; and L. J. Forman of Parkersburg. See the *Wheeling Intelligencer*, November 7 1911;   November 8, 1911.

29   Glasscock to Dr. M. H. Brown, 2 December 1911; Glasscock to Fuller Glasscock, 2 December 1911, both in Glasscock Papers.

30   Glasscock to H. C. Ogden, 11 November 1911, Glasscock Papers.

31   H. C. Ogden to Glasscock, 9 November 1911, Glasscock Papers.

when Glasscock returned to Morgantown,[32] a pleasant thought for a leader of a party under duress. For the present, however, Governor Glasscock focused his attention on the Republican Party that seemed to be adrift and headed in the wrong direction.

Glasscock and Ogden saw their faint hopes dashed when the State Committee in Parkersburg chose the statewide primary plan. Only six members voted for the Lilly measure. To the surprise of the governor, Chairman Matthews, who had earlier declared that he would support the district proposal, and had in fact done so at Charleston, changed his mind at Parkersburg. In explaining his action, Matthews admitted to Glasscock that he had been "drinking but denies stoutly any intention . . . [of] doing anything other than what he believed to be to the best interests of the party."[33] The federal and state officeholders did resign at the meeting, however. Although the makeup of the committee changed, its outlook remained quite consistent since outgoing members chose their successors.[34] Clearly, the conservatives conspired to maintain the status quo, as Elliott reported to Glasscock, "I have conclusive evidence that Elkins and the post master part of the committee, who are in touch at Washington, are doing all they can in an organized manner to prevent a reorganization of the committee and are loath to surrender any prestige or power they have as members of the committee for the welfare of the party."[35] The entire proceeding led Glasscock to wonder about the future prospects of his party. He lamented:

> I think the reorganization was a farcical and a monumental blunder, and if those people had had the best interests of the Republican party at heart I feel that they would not have acted as they did.
>
> It is unfortunate for us that leading Democrats of the State have more influence with our highest and most important committee than Republicans who have been voting the ticket for many, many years. This is a hard thing to say and yet I believe it is true.[36]

32 M. L. Brown to Glasscock, 23 August 1911; 18 November 1911; 22 November 1911, all in Glasscock Papers.
33 Glasscock to H. C. Ogden, 17 November 1911, Glasscock Papers.
34 *Charleston Daily Mail*, November 17, 1911.
35 C. D. Elliott to Glasscock, 11 August 1911, Glasscock Papers.
36 Glasscock to J. M. Jacobs, 17 November 1911, Glasscock Papers. No doubt, the reference to Democratic influence on the State Committee was aimed at Senator C. W. Watson and possibly former-Governor A. B. Fleming, both of the Fairmont Coal Company who certainly influenced the actions of local officeholders Howard Fleming, a Fairmont postmaster, and Sherman

Upon closer examination of the final Republican Party primary plan and after a period to reflect, Glasscock surmised that it was a good one and "in some respects exceptionally good."[37] The compromise agreement stated that each county would hold a primary election on June 4, 1912, to select nominees for governor, secretary of state, superintendent of free schools, auditor, treasurer, attorney general, and commissioner of agriculture. Voters would also nominate candidates for the House of Representatives from the congressional districts, circuit judges from the judicial circuits, members of the state Senate from the senatorial districts, and aspirants to the House of Delegates from the different counties. Finally, the people would choose Republicans for county offices including candidates for magisterial district offices.[38]

In addition to the statewide primary, the first held in the state, on different dates each magisterial district within a county would meet in mass meetings to elect two sets of delegates, sending one to Congressional District Conventions, which would select two delegates and two alternates to the Republican National Convention, and one presidential elector. The other set would be sent to the state convention to be held in Huntington on May 16, 1912, which would also select six representatives at large and six alternates for the national convention, plus three presidential electors. A critical step in the selection process, the results of these meetings would ultimately determine whether West Virginia would support Taft or Roosevelt in the national convention at Chicago. The state convention would also name two candidates to the West Virginia Supreme Court of Appeals. Finally, Republicans of each senatorial district would choose one official of the Republican State Executive Committee, and two members of the "colored race" chosen at large. All committeemen were to serve for a period of four years.[39]

In all, it was certainly a convoluted design that seemingly gave party members direct participation in the nomination process. It was also an example of the efforts of the reformers to proactively construct a party apparatus that provided transparency,

---

Denham, postmaster at Clarksburg. Glasscock and Adjutant General Elliott believed Senator Watson and some conservative Republicans were working together to prevent a more open and fair party primary, the passage of a state primary law, and a complete reorganization of the State Committee. After all, conservatives of both parties wanted no drastic change in the status quo or a weakening of their control over party machinery. See C. D. Elliott to Glasscock, 11 August 1911, Glasscock Papers.

37 Glasscock to W. R. Andrews, 18 March 1912, Glasscock Papers.

38 *Charleston Daily Mail*, November 17, 1911.

39 Glasscock to W. R. Andrews, 18 March 1912, Glasscock Papers.

rules, and procedures that would weaken factionalism, especially at the county level, and to create a uniform process for selecting party representatives.

The Republican reformers hoped that reformation and reorganization would lead to a rejuvenated membership and victory at the polls, but the process seemed incomplete because the conservatives still maintained much influence on the central committee. On May 16, 1912, when the state convention met in Huntington, the reformers, in a surprise move, secured enough votes in the convention as a whole to pass a resolution to increase the membership of the committee from sixteen to thirty-three.[40] At that time, the mood of the state was progressive, which meant that a majority of the new members would be of a reforming spirit. The humiliating defeat of the 1910 election provided the Republicans the impetus to incorporate more democracy into their party structure that would lead, they hoped, to victory in 1912.

Governor Glasscock had been a prime mover in advocating reforms, but his health failed at critical periods, and he was unable to exert his full energy. For this reason, Glasscock often lacked political clout, which, on many occasions, left him an ineffectual governor. In the summer of 1911, as his health worsened, Governor Glasscock again found himself deeply troubled over Republican politics within the state. Consulting with several leading party members, he learned that there was much sentiment for Federal District Judge Nathan Goff, a Republican, to run for the governorship in 1912. Former-Governor Atkinson believed that the Republicans should nominate the judge regardless of what he might say, and he was fairly certain that the "General will accept if the nomination is given him by acclamation."[41] Glasscock agreed, but when he wrote to Goff at a later date, assuring him that he could carry the state by a 50,000 majority, the judge indicated that he was not interested in entering state politics.[42]

40 *Charleston Daily Mail*, May 17, 1912. It was rumored that the conservative wing of the Republican Party, led by Davis Elkins, would attempt to add a preferential presidential primary and a preferential United States senatorial primary to the existing Republican plan. The progressives were not willing to go that far because of the lack of a strong primary law and a stronger corrupt practices act. Besides, these two primaries would be under the supervision of the State Committee, which was still suspect. In order to prevent this action the reformers, led by W. M. O. Dawson and William P. Hubbard, successfully spearheaded a movement to increase the membership of the State Committee, which in effect would make it more responsive to the progressives.
41 Glasscock to John W. Mason, 27 June 1911, 1911, Glasscock Papers. Nathan Goff, Jr. was judge of the Fourth U.S. Circuit Court composed of South Carolina, North Carolina, Virginia, Maryland, and West Virginia. See Ambler and Summers, *West Virginia, The Mountain State*, 292–93. See also Williams, *West Virginia and the Captains of Industry*, 246.
42 Glasscock to John W. Mason, 5 July 1911, Glasscock Papers.

Eventually C. W. Swisher of Marion County, C. W. Dillon of Fayette County, and Henry D. Hatfield of McDowell County, entered the race for the governorship. Glasscock, like many Republicans, did not approve of the timing of Senator Hatfield's announcement. It followed a late December 1911 conference in Washington, D. C. attended by former West Virginia Republican Committee members Sherman Denham and Virgil Highland of Clarksburg, Senators Scott and Elkins, and Hatfield, along with others, to discuss the political situation in the Mountain State. Soon after the meeting, Senator Hatfield announced his decision to run for governor, which left the impression that the conference had "fixed" the state ticket. Glasscock felt somewhat miffed at the proceedings and wrote to his brother:

> Confidentially, I have never intimated to anybody that I am for Hatfield, or that I expect to be for his nomination . . . and I presume that Hatfield is not expecting my support because he had never consulted me about it. I did not know of the Washington conference until it was given out in the newspapers.[43]

Yet, most political observers conceded that Hatfield would make a formidable candidate.[44] With the Norfolk and Western Railway behind him, he would be hard to beat. Dillon had strong support in Fayette and Raleigh Counties and areas above the Kanawha River. He was an attorney for the coal baron Sam Dixon of Fayette County, whose coal company controlled over seventy thousand acres of coal land in those two counties. Dixon dominated politics in Fayette County and parts of the southern counties.[45] In fact, jealousy existed between the leaders of the Pocahontas field and those of the Kanawha River district. Disregarding Senator Hatfield, Swisher also received substantial support from the southern part of the state, while Dillon received encouraging reports in the northern area. Yet, Senator Hatfield's strength seemed to cut across sectional lines.[46]

By mid-January 1912, perhaps sensing Glasscock's hostility, Hatfield wrote to the governor explaining his reasons for running:

43 Glasscock to S. F. Glasscock, 29 December 1911, Glasscock Papers. See also H. Roy Waugh to Glasscock, 20 December 1911; M. Horkheimer to Glasscock, 27 December 1911, both in Glasscock Papers.
44 H. C. Ogden to Glasscock, 30 December 1911, Glasscock Papers.
45 Conley, *History of the West Virginia Coal Industry*, 221–22.
46 Conley, *History of the West Virginia Coal Industry*, 221–22.

My tentative announcement was brought about by the persistent appeals of my friends. If I should consult my personal inclination, I would not under any circumstances enter the contest. My mind is in absolute keeping with my last two interviews, which I hope you have read. I am willing to do most anything to assure success for our party in the coming campaign. Of course, I am strong in this section and would get the largest vote ever cast for any candidate for the nomination, as well as break the record in the general election. The entire industrial section is very friendly toward me.[47]

The political pot was boiling, and Governor Glasscock concluded that it was a healthy sign that there were so many good Republicans vying for the gubernatorial nomination.[48] Adjutant General Elliott informed the governor that Senators Scott and Elkins had made a deal whereby Elkins would run for the United States senatorship and Scott for the governorship in the coming election. Elkins continued to desire a senate term of his own, but Scott, occupied with business affairs, chose not to become a candidate for office in 1912.[49] Hatfield remained the evident front-runner.

Soon, national events overshadowed politics in West Virginia. It was clear to Governor Glasscock that President Taft was losing popularity in the Mountain State. In June 1911, Taft's secretary, Charles D. Hilles, wrote to the governor asking for an assessment of the feelings of the people of the state with regard to the president and his administration. Glasscock replied that President Taft had lost support among West Virginia Republicans. Among other things, the governor confided that Taft's appointments had not been well received, as he explained:

I believe it is generally understood that I have a very kindly feeling for President Taft, but a careful canvass of the situation had thoroughly

---

47   Henry D. Hatfield to Glasscock, 17 January 1912, Glasscock Papers.

48   Glasscock to S. F. Glasscock, 28 December 1911, Glasscock Papers.

49   Senator Scott had become a leading force behind a new bank in Washington, D. C., for which M. Horkheimer, a businessman from Wheeling, and others underwrote much of the stock, with the condition that the senator would not run for the governorship of West Virginia. Horkheimer's purpose was twofold: to maintain Scott's health, and to keep him on the National Republican Committee. See M. Horkheimer to Glasscock, 27 December 1912; C. D. Elliott to Glasscock, 11 March 1911, both in Glasscock Papers.

convinced me that an overwhelming majority of the Republicans of West Virginia are for Roosevelt.[50]

Of course, Theodore Roosevelt had prepared quietly and subtly to reenter national politics since 1910. Soon after leaving office, Roosevelt heard from concerned progressives that President Taft was jeopardizing the reforms of his administration, especially in the area of conservation and his perceived support of the conservatives. When Taft fired Roosevelt's good friend Gifford Pinchot, head of the Division of Forestry, for insubordination, Roosevelt was incensed. By the summer of 1910, Roosevelt defended his progressive record and his vision for America, calling it "the New Nationalism," as espoused by the author Herbert Croly. In August, at Osawatomie, Kansas, in a frontal attack at the conservatives, the former president stated, "The essence of any struggle for liberty has always been, and must always be to take from some one man or class of men the right to enjoy power, or wealth, or position, or immunity, which has not been earned by service to his or their fellows."[51] Roosevelt had not yet tossed his hat in the ring for the 1912 presidential election, but it was in his hand.

Before concluding that Taft had negative support in West Virginia, Glasscock had closely examined the political situation. He found that in his own administration the secretary of state, the auditor, the treasurer, the state superintendent of free schools, and the attorney general agreed that Roosevelt was the only Republican who could carry the state. Former-Governors White and Dawson were of the same opinion. Glasscock also had access to several fragmentary straw votes taken in different parts of West Virginia that showed substantial support for Theodore Roosevelt.[52]

Regardless of the popularity of the former president, several influential Republicans refused to abandon Taft. Their ranks included former U.S. Senator Davis Elkins, former Congressman James A. Hughes, and Isaac T. Mann, a coal baron from Bramwell. On the other hand, former Congressman William P. Hubbard and former State Auditor Arnold C. Scherr supported Roosevelt.[53] The struggle strongly resembled the old "stand-pat-insurgent" fight, placing the governor squarely on the side of the insurgents.

---

50   Glasscock to Charles D. Hilles, 17 June 1911, Glasscock Papers.
51   Harbaugh, *Power and Responsibility*, 391.
52   List of polls, signed by Glasscock, February 8, 1912, Glasscock Papers.
53   Glasscock to Pierre De Pew, 8 May 1912, Glasscock Papers.

County	Roosevelt	Taft	La Follette
Braxton	51	3	1
Clay	31	4	—
Greenbrier	221	21	10
Jackson	46	11	2
Marshall	32	1	2
Monongalia	16	1	—
Monroe	105	—	—
Raleigh	91	2	1

Although there seemed to be much support for Roosevelt, he still had to be careful to enter the contest without alienating too many party members on the state and national levels. In other words, he did not want to appear too aggressive. On January 19, 1912, Glasscock publicly endorsed Roosevelt's candidacy. In his statement, he outlined the way in which the former president would probably accept the nomination:

> I am certain Roosevelt will not seek the nomination or work for it in any way, directly or indirectly, and I believe he would not accept it if it came to him as result of intrigue for his personal benefit. But if it comes to him as a result of a genuine popular movement, because the people as a whole believe that he is the best man for the job, then I am sure he will accept.[54]

The Roosevelt boosters and the governors who supported his nomination pondered the best means of providing the former president a way to announce his candidacy. Former Governor John Franklin Fort of New Jersey, apparently acting on his own initiative, suggested that the pro-Roosevelt governors ask him to accept the nomination. Governor Glasscock gladly gave his consent to the plan, "So far as I am concerned I am willing that you shall prepare the letter and present it to the Colonel with my signature." In the meantime, Roosevelt had devised a similar plan by which Frank Knox, the Republican State Chairman of Michigan, was to take a letter to the gover-

---

54   *Wheeling Intelligencer*, January 19, 1912.

nors for their signature,[55] urging Theodore Roosevelt to become a candidate.[56] When the scheme was leaked to the press, it was evidently shelved. In fact, when Governor Glasscock arrived in New York on January 25 for a luncheon with Roosevelt, the press speculated that an announcement was imminent. None, however, was forthcoming. To Nicholas Longworth, Roosevelt exclaimed, "Nick, I have to come out."[57]

Governor Chase Osborn of Michigan solved the problem when he issued a call for a conference of "representative" Republicans to meet in Chicago in early February. Ever loyal to the former president, Glasscock, his personal stenographer, and William S. Edwards, a Kanawha County Republican and politician, left on February 9 for Chicago. At the conference, Governor Glasscock along with governors from Wyoming, Nebraska, New Hampshire, Michigan, and Missouri, signed a formal letter calling upon Roosevelt to announce his candidacy.[58] On the February 24, Theodore Roosevelt answered affirmatively the governors' plea with a letter to each; on February 26, he announced to the press that he would seek the nomination.[59] The seven governors, whom Taft's followers called the "war governors" and the Democrats labeled "the seven little governors who put Roosevelt in a hole," were successful in presenting to "Teddy" a means by which he announced his intentions.[60]

---

55   John Franklin Fort to Glasscock, 19 January 1912; Glasscock to J. F. Fort, 22 January 1912, both in Glasscock Papers.

56   Roosevelt was eager to start the campaign, because he felt the time was right. In the spring of 1911, the support of the newly created National Progressive Republican League was behind Senator Robert La Follette of Wisconsin. His candidacy for the presidential nomination of the Republican party, however, never really got off the ground because Roosevelt withheld his wholehearted support. By January 1912, the big money men such as the publisher Frank Munsey, had switched allegiance to Roosevelt, leaving La Follette near a nervous breakdown. See George E. Mowry, *Theodore Roosevelt and the Progressive Movement* (New York: Hill and Wang, 1960), 172–74 and 207.

57   Paul Douglas Casdorph, "Governor William E. Glasscock and Theodore Roosevelt's 1912 Bull Moose Candidacy," *West Virginia History*, 28 (October 1966): 9. See also *Charleston Daily Mail*, January 26, 1912; January 27, 1912. David Burton, *Theodore Roosevelt*, (New York: Twayne Publishers, Inc., 1972), 189.

58   *Charleston Daily Mail*, February 13, 1912; Glasscock to Governor Chase S. Osborn, 9 February 1912, Glasscock Papers. See also Harbaugh, *Power and Responsibility*, 415.

59   Henry F. Pringle, *Theodore Roosevelt: A Biography* (New York: Harcourt, Brace & Co., 1931), 555–56; *Charleston Daily Mail*, February 24, 1912; February 26, 1912.

60   *Charleston Gazette*, January 30, 1912.

Anticipating a vigorous campaign, Governor Glasscock urged sympathetic party members to organize Roosevelt clubs throughout the state. In particular, the governor worked closely with Colonel William S. Edwards, who had served many years in the legislature,[61] and former Governor Dawson. Dawson, highly motivated and energetic, headed a movement to hold a statewide meeting of Roosevelt people in Parkersburg, scheduled for February 29.[62] Evidently, because of the large number of federal office holders in Wood County, Taft sentiment ran high along with significant anti-Roosevelt feelings. By holding the "love feast" in the lion's den, so to speak, the Roosevelt boosters meant to show they were very serious about their candidate.[63]

The call for the Parkersburg rally received little attention in the state press, which was no surprise since most of the Republican newspapers remained loyal to Taft. H. C. Ogden's *Wheeling Intelligencer* typified this loyalty. Ogden printed an editorial that partially explains why so many progressive Republicans remained Taft supporters. In it, the editor asked why there was a need to call a former president from retirement. In what danger were the American people? He continued:

> The American people were never more prosperous than they are to-day. Wages are higher and hours of work shorter. The country is at peace. The treasury is overflowing. All our great works are being successfully carried on. Why, then, the hysterical assumption that there is one man and only one man among our 15,000,000 voters to whom the duties and powers of the Presidency can be safely entrusted?[64]

In addition to the *Intelligencer*, the two Parkersburg Republican papers, the *Parkersburg Dispatch-News* and the *Parkersburg State Journal*, criticized the Roosevelt movement. On the other hand, at least half the weekly newspapers stood by Roosevelt. In Glasscock's opinion, the *Huntington Herald-Dispatch* and the *Fairmont West Virginian* had been neutral up to that time and had treated the colonel fairly. The

---

61 *Charleston Gazette,* January 30, 1912.
62 W. M. O. Dawson to Glasscock, 8 February 1912; Glasscock to Stephen Mason, 31 January 1912, both in Glasscock Papers.
63 Glasscock to Amos Bright, 19 February 1912, Glasscock Papers. See also Glasscock to Howard Sutherland, 21 February 1912, Glasscock Papers.
64 *Wheeling Intelligencer,* January 20, 1912.

Sistersville Oil Review and the *Morgantown Post-Chronicle* were "out and out" Roosevelt newspapers.[65]

In order to counteract the poor publicity, Glasscock sought aid from the Roosevelt committee in New York. On a number of occasions, he had copies of the *Chicago Tribune* sent to West Virginia, because it was pro-Roosevelt in sentiment. In addition, the governor also received printed copies of Roosevelt's speeches. For example, Glasscock requested 50,000 copies of Roosevelt's New York speech of mid-March 1912, which he thought was "the greatest that has been delivered in this country in my time, and is the best campaign document that we can circulate."[66] Governor Glasscock also obtained copies of the colonel's Columbus speech, and 50,000 copies of an article entitled "Catching up with Roosevelt," which appeared in *Munsey's Magazine*, in addition to 50,000 of another article entitled "Roosevelt's Broadside."[67]

With Republicans subjected to all types of propaganda, it was no surprise that many party members had mixed emotions. While most still held Roosevelt in high esteem, they could not understand why their former chief wanted to take the nomination from its rightful owner, President Taft.[68] On February 28, the day before the statewide meeting of Roosevelt supporters, a Taft club quietly organized at the Chancellor Hotel in Parkersburg, where a subdued mood enveloped the gathering.

From all indications, the announcement made on Monday of the candidacy of ex-President Theodore Roosevelt for the nomination for the presidency cast a gloom over the supporters of President Taft so strong that they could not conceal it; the speakers at this meeting gave expression to these feelings.[69]

By way of contrast, the statewide organization for Roosevelt was a jubilant affair, generating much enthusiasm among the former president's followers. On hand for the festivities, Glasscock arrived at Parkersburg with Adjutant General Elliott and other notables, described by the local press:

---

65   Glasscock to Dr. T. F. Lanham, 12 March 1912, Glasscock Papers.

66   Glasscock to Samuel B. Montgomery, 27 March 1912, Glasscock Papers.

67   Oliver Carpenter to Glasscock, 26 February 1912; 25 March 1912; Glasscock to Oliver Carpenter, 1 March 1912, all in Glasscock Papers.

68   Henry F. Pringle, a student of this period and a biographer of both Theodore Roosevelt and William H. Taft, was critical of Roosevelt for betraying Taft and distorting his administration. See Henry F. Pringle, *The Life and Times of William Howard Taft*, (New York: Farrar & Rinehart, Inc., 1939), 2:765. Hereafter cited as Pringle, *The Life and Times of William Howard Taft*.

69   *Parkersburg Sentinel*, February 28, 1912.

Theodore Roosevelt on the 1912 Campaign Trail.
Courtesy of the Theodore Roosevelt Collection of Harvard College Library, Cambridge, MA.

The widely heralded Roosevelt meeting, to which many boosters for the former President have been looking forward for the past ten days, materialized this afternoon amid great noise, which characterized the former occupant of the White House. The meeting was advertised to begin at 1:30, and a few minutes before that time the Citizens Band escorted from the Chancellor Hotel W. E. Glasscock, Adjutant General Elliott and the Roosevelt clans to the Auditorium Theater, many local supporters of the candidacy of Roosevelt joining in line.[70]

At the theater packed with Roosevelt supporters, Governor Glasscock and Senator D. B. Smith of Huntington appeared on the stage, standing between the portraits of Teddy and Abraham Lincoln. Senator Smith began the proceedings by nominating former Congressman William P. Hubbard as chairman of the meeting. Hubbard

70   *Parkersburg Sentinel*, February 29, 1912.

delivered a harangue against the non-accomplishments of President Taft and criticized the editorial stand of the *Wheeling Intelligencer*. He concluded his remarks with the observation that Roosevelt had carried the state by a 31,000 majority in 1904 and Taft by only 25,000 in 1908.[71]

Former Governor A. B. White gave the most blistering speech of the session as he chastised the Republican newspapers of the state for abusing the Roosevelt people because of a difference of opinion. White particularly singled out the *Parkersburg Dispatch-News*, because it "had been classifying all those Republicans favoring the initiative, referendum and recall, as persons with socialistic and anarchistic ideas."[72] Glasscock was especially pleased with this speech and thanked Governor White for his remarks about the local newspapers, which "would feel the rebuke very keenly."[73]

Following the speeches, former Governor Dawson made a motion that carried, suggesting the appointment of three committees composed of one member from every senatorial district. In quick succession, the leadership created a committee on resolutions, followed by a committee to organize the Roosevelt movement in West Virginia, and, lastly, a committee on permanent organization, chaired by W. M. O. Dawson who was known for his organizational skills. Other members included Houston G. Young of Clarksburg as secretary and William S. Edwards of Charleston as treasurer. Glasscock's good friend and fellow townsman, penitentiary warden M. L. Brown, represented the Eleventh Senatorial District on the Resolutions Committee. Finally, the selection of chairmen for each county, given the authority to select precinct workers, completed the organization.

Elated over the success of the rally, Governor Glasscock noted that "it was a wonderful thing, the like of which I never saw and never expect to see again."[74] Glasscock also marveled at the fact that so many men had traveled hundreds of miles to be there, "paying their own expenses and having no object in view except the good of the party and the country."[75] Glasscock immediately sent a message of good tidings to Roosevelt in New York:

> West Virginia State meeting of Roosevelt Republicans yesterday the greatest I ever saw. About one thousand representative Republicans present representing every senatorial district and nearly every county in the State. It

---

71 *Parkersburg Sentinel*, February 29, 1912.
72 *Parkersburg Sentinel*, February 29, 1912.
73 Glasscock to A. B. White, 8 March 1912, Glasscock Papers.
74 Glasscock to Sol Mayer, 1 March 1912, Glasscock Papers.
75 Glasscock to Sol Mayer, 1 March 1912, Glasscock Papers.

was the greatest tribute ever paid by West Virginia Republicans to any man, and your followers are most enthusiastic and confident we effected a State organization with ex-Governor Dawson at the head and adopted strong resolutions, copy of which I will send you later.[76]

In reply, in early March, Roosevelt informed Governor Glasscock that "my hat is in the ring, and the fight is on." The colonel further commented that the issues were now before the people, and "I think that the people will come out on top."[77] With the completion of the Roosevelt organization, the progressives were ready for the fight, at least in West Virginia.

Governor Glasscock stayed in contact with the Roosevelt headquarters almost daily. Asked to speak outside the state, he declined, stating, "all the time that I can give to the campaign I shall spend in West Virginia."[78] About mid-March, Glasscock went to New York to confer with Roosevelt. After the meeting, the governor described a portion of his visit in a letter to his brother in Bellingham, Washington:

I saw Teddy in New York last week and he is as full of fight as any man you ever saw, and it was a real inspiration to be in his presence for a few minutes. I spent about three hours with him the other night and came away feeling mighty good.[79]

Although ecstatic over the success of the early period of organization, Glasscock knew the stress was beginning to catch up with him. He had become slightly ill in January and had not fully recuperated. In fact, he had traveled to New York twice and once to Chicago and with his delicate health, his aches and pains accumulated. In addition to his travels and efforts to organize the progressives in West Virginia, he found it difficult to keep up with his duties in Charleston. Governor Glasscock wearily explained, "I have used about all the energy I have, and must let up a little or else I will have to lay up for repairs."[80] Little did the governor know how much energy and good health he would need for what lay ahead toward the end of May. The Democratic press had even charged the governor with looking for a higher office, perhaps the vice presidency,

---

76 Glasscock to Theodore Roosevelt, 1 March 1912, Glasscock Papers.
77 Theodore Roosevelt to Glasscock, 2 March 1912, Glasscock Papers.
78 Glasscock to Edwin W. Sims, 28 February 1912, Glasscock Papers.
79 Glasscock to S. A. D. Glasscock, 21 March 1912, Glasscock Papers.
80 Glasscock to B. H. Madeira, 21 March 1912, Glasscock Papers.

because of his avid support for Roosevelt. In answer, Glasscock frankly explained that he was not a candidate for anything, "and in fact am very anxious to retire to private life." He further explained that his tenure of office had been a "wonderful strain" on him physically as well as financially.[81]

Decided perhaps at the second New York meeting in March, Roosevelt scheduled a visit to West Virginia. The delegate elections had already begun and Glasscock wanted the colonel to visit the state before April 6, because Berkeley, Wood, and Summers Counties would select their delegates at that time.[82] When Roosevelt entered the Mountain State on April 2, throngs of well-wishers jubilantly greeted the former president at the different stops along the way, especially at his two main appearances in Huntington and Parkersburg. Traveling aboard the C&O special, the former president made several whistle stops along his itinerary, as Glasscock described:

> Colonel Roosevelt passed through Charleston today and was met at the station here by 4,000 or 5,000 people. This morning he spoke at Hinton to 5,000 and afterwards at Montgomery to about 3,000 . . . I think the meetings at Huntington tomorrow afternoon and at Parkersburg tomorrow night will be among the biggest ever held in this State.[83]

Due to the support of its governor, a visit to the Mountain State seemed fitting and proper. After his appearance in Huntington, the "Roosevelt Special" made a stop at Point Pleasant and at Ravenswood, where a crowd of nearly 1,000 people met it and former Governor White, Governor Glasscock and other dignitaries boarded for the ride to Parkersburg. A visit to Parkersburg, filled with Taft followers, naturally suited the audacious former president. In that city, a large gathering consisting of fans and the curious greeted the party before leaving for the courthouse square, where Roosevelt delivered a short address, complimenting the people of the city for having eliminated the grip of the politicians and for adopting a commission form of government. From there, the dignitaries ushered the former president to the Auditorium Theater where he gave his principal speech of the evening. The colonel urged the citizens to attend the mass meeting held later in their city to elect delegates to the state convention; he again spoke of Parkersburg's form of government:

81 Glasscock to Harvey W. Harmer, 27 March 1912, Glasscock Papers.
82 Glasscock to J. Bruce Hess, 2 April 1912, Glasscock Papers.
83 Glasscock to Edwin W. Sims, 6 March 1912, Glasscock Papers.

I need not have to say much in Parkersburg about my principles, as you are a little bit ahead of what I advocate. You have the initiative, the referendum, and recall. I have advocated the first two, but I have advocated the recall only in a qualified form, so that I find myself trying to catch my breath in order to catch up with you. I have never advocated anything quite as radical as you have applied in Parkersburg, but if you would believe all that you read about me then you would think I am trying to upset the whole Constitution of the United States.[84]

In concluding his remarks, Roosevelt asked for social and industrial justice, saying, "we cannot get this unless we get political justice and you can't get political justice unless you dethrone the political bosses and the political politicians."[85] Although it would be difficult to define "political politicians," in all it was a rousing speech, hammering on familiar themes to West Virginians and one which left the Roosevelt boosters well satisfied.

Governor Glasscock worked hard in order to secure a solid Roosevelt delegation to the National Convention in Chicago. He persuaded several Republicans, representing different county committees and congressional districts, to petition the state Republican Executive Committee to place the names of presidential candidates on the June 4 primary ballot. Most of the delegates would have already been selected by that time, "but the object is to instruct them by the result of the June Primary."[86] Perhaps, because of the late notice, the plan never materialized. The governor also worried about the turnout at the magisterial district mass conventions because they could easily be "packed" with the wrong kind of Republicans. In anticipation, Glasscock, doing a little "packing" of his own, urged "his" people to attend their respective meetings. Leaving no stone unturned, he wrote to a friend in Fairmont asking him to go to the Italian Consular Agent in that city to "tell him for me that anything that he can do for you next Saturday in your district mass conventions will be very much appreciated by me."[87] There were many Italians in that area and their votes could be crucial.

84   *Parkersburg Sentinel*, April 5, 1912.

85   *Parkersburg Sentinel*, April 5, 1912.

86   Glasscock to Dr. W. R. Andrews, 18 March 1912, Glasscock Papers. See also Glasscock to Dr. J. W. McDonald, 21 February 1912; Glasscock to W. P. Hubbard, 21 February 1912, both in Glasscock Papers.

87   Glasscock to Ira L. Smith, 17 April 1912, Glasscock Papers. See also Glasscock to Luther Knight, 11 March 1912, Glasscock Papers.

With the conclusion of delegate selections in Ohio County, one of the last counties to meet, it was evident that West Virginia would send a solid Roosevelt delegation to the Republican National Convention. Members of the Mountain State GOP watched the states that held primary elections with particular interest. Roosevelt carried Maryland. He then swept Illinois by 139,436; New Jersey by 17,213; Pennsylvania by 105,899; and California by 69,218. Tension mounted as Glasscock anxiously waited for the result of the Ohio election, Taft's home state, as he explained to a member of the Roosevelt Executive Committee:

> The Roosevelt Republicans of West Virginia are feeling more jubilant now than ever before, but we are extremely anxious with reference to the campaign in Ohio and sincerely hope that Colonel Roosevelt will spend as much time there as possible. I think everyone realizes that if the Colonel can break even in Ohio that it is all over but the shouting and we can do that part of the job in Chicago.[88]

In fact, Roosevelt carried Ohio by 47,447 votes. Glasscock stayed up until nearly one o'clock in the morning waiting for word from that state. Upon hearing the news, the governor felt "confident that nothing can keep Roosevelt from being nominated, Hurrah for Teddy!"[89] Theodore Roosevelt had been successful in every primary except two, and in those states, La Follette had won. President Taft had won only in those states where the traditional convention method selected the delegates, which ensured a formidable array of Taft support at Chicago. The fight was not over.[90]

On May 16, West Virginia Republicans held their State Convention in Huntington and, as expected, elected six Roosevelt delegates at large, and six alternates to go to the National Convention. Glasscock was prominent at the meeting and was chosen to go to Chicago where he would serve as chairman of his state's delegation of sixteen members, which included ten selected at the Congressional District Conventions. For Glasscock, the result of the delegate selection process was clear evidence that West Virginia was progressive in sentiment and the Republican Party had charted the right course. After the Huntington convention adjourned, Governor Glasscock was jubilant about the future of his party. He wrote: "Wasn't that a good convention? Did you notice how

---

88   Glasscock to O. K. Davis, secretary of Roosevelt Executive Committee, 9 May 1912, Glasscock Papers.

89   Glasscock to W. C. Grimes, 22 May 1912, Glasscock Papers.

90   Pringle, *The Life and Times of William Howard Taft*, 796–97.

many young men there were there? It means new life and new blood in the Republican party in November."[91]

Although the successful Roosevelt organization swept through West Virginia, it did not prepare the Mountain State delegation for what they would encounter in Chicago at the National Convention, dashing the hopes of many progressive Republicans. Since the Taft people had control of the National Committee, they successfully contested a large number of Roosevelt delegates. This act appalled Governor Glasscock, but he was determined to stand "by T. R. to the last ditch."[92] One West Virginia delegate later wrote that the events in Chicago had shown "to what absurdities the method of nominating by delegate conventions can be carried."[93] Another member stated that he had "lost all interest in the Chicago Convention after the seventy-eight contesting Roosevelt delegates were all excluded . . ."[94] Upon his return home, Glasscock wrote to a friend about his experience in the Midwest:

> I think that the Chicago Convention will teach the people of this country one important lesson if nothing else, and that is that hereafter nominations must be made at primary elections for offices from President to constable, and in my judgment, there will never be another national political convention after this year.[95]

Proving that control of party machinery is crucial for success, the Republicans in Chicago nominated Taft. Also showing that national conventions do not always bind party members, the Roosevelt people bolted the Republican Party and formed their own, the Progressive, popularly known as the "Bull Moose" Party. Following this course of action, Glasscock had a great mental struggle—"the hardest one I ever had in my life."[96] While he concluded, "I cannot and will not vote for President Taft,"[97] neither could the governor join a third party, which would have meant political suicide for the state Republican ticket. Glasscock openly urged

91 Glasscock to W. C. Grimes, 22 May 1912, Glasscock Papers. See also the *Charleston Daily Mail*, May 17, 1912.
92 John T. Cooper to Glasscock, 17 June 1912, Glasscock Papers.
93 Glasscock to Elmer F. Goodwin, 27 June 1912, Glasscock Papers.
94 W. R. Andrews to Glasscock, 25 June 1912, Glasscock Papers.
95 Glasscock to Henry S. Green, 27 June 1912, Glasscock Papers.
96 Glasscock to Henry S. Green, 27 June 1912, Glasscock Papers.
97 Glasscock to James Adams, 11 July 1912, Glasscock Papers.

Republicans to "give to the State, Congressional and local candidates nominated by the Republican Party" their full support. He, however, did not endorse Taft.[98] As he explained to a Roosevelt supporter in New York, "To be frank with you I still claim to be a Republican, but I don't endorse the Chicago steal and am not going to do so. I was for Roosevelt before the Chicago convention and I am still for him."[99]

In the first statewide party primary in West Virginia held for state offices, Henry D. Hatfield, who had won the Republican nomination for governor on June 4, also urged Glasscock to remain loyal to the GOP and not to join a third party. Hatfield explained to the governor that he planned to carry on the battle for a primary election law "for the election of President to Constable." The aspirant further stated that he would "serve the Republican party first; personal ambition of man last; will stand in the middle of the road, and insist upon a majority rule on all occasions." As to the recent crisis in the party, Senator Hatfield explained that Glasscock could "depend upon me and my support in carrying out the will of the people of West Virginia as to the Presidential contest," which meant that he would try to remain neutral.[100]

On July 18, the dissidents issued a call for the formation of a state Progressive Party, which would meet in Charleston on July 30. There the Progressives would select delegates and alternates to the Progressive Party Convention, which would meet in Chicago on August 5. Although Glasscock took no part in the proceedings, former Governor Dawson, William S. Edwards, and Adjutant General Elliott attended. The state Republican candidates, meanwhile, made a plea for party harmony for the sake of the ticket.[101]

In convention at Charleston, the Progressives drew up an elaborate, far-reaching platform. It condemned the Republican National Committee for conspiring to take the nomination from Roosevelt. It commended the action of the state's sixteen delegates to the Chicago Convention, and endorsed the administration of Governor Glasscock. The platform further asked for more governmental influence within the economic sector of society. It called for the enactment of female suffrage; initiative, referendum, and recall;

---

98   Glasscock to H. F. West, 11 July 1912; Glasscock to P. H. Anderson, 11 July 1912, both in Glasscock Papers. See also the *Charleston Daily Mail*, July 22, 1912.
99   Glasscock to Hon. Wm. C. Priestly, 28 September 1912, Glasscock Papers.
100   H. D. Hatfield to Glasscock, 8 June 1912, Glasscock Papers.
101   *Wheeling Register*, July 19, 1912. Also on July 18, 1912, the regular Republicans quietly met in Parkersburg and organized a new executive committee. Although they pledged support for the national ticket, the members largely ignored the formation of a third party, careful not to cause a further rift in the state GOP.

uniform presidential primaries held on the same day in all states; and nomination of all candidates by all political parties in this state by primary elections, at public expense.[102] The state platform very closely followed the national Progressive platform to the delight of women seeking the right to vote. Especially on the national level, the reformers incorporated women into all of their main activities rather than relegating them to the sidelines. Even the renowned feminist Jane Addams seconded Roosevelt's nomination at the Bull Moose Convention.[103] Although these planks attracted many Republicans in West Virginia, prospects for success at the polls were indeed bleak.

Progressives eased the anxiety of the state Republican candidates when they later agreed to allow those candidates chosen at the June 4 primary to go on their ticket, placing them on the Progressive ballot without mentioning the name Republican. This act secured success for the Mountain State GOP. Voters elected Henry D. Hatfield the eighth Republican governor of West Virginia, and the state prohibition amendment passed by a sizable majority. In the end, Democratic presidential candidate Woodrow Wilson carried West Virginia with a vote of 113,097. Roosevelt received 94,360 and Taft, 56,754.

On the national and state levels, the combined vote of Roosevelt and Taft surpassed Wilson's, proving Roosevelt's popularity among the voters.[104] The outcome vindicated Glasscock's earlier view that the colonel was the only Republican who could carry the party to victory. Losing the presidency was no surprise, but many observers did not expect the GOP to maintain control over the state government. Even former Democratic Governor W. A. MacCorkle marveled at the way W. M. O. Dawson had handled the situation:

> He [Dawson] showed his consummate ability in the management of party
> politics when he had followed President Roosevelt into the Bull Moose

---

102 *Wheeling Register*, July 30, 1912; July 31, 1912.

103 Allen F. Davis, *American Heroine: The Life and Legend of Jane Addams*, (New York: Oxford University Press, 1973), 238.

104 Glasscock to P. H. Anderson, 11 July 1912; Glasscock to W. A. White, 2 December 1912, both in Glasscock Papers. See also Casdorph, "William E. Glasscock," 15. In order to complete the election returns, it should be noted that Eugene V. Debs, the Socialist presidential candidate, polled 14,819 votes in West Virginia during the election of 1912; he had received 3,679 in 1908. Debs enjoyed wide support in those counties that were experiencing labor disputes. For example, in Kanawha County, he received 3,380 votes in 1912 and only 464 in 1908. See the *Wheeling Register*, November 30, 1912.

Party. He was chairman of that organization in this state, and his ability showed itself in his management of the Republican candidates so that the Bull Moose did not nominate candidates for the state offices but only for the county offices. Thus by his manipulation he was able to manage the Bull Moose party and at the same time allow the Republicans to hold the state offices.[105]

Governor Glasscock had entered the campaign of 1912 with much energy. He expressed a zeal and a tone of "high spirits" in his correspondence that had been absent during most of his tenure. Sincere in his belief that Roosevelt was the most viable GOP candidate for the presidency, it is evident that Glasscock enjoyed the role he played in Roosevelt's return to national politics, never swaying in his support for the former president. Strong Republicans had lost in the mid-term elections of 1910, and there had been no clear evidence that Taft could stem the tide. Governor Glasscock had also grown cool toward President Taft, believing the president had not been a forceful leader and had not held certain members of his administration in line who had attempted to prevent the passage of reform legislation. Since the governor had chosen the "insurgent" path, it is understandable that he would support a Progressive candidate, one who he thought could carry the nation and the state.

105 William A. MacCorkle, *Recollections*, 451.

GOVERNOR GLASSCOCK
AND VIOLENCE IN WEST VIRGINIA

" . . . he who lives by the sword must perish by the sword."[1]

OVERNOR GLASSCOCK, a religious man of peace with a strong urge to cru-
sade against the social and economic ills of society, spent much of his time
and strength reacting to racial and industrial violence in West Virginia.
The governor stood firmly on the side of law and order during these critical times,
though critics sometime questioned his impartiality, especially during labor-management strife. There could be little criticism over the intentions of his actions, however,
when it came to preventing the horrendous crime of lynching, which predominantly
involved blacks.

Governor Glasscock would prove time and again that he would spare no cost,
although some did object, to prevent the commission of heinous crimes, even to the
point of placing himself in danger. In every incident, the governor not only used force
to instill order, but he also genuinely attempted to bring the guilty parties to justice. He
wanted to show violators that modern society could not and would not tolerate such
immoral behavior that hindered the natural flow of civilized society. Glasscock believed
that mob violence was simply incompatible with modern times and must be dealt with
quickly and harshly by an active government. He was not the first governor, however,
to speak out against lynching and discrimination. In his 1903 message to the legislature,
former Governor A. B. White called lynching "a cowardly crime, subversive of social
order, and productive of no good result."[2] As a young journalist, former Governor
Dawson wrote that "The Republican Party elevated the colored individual from being
a *thing* to a *man*, with all the rights that belong to manhood; the Democratic party

---

1　Glasscock to Prosecuting Attorney J. R. Pendleton, 5 September 1912, Glasscock Papers.
2　Burckel, "Governor Albert B. White and the Beginning of Progressive Reform, 1901–05," 7.

resisted that sacred work with armed and wicked rebellion." However, Glasscock put force behind his words.[3]

Soon after Glasscock's inauguration, Joe Brown, a white man, was lynched at Whitmer, in Randolph County, for allegedly killing Chief of Police Scott White.[4] It was the fourth lynching in that county in eight years, and the governor let it be known that he wanted those guilty of such violence arrested, tried, and punished. Judge Frank Cox of Morgantown agreed with Glasscock and suggested that the Brown case was a good opportunity for the governor to demonstrate the power of the state over mob action. Cox stressed this point with particular vigor because "no woman was involved," which always aroused public sentiment, and because the episode had occurred in the northern half of the state.[5] The judge could have also added that this was a good case to take a firm stand against vigilante action because no blacks were involved, which usually increased emotions among whites.

Following the lynching, Glasscock offered to aid the sheriff and prosecuting attorney of Randolph County, recognizing that the perpetrators probably would not be apprehended because public sentiment was so strong against the victim.[6] In fact, Glasscock's friend, Professor J. G. Knutti of Shepherd College, informed the governor that the whole community had been afraid of Brown. He was a man who "was said to have killed a dozen Italians in his time, at different times and in various ways, just simply because they had dared to oppose his wishes."[7] Since no one would testify, there was little to be done, but Glasscock had emphasized his stand against mob rule.

In early November 1909, the governor faced a similar problem. Three African-Americans, Scott Lewis, Hank Johnson, and Charles Lewis, allegedly committed an "outrage" on Mrs. Albert Rockhold of Gassaway. The posse killed one of the men during the apprehension and lodged the other two in the jail at Gassaway. Tempers flared as a crowd milled around the jail. An observer at the scene wired the governor of the possibility of an attempted lynching. Glasscock, his private secretary E. L.

---

3   Don Blagg, Unfinished biography of W. M. O. Dawson, W. M. O. Dawson Papers.

4   *Charleston Gazette*, March 21, 1909; *Wheeling Intelligencer*, March 22, 1909; *Wheeling Register*, April 9, 1909.

5   Frank Cox to Glasscock, 20 March 1909, Glasscock Papers. See also C. Vann Woodward, *The Strange Career of Jim Crow*, 87. While lynching reached its zenith during the 1880s and 1890s it had decreased during the first decade of the new century. The proportion of lynching in the South, however, had increased in the early 1900s, with blacks most often the victims.

6   Glasscock to Frank Cox, 23 March 1909, Glasscock Papers.

7   J. G. Knutti to Glasscock, 23 March 1909, Glasscock Papers.

Boggs, and Captain J. I. Pratt of the National Guard, immediately left Charleston for Gassaway.[8]

Upon his arrival that evening, Governor Glasscock found the situation untenable and called out Company A, Gassaway's detachment of the National Guard. In an effort to calm the people, Glasscock mounted a stand made of packing cases and addressed the crowd of about 200 men. The victim's husband stood at his side as the governor remarked, "Here is the man most injured, whose wife was brutally assaulted, and he does not want these men lynched. He desires the law to take its course."[9] Impressed with his words and actions, along with a show of force, the crowd did not attempt to lynch the men, who were soon taken to a jail in Sutton where calmer tempers prevailed. The two alleged criminals were later acquitted of all charges and released.[10]

Although Glasscock was pleased with the outcome, another related incident bothered him; newspaper reports stated that the soldiers of Company A, if ordered to fire into an angry mob to save lives, had agreed not to fire upon their fellow citizens.[11] Glasscock later denied this, saying he was angry because the captain was intoxicated; furthermore, he doubted the necessity of a company at Sutton and one at Gassaway. He decided to close out the Gassaway detachment of the National Guard.[12] On November 10, Governor Glasscock announced that Company A of the 2nd West Virginia Infantry would be mustered out "not because of any mutiny on their part or refusal to do their duty, but because they proved themselves unprepared to efficiently meet an emergency the first time they were called into active service."[13] In other words, the soldiers had displayed an evident lack of discipline, but they were to receive honorable discharges so that no one would "be hurt."[14] Thus ended the only conflict between the governor and the soldiers themselves during his administration.

The prospect of another lynching presented itself in August 1910, after an African-American, Thomas Wayne, allegedly assaulted John Ailiff of Fayette County and raped and killed his sixteen-year-old wife. A railroad detective apprehended Wayne and took

8 *Wheeling Intelligencer*, November 4, 1909; *Charleston Gazette*, November 5, 1909; John Baker White to Glasscock, 11 December 1909, Glasscock Papers.

9 *Wheeling Intelligencer*, November 5, 1909.

10 *Charleston Gazette*, March 20, 1910.

11 Glasscock to G. W. Atkinson, 6 November 1909; Glasscock to Cary C. Hines, 26 November 1909, both in Glasscock Papers.

12 *Charleston Gazette*, November 11, 1909.

13 Glasscock to R. G. York, 10 November 1909, Glasscock Papers.

14 Glasscock to R. G. York, 10 November 1909, Glasscock Papers.

him by train to Hinton, placing him under arrest. On August 17, a mob of about 800 people gathered in that city to lynch the hapless defendant. Reacting quickly, Glasscock ordered four companies of the National Guard to the scene of unrest and sent his private secretary, Boggs, to supervise the activity. The *Hinton News* wrote that it was the first time in the history of the city that guards were needed to preserve the peace, "but with the soldiers here, there was a general feeling that the state meant to stand by the county and city officials, and if possible, prevent the lynching of the negro [sic]."[15]

For purposes of security, the guard transported the defendant from Hinton to Huntington. On August 29, mobs appeared in the streets of Huntington and Glasscock called out Company I, under the command of Adjutant General Elliott. Tension ran high in Huntington for several nights, but no violence occurred. Wayne, nearly lynched in Hinton, was placed on trial in mid-March and was soon convicted and consequently hanged on December 23, 1910.[16]

Following the Wayne incident, Governor Glasscock wrote to Senator Stephen B. Elkins that he "was not doing much nowadays except trying to protect prisoners in jail."[17] The governor also complained that the state was getting a reputation it did not deserve, and he intended to prevent further violence if he had to call out all the members of the National Guard. The resolve of the nonviolent chief executive was soon tested when, on December 27, 1910, he quickly dispatched the Weston and Clarksburg companies of the Guard to Weston, in Lewis County, to protect William Furbish, a black man, who allegedly attacked a Miss Anglin.[18] The soldiers transported the defendant with haste to Clarksburg, preventing a lynching. In connection with this case, Governor Glasscock corresponded with Circuit Court Judge Charles Lynch of Clarksburg. Perhaps meddling where he had no legal right, the governor suggested that Furbish's trial not be held in Weston, because "I am not a believer in mob law and neither do I believe in legalized lynching. You know what I mean by the term 'legalized lynching.'"[19]

Soon after the mob action, Glasscock received word that the Weston officials intended to prosecute the leaders, and he confided that "It is time for our people to learn that the law must be respected and that violators, whether white or black, will be

15 *Hinton News*, August 17, 1910, clipping in Glasscock Papers.

16 Glasscock to Judge Charles W. Lynch, 31 December 1910, Glasscock Papers.

17 Glasscock to Senator S. B. Elkins, 30 August 1910, Glasscock Papers.

18 *Wheeling Intelligencer*, December 28, 1910.

19 Glasscock to C. W. Lynch, 31 December 1910; C. W. Lynch to Glasscock, 11 January 1911, both in Glasscock Papers.

punished."[20] Although he was unhappy with the lawlessness of 1910, Glasscock pointed out that through his actions four persons whom the mob attempted to hang eventually received fair trials—two were found not guilty and two of them guilty.[21] William Furbish was found guilty and sentenced to hang.[22]

The last lynching to take place in the state during Glasscock's administration occurred on September 5, 1912. The governor received a telegram from Assistant Prosecuting Attorney W. R. Ross of Mercer County, warning that a lynching was imminent. Ross reported that a mob had forcibly seized an African-American boy, Robert Johnson, accused of rape by a deputy sheriff at Rock, in the same county. The young man was escorted to Princeton, where a mob intended to hang him. Governor Glasscock ordered a company of National Guard from the strike zone on Paint and Cabin Creeks to the scene by way of the Virginian Railroad. In the meantime, the governor wired Prosecuting Attorney J. R. Pendleton of Princeton the following message to read to the mob if necessary:

> I earnestly hope you may be able to save your county and the State the disgrace that follows any lynching. Certainly the good people of Mercer County will not take the law into their hands and in so doing make themselves guilty of murder. Every man who participates in a lynching will bring to himself and family, if he has one, the disgrace that attaches to crime. Let us also remember that he who lives by the sword must perish by the sword.[23]

Regrettably, the governor and the county officials failed to halt the violence. The young man was hanged by the mob in Princeton and his body riddled with bullets. The assaulted girl's father, in a drunken state, identified the alleged assailant as the man who had attacked his daughter. The mob used no disguises and the local officials hoped to prosecute the leaders,[24] moving quickly to bring them to justice. Shortly after the incident, a grand jury convened, but later adjourned without returning any indictments. This was not only one of the most brutal cases of lynching in West Virginia, but it was

20   Glasscock to Charles P. Swint, 2 January 1911, Glasscock Papers.

21   Glasscock to Mme. E. E. Minott, 26 March 1912, Glasscock Papers.

22   *Wheeling Intelligencer*, February 11, 1911.

23   Glasscock to Prosecuting Attorney J. R. Pendleton, 5 September 1912; see also W. R. Ross to Glasscock, 5 September 1912, both in Glasscock Papers.

24   J. R. Pendleton to Glasscock, 6 September 1912, Glasscock Papers.

also one of the most tragic, because later it was reported to have been a case of mistaken identity.[25] As in so many of these affairs, the guilty persons went unpunished.

It is ironic to note that the Criminal Court Judge J. Frank Maynard of Bluefield, acting with the governor's permission, hired Baldwin-Felts detectives to aid in the investigation.[26] This agency had also supplied mine operators with guards, which, in turn, agitated the miners and led to the stationing of the National Guard in the strike area. Had the Mercer County contingent of the state militia been home, perhaps the lynching could have been prevented. In the end, an angry governor complained not only about the violence in the state but also that the detective agency had charged too much for too little, "I think your account is unreasonable but under the circumstances suppose I have nothing left to do but pay it."[27]

Governor Glasscock never hesitated to use the National Guard in order to curb violence, and he was satisfied with the conduct of the soldiers in nearly every instance except at Gassaway. As he explained, "I have never known them to fail to do their duty promptly and efficiently."[28] In the matter of lynching and mob violence, Glasscock proved to be a chief executive who could take decisive action. Although some residents criticized him for meddling in local matters and needlessly spending large sums of money, law-abiding citizens applauded the governor's actions. It is evident that Governor Glasscock took a strong moral stand on human life, regardless of race.

Toward the end of his administration when the ailing governor thought he could turn his attention to pressing domestic issues, he was once again forced to confront a growing threat of violence not far from the state's capital. This was a different type, however, involving large numbers of citizens. It necessitated calling out the West Virginia National Guard on a number of occasions and three declarations of martial law. Industrial strife on the banks of the tranquil Kanawha River and the hollows of Kanawha County led to large-scale military operations in order to protect life and property, the likes of which had not been seen since Civil War days. The miners' strike, which lasted from April 1912 to May 1913, centered on Paint and Cabin Creeks in

25   William P. Bynum to Glasscock, 19 September 1912, Glasscock Papers.

26   J. Frank Maynard to Glasscock, 11 November 1912; Glasscock to Judge Maynard, 12 November 1912, both in Glasscock Papers.

27   Glasscock to W. G. Baldwin, 12 November 1912, Glasscock Papers.

28   Kyle McCormick, "The National Guard of West Virginia During the Strike Period of 1912–1913," *West Virginia History*, 22 (October 1960): 35. Hereafter cited as McCormick, "The National Guard of West Virginia."

Kanawha County. Before it was settled, it affected 90% of the mines in Kanawha County, 35% in Fayette, 50% in Boone, 40% in Raleigh, and 25% in Logan.[29]

Historians of the American labor movement have characterized non-union West Virginia as "a pistol pointed at the heart of industrial government in the bituminous coal industry" in the early twentieth century.[30] By this they meant that the state was rapidly becoming a major producer of cheap coal, because of a number of natural advantages that it enjoyed: (1) the presence of larger and softer veins of coal; (2) mountainous topography which permitted inexpensive drift entry, rather than costly shaft mining; (3) relatively low freight rates; and (4) the advantage of a non-union condition that led to a great expansion of coal production.[31] Western Pennsylvania, Ohio, Indiana, and Illinois, which together with West Virginia comprised the Central Competitive Field, were shocked at West Virginia's rapid output of inexpensive coal. Production had surged from 609,000 tons in 1870 to 60,000,000 in 1911; the real quantum leap occurred at the turn of the century when the Mountain State surpassed Ohio in the extraction of minerals. West Virginia, however, was peculiar in that it was able to market only 10% of its coal inside the state while shipping 90% outside. Transporting much of this product to the Great Lakes, it competed with other coal producing states. These states viewed with alarm West Virginia's increasing share of that trade,[32] which would climb from 1% in 1898 to 23% by 1913.

In the face of such competition, the unionized operations of the other Central Competitive states sought to inhibit Mountain State coal production by pressuring the Interstate Commerce Commission to grant the northern states a railroad rate differential in their favor. For example, Pennsylvania interests had been successful in receiving a rate differential of 9 1/4 cent advantage per ton in the Lake Trade on a Pittsburgh Plus basis, which discriminated against West Virginia. In 1912, this rate even increased to 19 cents per ton of coal transported by way of Lake Erie. To the consternation of

29   Elizabeth J. Goodall, "The Charleston Industrial Area: Development, 1797–1937," *West Virginia History*, 30 (October 1968): 380–381.

30   Selig Perlman and Phillip Taft, *History of Labor in the United States, 1896–1932* (New York: Macmillan, 1935), 326.

31   John M. Barb, "Strikes in the Southern West Virginia Coal Fields, 1912–1922" (master's thesis, West Virginia University, 1949), 39. Hereafter cited as Barb, "Strikes in the Southern West Virginia Coal Fields." See also Lawrence R. Lynch, "West Virginia Coal Strike," *Political Science Quarterly*, 29 (December 1914): 626–27. Hereafter cited as Lynch, "West Virginia Coal Strike."

32   Lynch, "West Virginia Coal Strike," 658. See also John T. Harris, ed., *West Virginia Legislative Hand Book and Manual and Official Register 1924* (Charleston: Jarrett Printing Company, 1924), 395–416.

the northern competitors, West Virginia coal was still cheaper.[33] It was also evident that the other competitive operators had encouraged union organizers to go into West Virginia to organize labor, which they hoped would lead to higher wages and expensive Mountain State coal.[34] Pittsburgh operators further declared that the decision to open up West Virginia was an "economic blunder," because "Lake Traffic" could not use more coal than produced by Pennsylvania and Ohio.[35] Desperate economic conditions called for equally desperate actions, making an ally of a formidable opponent and causing labor to become a pawn in the ensuing conflict. Northern operators were intent on curbing or killing the flow of southern coal, particularly from the Kanawha Field, and just as determined to remain competitive.

On January 28, 1898, with the signing of an agreement between the operators of the Central Competitive Field and leaders of the United Mine Workers of America, competition for markets now involved union and non-union mines. Northern coal owners agreed to recognize the UMW if they promised to begin in earnest the drive to organize the southern miners of West Virginia. Of course, that was no problem for the miners' organization, which was always happy to enlarge its family and had already planned a drive to unionize the southern workers. With the extension of rail lines into the heart of the Mountain State coalfields, northern operators knew that their monopoly of the Lakes Trade would soon be broken. With the tremendous growth of the coal industry below the Ohio River and the growing number of miners, the UMW recognized an urgent need to unionize the southern coalfields, which, like a pistol pointed at the union, could affect their bargaining power.[36] After all, because of its ability to burn cleaner, hotter, and to be stored longer, demand for West Virginia coal steadily increased with such customers as the U.S. Navy. Washington D. C. also favored this fuel because of that city's strict laws against smoke pollution. The leaders of this industry envisioned a bright future.[37]

33   P. L. Donahue, S. L. Walker, and Fred O. Blue, *Report of West Virginia Mining Investigation, 1912* (Charleston: Tribune Printing Co., 1912), 9. Hereafter referred to as Donahue, Walker, and Blue, *Mining Investigation, 1912.* Also see Joseph T. Lambie, *From Mine to Market,* 302–05.

34   Lynch, "West Virginia Coal Strike," 659–60. See also U.S. Bureau of the Census, *Extra Census Bulletin, Coal Production of the United States, No. 10,* Washington DC: Government Printing Office, 1891, 1–13; Stuart Seely Sprague, "Unionization Struggles on Paint and Cabin Creeks, 1912–1913," *West Virginia History,* 38 (April 1977): 199. Hereafter cited as Sprague, "*Unionization Struggles.*"

35   Sprague, "Unionization Struggles," 199–200.

36   Sprague, "Unionization Struggles," 212.

37   David Alan Corbin, *Life, Work, and Rebellion in the Coal Fields,* (Chicago: University of

The Mountain State, of course, was not new ground for union activities. In fact, the first organizing meeting of the United Mine Workers of America took place at Wheeling on April 21, 1890, creating West Virginia as District 17 which was affiliated with the American Federation of Labor. By 1902, union organizers had been moderately successful in recruiting the bituminous miners, but eventually the operators refused to recognize the union and to meet in joint conferences. In a 1902 convention at Huntington, union members met and determined to force the operators to accept their organization. Over the objection of John Mitchell, president of the UMW, who feared that the southern miners were yet not well organized, the delegates ordered a strike, in part to support the miners who were on strike in the northern coalfields. The workers prepared a new wage scale to replace the old one and called for a joint conference of labor and management. The coal owners rejected the offer and a strike ensued. In the end, this action accomplished little; the operators refused to recognize the union, and the men had lost most of their labor organizations throughout the state, except in the Kanawha District. In that area, the miners won recognition and a number of important concessions.[38]

The Kanawha District became a bastion of unionism in West Virginia, and the miners and the operators scheduled biennial joint conferences to discuss wage scales and other working conditions. The district was divided into a number of sub-districts, which included Paint Creek and Cabin Creek, both located near Charleston. In 1912, Kanawha County mines employed a workforce of 6,803 miners (4,958 white and 875 black, along with 486 Italians, 154 Hungarians, 85 Poles, and others).[39] About 60% of the mines in this area were small, with an annual average production of 45,480 tons of coal, necessitating a close watch over operating expenses. On the other hand, the larger mines, usually owned by out-of-state interests, annually produced about 162,877 tons. Absentee ownership was common. For example, two such men were Charles M. Pratt of Brooklyn, New York, a former United States Senator with close ties to John D. Rockefeller and the Standard Oil Company, and George M. Wetmore of Rhode Island, who together owned 33 square miles of land on Paint Creek.[40] In 1901, Pratt's

Illinois Press, 1981), 5. Hereafter cited as Corbin, *Life, Work, and Rebellion*.

38   Lynch, "West Virginia Coal Strike," 628; Barb, "Strikes in the Southern West Virginia Coal Fields, 1912–1922," 39–40. See Ambler and Summers, *West Virginia: The Mountain State*, 445–47. See also Corbin, *Life, Work, and Rebellion*, 48–49.

39   Otis K. Rice, *Charleston and the Kanawha Valley*, (Woodland Hills, California: West Virginia Historical Society, 1981), 70–71.

40   Lynch, "West Virginia Coal Strike," 628–29. Taking another view, it is interesting to note that

Land Company leased fifteen thousand acres to the Paint Creek Colliery Company, which had eleven mines operational by 1902. On the right fork of Cabin Creek, the Consolidated Coal Company ran twenty-two mines. On the left fork, the Carbon Fuel Company led by C. A. Cabell, sometimes referred to as the boss of Cabin Creek, and others of Charleston operated ten mines.[41]

Working in any mine was hard and dangerous, but it appeared that conditions on the two creeks were much better than other mines in the area because of recent development in the region and new machines. Coal loaders usually loaded about ten to fifteen tons a day at 33 cents per ton, while the company received 90 cents a ton for ordinary coal and up to two dollars for special grades. It seemed both operators and miners worked together fairly well, taking advantage of profits and wages. Romance had even blossomed between some miners' daughters and mine guards.[42] A contemporary wrote:

> Up to the strike in 1912 our relations were very pleasant. Nothing out of the ordinary run of things happened during this period. The mines were working regularly and everybody seemed happy. The miners and the guards were on good terms and lived together in the same neighborhood, visited each other and acted in much the same manner as other neighbors in mining communities.[43]

A closer look at industrial relations, however, revealed a layer of discontent beneath the surface of tranquil work relations. While harmony seemed to exist in day-to-day routines, many miners complained that the companies increasingly ignored union rules. In 1900, the headquarters of the UMW had moved to Montgomery, WV, in the heart of the Kanawha coalfield, intensifying efforts to organize the miners. Union organizers had won several early victories such as recognition of the UMW as a bargaining agent and acceptance by the operators of the check-off clause, which meant, in the view of

---

out of a population of 20,000 people in both areas, 50% were foreign born, 25% black native born, and another 25% white native born.

41 Sprague, "Unionization Struggles," 186–87.

42 Sprague, "Unionization Struggles," 187. See also Charles Bierne Crawford, "The Mine War on Cabin Creek and Paint Creek, West Virginia in 1912–1913" (master' thesis, University of Kentucky, 1939), Foreword, passim. Hereafter cited as Crawford, "The Mine War." Crawford worked in the mines on Cabin Creek as a young man until an accident. He later became a teacher, justice of the peace, and a postmaster in the area of the 1912–1913 strike.

43 Sprague, "Unionization Struggles," 187.

the union, mandatory dues paid by every worker, whether they belonged to the union or not. In 1904, however, the operators denied this broad interpretation, insisting on only union members' wages being checked-off, urging settlement of the impasse by arbitration. The union refused to accept these demands. A strike followed that lasted ten days. By the fall of 1904, mainly because of a lack of unity among the miners, a breakup of the union on Cabin Creek occurred.[44]

In contrast to mines on Cabin Creek, the Paint Creek mines remained unionized and enjoyed a slightly higher wage scale. Eventually, the men at the latter mines became dissatisfied because the check-off system had fallen into disuse. At the UMW's 1912 conference, the union asked for four things: (1) the Cleveland wage advance (the Ohio operators had given their miners an increase of five cents a ton and an advance of 5.26% for inside labor); (2) a uniform work day of eight hours; (3) pay every two weeks; and (4) an unlimited check-off. Management refused, offering to renew the old scale and working conditions. In turn, the union dropped all demands except the Cleveland wage advance, which the operators rejected. The owners intended to make a stand, while the union was clearly determined to intensify its efforts to increase its membership. Caught in the middle, the miner wanted to improve his standard of living and working conditions. After all, in a society where only the Bible was read more than the Sears catalogue, workers wanted their fair share.

Talks continued until April 18, 1912, when negotiations were broken off, and the miners went on strike throughout the Kanawha District, except on non-union Cabin Creek. There was little violence, and on May 1, all the union mines except those on Paint Creek accepted a compromise agreement of one-half the Cleveland advance. The operators on Paint Creek refused the offer because of the non-union conditions on nearby Cabin Creek, which made their coal cheaper and more competitive. The trouble, therefore, was centered on Paint Creek and both sides prepared for a long struggle.[45]

Relations between management and labor rapidly deteriorated on Paint Creek, an area previously considered prosperous, contented, and happy.[46] Since 1910, companies had used mine guards on Cabin Creek to prevent union interference; however, none had been employed on Paint Creek. Because of the alleged possibility of danger

44　United States Senate, *Hearings before a Subcommittee of the Committee on Education and Labor*, 63rd Congress, 1st Session, 1913, 111–13. Hereafter referred to as *Hearings*. Sprague, "Unionization Struggles," 186–87.
45　Dale Fetherling, *Mother Jones, The Miners' Angel* (Carbondale: Southern Illinois Press, 1974), 85–86. Hereafter cited as Fetherling, *Mother Jones*. Lynch, "West Virginia Coal Strike," 630–32.
46　Ben Davis to Glasscock, 21 December 1910, Glasscock Papers.

to individuals and destruction of property, Paint Creek operators hired guards from the Baldwin-Felts Detective Agency. Sometimes called "thugs" or professional strike-breakers, former Attorney General Howard B. Lee described them as "fearless mountain gunmen, many with criminal records, whose chief duties were to keep the miners intimidated."[47] Soon afterward, Governor Glasscock began hearing about confrontations between the miners and the operators' private police force in the strike zone.

The first contingent of mine guards arrived on Paint Creek in early May. On May 8, the companies served the first eviction notices on the striking miners, giving the families ten days to vacate the company houses. Homeless families began to move to Holly Grove near Paint Creek Junction, where they encamped in tent colonies. The union provided them with food and shelter, but it could not guarantee safety from violence. The company guards and the dispossessed workers naturally held deep animosities toward each other, but actual hostilities did not break out until May 29, when a group of miners fired from the surrounding hills on the mine guards in Mucklow Village on Paint Creek. Alarmed, the operators erected a fort with a machine gun in the village. Soon afterward, another battle occurred in the woods surrounding Mucklow, killing one man. Glasscock learned that the victim was an employee of a union mine located twenty miles from the strike area.[48] Still hoping the local courts could settle the conflict, he gathered information about the incident. The governor, however, found it difficult to discover the cause of the trouble or which parties was to blame, as rumors were rampant and newspaper accounts often exaggerated. Kanawha County officials, however, asked for no assistance and, under the law, the governor had no legal right to interfere as long as the local officers controlled the situation.[49]

Around August 1, Governor Glasscock, who was recuperating from an acute attack of rheumatism in a Huntington hospital, received news that the strike was nearly out of hand. Mucklow was again under siege. The *Charleston Daily Mail* reported "A Regular Hurricane Of Bullets Awakened The Echoes At Mucklow." Shots fired reportedly ranged from several hundred to 100,000 as written by the press. Inflammatory quotes such as " . . . there is murder in the hearts of many of those who would as lief pick off a mine

47 Howard B. Lee, *Bloodletting in Appalachia* (Morgantown; West Virginia University, 1969), 11. Hereafter cited as Lee, *Bloodletting in Appalachia*.
48 *Hearings*, 111–13, 361–63. See also Walter B. Palmer, "An Account of the Strike of Bituminous Miners in the Kanawha Valley of West Virginia, April, 1912 to March 1913." West Virginia Collection, West Virginia University Library, Morgantown, WV; Crawford, "The Mine War," 36–38.
49 Glasscock to Royal Consular Agent of Italy, 22 July 1912, Glasscock Papers.

guard or mine official as he would eat his dinner" only added fuel to the volatile crisis. The "Hurricane Of Bullets" claimed the lives of four mine guards and twelve miners. The death of four mine guards was probably accurate, but it is difficult to know for sure about the miners because they usually quickly removed the wounded and buried the dead in order to deny the companies that information.

Many felt the importation of sixty Kentucky strikebreakers to Cabin Creek less than a week before the fight ignited an already tense situation. Unable to control the violence, the sheriff wired for help, and Glasscock sent one company of the National Guard to patrol the two creeks. Seeing that it was impossible for one company to control an area twelve or fifteen miles in length, the governor ordered more troops to the strike zone and continued to do so until the entire West Virginia National Guard, totaling about 1500 troops, costing the state about $3,000 a day, patrolled the two creeks.[50] By the latter part of July 1912, Governor Glasscock found it necessary to spend about ten days in the hospital at Huntington. He explained, "I have been going under the whip all year, and the time came when I could not stand it any longer."[51] With no solution in sight, the ailing governor surmised, "I am fully convinced that General Sherman knew exactly what he was talking about when he said that war was something that I do not care to repeat."[52]

Reports of the governor's failing health worried his family and friends, prompting Dr. M. H. Brown of Morgantown to advise him to slow down. Glasscock replied that he was trying "to take as good care of myself as possible and will follow your directions and take some cod liver oil and strychnia." Fuller, the governor's brother, concerned over the same reports, wrote that he had heard "you are taking the strike entirely too seriously. You are not responsible for it."[53] This was sage advice from concerned spectators, but of little comfort to a frail, sick, conscientious chief executive who saw the situation spinning out of control.

....

50 For Governor Glasscock's message see *West Virginia House Journal and Bills*, 1913, 86–87. Hereafter referred to as *House Journal and Bills*. Sprague, "Unionization Struggles," 190–93. Kenneth R. Bailey, "'Grim Visaged Men' and The West Virginia National Guard in the 1912–13 Paint and Cabin Creek Strike," *West Virginia History*, 41 (Winter 1980): 112–113. Hereafter cited as Bailey, "Grim Visaged Men." See also *Report of the Adjutant General, 1911–1912*, West Virginia Division of Culture and History, Charleston, West Virginia, 233.

51 Glasscock to A. E. Sutherland, 25 July 1912; see also H. E. Hatfield to Glasscock, 24 July 1912, both in Glasscock Papers.

52 Glasscock to C. W. Cramer, 23 August 1912; see also Glasscock to George C. Baker, 10 August 1912, both in Glasscock Papers.

53 S. Fuller Glasscock to Glasscock, 25 September 1912, Glasscock Papers.

Glasscock did not issue a proclamation of martial law, which he considered a last resort, but he was ready to make the declaration at a moment's notice if necessary. From Huntington, the governor sent a copy of the "Proclamation of Martial law in Cabin Creek District," along with the sheriff's request for such action to his private secretary, H. P. Brightwell, in Charleston.

Glasscock further instructed his secretary to have the sheriff and the secretary of state sign the document in order to save time, but it was to be done secretly:

> Now do not forget one thing. I want no record made of the issuance of this letter either in the Secretary of State's office or anywhere else until it is ascertained that it is absolutely necessary to issue the Proclamation, but it would be well to have everything ready so that in case it is necessary to do something there will be no delay.[54]

The miners welcomed the arrival of the National Guard, thinking their presence would negate the need for the hated mine guards. Unfortunately, the private police remained on duty, though the soldiers stabilized the situation. With peace restored, the governor gradually withdrew the guard.

At this time, the attention of the union "agitators" turned to the mines on Cabin Creek, which had not been on strike. The octogenarian union organizer Mary Jones, a self-proclaimed "hell raiser" whom the miners affectionately called "Mother," had a great deal of influence with the workers. On August 1, 1912, at a mass rally of miners on the Charleston levee, Mother Jones denounced the governor for not removing the company police:

> Your Governor has stood for it. He went off to Chicago and left two Gattling [sic] guns with the bloodhounds to blow your brains out. Now boys, you are in this fight. I want to say to you the Governor is sick, poor fellow. (From the crowd: I hope he is dead. I do[.])
>
> Let the Governor alone today. We have arranged a mass meeting in Montgomery, also the citizens, merchants, lawyers, doctors and all—in Montgomery for four o'clock Sunday afternoon. Come down there and then we will do business with the Governor. You must have a system, you must have

---

54   Glasscock to H. P. Brightwell, 29 July 1912, Glasscock Papers.

An angelic hell raiser: Mother Jones. Courtesy of the Otis K. Rice Collection of the West Virginia Institute of Technology, Montgomery, WV.

a voice behind you. When you are going to do business with these big fellows you have got to have ammunition.[55]

West Virginia prosecuting attorney Reese Blizzard allegedly once referred to Mother Jones as "the most dangerous woman in America."[56] Perhaps she lived up to her reputation when, after a speech in Charleston, she so aroused the passions of the men

55   Mother Jones's speech at Charleston, August 1, 1912, Mary Jones Papers, West Virginia University Library.
56   Elliott J. Gorn, *Mother Jones; The Most Dangerous Woman in America* (New York: Hill and Wang, 2001), 95–97. Hereinafter cited as Gorn, *Mother Jones*. Charles Crawford, a former miner and eyewitness to these events stated, "in my estimation the efforts to Unionize the Cabin and Paint Creek coal fields were not of local origin, and that the causes of discontent were the creation of agitators who came into the fields." See Crawford, "The Mine War," Conclusion, 7.

that they bought large quantities of rifles and ammunition. On the next day, Governor Glasscock returned from Huntington stating that he would have come sooner if he had known the miners were there to see him.[57] Mary Jones, however, was not in the city. She had gone to Cabin Creek or "Old Russia" as she called it, to organize the miners, urging her "boys" to "Pray for the dead and fight like hell for the living."[58] The miners' angel, for all of her salty language and spirited demeanor did not hesitate to enlist the help of the Lord in her efforts to organize:

> The labor movement was not originated by man. The labor movement, my friends, was a command from God Almighty. He commanded the prophets thousands of years ago to go down and redeem the Israelites that were in bondage and he organized the men into a union and went to work.[59]

With his health improved, Glasscock made a tour of the strike zone, where he found the soldiers well and happy. While visiting with the guard, he met with several men from his hometown, Morgantown, and talked with Charles Baker, son of the governor's friend, George C. Baker. Many soldiers of Company L of Morgantown reported that they had enjoyed their duty at Paint Creek Junction, which was mainly to guard incoming and outgoing trains. According to the *Morgantown Post-Chronicle*, "One member of the company stated that he would not have missed the trip for an hundred dollars."[60] Lieutenant Baker, however, struck a serious note when he confided that if the National Guard were pulled out there would again be violence. Many others had made the same conclusion since the operators had built three forts and equipped them with six machine guns. Peace prevailed, though, and Glasscock ordered several companies home by mid-August, leaving four to maintain peace.

Governor Glasscock felt he had done everything he could except to order martial law. In the beginning of the conflict, he had unsuccessfully encouraged the settlement of the dispute in court. He also concluded that many of the county officials had not done their duty; otherwise, there would have been no trouble. The attitude of the operators

---

57   *Charleston Gazette*, August 3, 1912.

58   Mary Jones, *The Autobiography of Mother Jones* (Chicago: Charles H. Kerr & Co., 1925), 148; Gorn, *Mother Jones*, 169ff.

59   Philip S. Foner, ed., *Mother Jones Speaks* (New York: Monad Press, 1983), 196.

60   *New Dominion* (Morgantown), August 26, 1912, clipping in Glasscock Papers. See also *Charleston Gazette*, August 9, 1912.

Mine guard "thugs." Courtesy of the Otis K. Rice Collection of the West Virginia Institute of Technology, Montgomery, WV.

also displeased the governor. Before the hostilities, he had entreated management and labor to meet together to work out their differences, but the operators refused. Glasscock then asked each side to visit him separately to discuss their demands, but again the owners declined, maintaining they had nothing to settle.

When Glasscock ordered the troops to Paint Creek in July, he had asked the employers to remove their guards from the area patrolled by the soldiers; they rejected that suggestion, which possibly could have prevented a further escalation of violence.[61] Since management and union felt they were fighting for their very existence, nonviolence appeared to be an elusive goal, especially combined with the inadequacies of local and state law.

In the meantime, the stalemate further heightened emotions among the miners. On August 16, perhaps 3,000 strong, they held a mass meeting in Charleston. The men paraded through the streets and, later, in a speech, Mother Jones again ordered the governor to remove the mine guards. She left little to the imagination when she threatened Glasscock:

61   Glasscock to George C. Baker, 25 September 1912, Glasscock Papers.

You can expect no help from such a goddamned dirty coward . . . whom, for modesty's sake, we shall call 'Crystal Peter.' But I warn this little Governor that unless he rids Paint Creek and Cabin Creek of these god-damned Baldwin-Felts mine-guard thugs, there is going to be one hell of a lot of bloodletting in these hills.[62]

Mother Jones then admonished her "boys" to "Arm yourselves, return home and kill every goddamned mine guard on the creeks, blow up the mines, and drive the damned scabs out of the valleys." In compliance and using union money, the striking miners bought all the guns and ammunition in the Charleston stores. They also ordered six machine guns, 1000 high-power rifles, and 50,000 rounds of ammunition.[63] Alarmed, several Charleston businessmen held a conference with Glasscock to discuss the turn of events. Shortly after the meeting, the governor issued a Peace Proclamation to the Cabin Creek District, which also included Paint Creek:

Now, therefore, I, William E. Glasscock, Governor of the State of West Virginia, do hereby call upon all persons in said Cabin Creek District to preserve the peace and abide by the laws of this State and I warn all Persons, not members of the National Guard, who have arms, to lay them aside; and I warn all persons to refrain from gathering together in riotous or unlawful assemblies, from assembling or marching as armed bodies, and from obstructing the public highways and from uttering inflammatory speeches calculated to incite riot, violence or injury to persons and property.[64]

The combatants largely ignored the governor's plea. In his message to the legislature of 1913, Glasscock stated, "the answer of the operators to this proclamation was the purchase of additional guns and ammunition and the erection of forts."[65] This prompted the governor to appoint a commission to investigate conditions on Paint and Cabin Creeks, mainly because the information he was receiving was so contradictory. Glasscock urged labor and management to select two individuals each to serve on that body, with a third to be chosen by a disinterested party. The miners complied, but

---

62   Lee, *Bloodletting in Appalachia*, 88–89. See also Gorn, *Mother Jones*, 174.

63   Lee, *Bloodletting in Appalachia*, 27.

64   Glasscock to William G. Conley, 20 August 1912, Glasscock Papers. See also *House Journal and Bills*, 88–89 and *Hearings*, 364, 367.

65   Glasscock to George C. Baker, 25 September 1912, Glasscock Papers.

the operators refused,[66] as their acceptance would have been a tacit recognition of the union. On August 28, tired of further delay, the governor selected three men to compose the investigating committee: the Right Reverend P. J. Donahue, Catholic bishop of Wheeling, as chairman; Captain S. L. Walker of the state militia from Fayetteville; and Fred O. Blue, the State Tax Commissioner, from Charleston, whom the *Socialist and Labor Star* ridiculed as a "Catholic priest, a tin soldier, and a politician."

The governor's verbatim instructions were fourfold:

1. They were to inquire into and report upon the 'guard system' as in force and practice in the coal fields of this State.
2. The mining conditions generally in the coal fields of the State, and particularly on Paint and Cabin Creeks, including their home life, sanitary conditions, and generally how their home life compares with that of laborers engaged in other kinds of work.
3. They were asked to report upon anything else that seem pertinent and proper in order that the legislature, as well as myself, might be fully informed as to the cause of the disagreement between the miners and operators and the best method to prevent future disturbances of a similar character.
4. They were asked to make such recommendations for remedial legislation as might be suggested to them by existing conditions.[67]

While the commissioners investigated the conflict in August, several ominous events occurred. Newspaper stories reported that "transportation men," strikebreakers, had been sent to a couple of Boone County mines. Despite the efforts of the UMW to keep the miners working, 1500 men walked off the job at Boomer in Fayette County. Discontent seemed pervasive, and although guns and ammunition had been confiscated in large quantities from both sides, common sense dictated that many remained.[68] Indeed, Jones and others advised the strikers to hide or bury their weapons in the woods for later

---

66 *House Journal and Bills*, 88.

67 *House Journal and Bills*, 88–89. See also Eugene V. Gartin, "The West Virginia Mine War of 1912–1913: The Progressive Response," *North Dakota Quarterly*, 41 (Autumn, 1973): 24. Hereafter cited as Gartin, "The West Virginia Mine War."

68 In all, the National Guard collected 2,360 weapons in the strike zone. The guns were of all types, including 6 machine guns, 482 pistols, 453 repeating rifles, 84 old-style mountain rifles, 301 small repeating rifles, and 1136 shotguns of different types. See McCormick, "The National Guard of West Virginia," 34.

Some of the weapons confiscated from the strike zone. Courtesy of the Otis K. Rice Collection of the West Virginia Institute of Technology, Montgomery, WV.

use.[69] Additional reports that "scabs" had been sent to Paint Creek and headlines in the *Clarksburg Daily Telegram* that read "Failure To Agree Means Battle In Strike Zone" and "Blood Will Be Spilled Tonight" only increased anxiety. As one miner concluded, "I have never had to kill a man and hope never to be compelled to kill one, but I would kill a dozen of these guards as I would so many rats."[70] At a mass rally at Cabin Creek Junction, Mother Jones echoed the intense hatred for the mine guards when she held the blood-soaked coat left behind by a wounded "thug." She cried out, "This is the first time I ever saw a goddamned mine guard's coat decorated to suit me." Jones then had the garment cut into small pieces and distributed to the miners to wear on their lapels.[71]

By the end of August, as the commissioners were making their investigation, violence broke out at Dry Branch, on Cabin Creek, where there had previously been no battles. An attempt to arrest a check weighman at Kayford led to the death of Deputy

69   Edwin E. Hoffman, *Fighting Mountaineers: The Struggle for Justice in the Appalachians* (Boston: Houghton Mifflin Co., 1979), 111. Hereafter cited as Hoffman, *Fighting Mountaineers.*

70   Sprague, "Unionization Struggles," 203.

71   Lee, *Bloodletting in Appalachia,* 29.

Sheriff T. J. Hines, serious injury to a miner, plus the destruction of railroad track. Governor Glasscock also received word that union organizers planned a large demonstration on Cabin Creek to encourage those working miners to strike. The commission reported the situation as it appeared at that time:

> Wild eyed men, seventy five per cent of them with usually cool Anglo-Saxon blood in their veins and with instincts leading to law and order inherited down through the centuries, gradually saw red, and with minds bent upon havoc and slaughter marched from the union district across the river like Hugheston, Cannelton and Boomer, patrolled the woods overhanging the creek bed and the mining plants, finally massing on the ridges at the headwaters and arranging a march to sweep down to the junction. Meanwhile, the operators hurried in over a hundred guards heavily armed, purchased several deadly machineguns and many thousand rounds of ammunition. Several murders were perpetrated and all who could, got away, men and women and children fled in terror and many hid in cellars and caves.[72]

When Governor Glasscock learned that for the first time union miners had crossed the Kanawha River in large numbers in support of their union "brothers" and that as many as 1500 armed men were in the hills on the night of September 2, he issued a proclamation of martial law and appointed a military commission to try all offenders. In an effort to instill law and order among the combatants, the commission quickly arrested violators on charges ranging from unlawful congregation to inciting a riot. Evidently, it was easier to incarcerate groups of miners than mine guards, who probably exercised restraint and used low visibility in the presence of the soldiers. While some guards were detained, the soldiers mainly arrested about sixty-six striking miners, who were generally given milder sentences during the first period of martial law, but the sentences were still demeaning to those who desired the constitutional right of a speedy trial in the civil courts. Penalties ranged from digging ditches to sixty days in the bullpen at Pratt. Trying civilians in a military court during peacetime caused Glasscock to receive some of the harshest criticism during his administration. He, however, acting at the behest of concerned citizens in nearby towns, felt strong actions on the part of the state government were necessary to quell the violence. Mother Jones, perhaps

---

72   Donahue, Walker, and Blue, *Mining Investigation, 1912*, 10–11, see also the *Charleston Gazette*, August 31, 1912. Sprague, "Unionization Struggles," 194–195.

testing the resolve of the guard, was arrested at Eskdale, the local strike headquarters, for reading to the miners the Declaration of Independence. One of the young soldiers, placed in a difficult position himself, later stated, "Hell's fire, was that what you were reading? I thought you was incitin' a riot."[73]

Before this crisis, between 1877 and 1902, the West Virginia National Guard had been called out seven times to quell industrial disputes. A military commission to try civilians while the civil courts were functioning had never before occurred in West Virginia, leading to strong rebukes not only locally but also nationally.[74] In his message to the 1913 legislature, Glasscock explained:

> ... I hesitated long before deciding to resort to this method of handling the situation, but believing that not only the lives of the people who lived on these creeks but the lives of the soldiers as well, and all property on these creeks, were in absolute danger, and that unless something was done that would enable us to handle the situation better than we could possibly do without martial law, and after consultation with others who accompanied me on some of these trips and became more or less familiar with the actual conditions up there I decided to declare martial law ... [75]

In an effort to end the bloodshed, the soldiers disarmed the mine guards and the miners. With the National Guard in control and peace restored, the companies, fearing this would happen, finally agreed to release their private police. On October 14, the state militia withdrew and martial law ended after devising a new guard system to protect private property. Special police, selected by the operators with the approval and supervision of the military commission, now patrolled the strike area.[76] Pleased with the work of the National Guard, Governor Glasscock congratulated Adjutant General Elliott on the "splendid work" he and his men had performed in disarming the two camps and ending the violence.[77] With the "thugs" removed from the troubled region, Glasscock had reason to hope for a prompt settlement.

---

73   Hoffman, *Fighting Mountaineers*, 112. See also Lee, *Bloodletting in Appalachia*, 33.

74   Merle T. Cole, "Martial Law in West Virginia and Major Davis as 'Emperor of Tug River,'" *West Virginia History*, 42 (Fall 1981): 120–21. Hereafter referred to as Cole, "Martial Law."

75   *House Journal and Bills*, 87.

76   Bailey, "Grim Visaged Men," 120.

77   Glasscock to Adjutant General Elliott, 4 September 1912, Glasscock Papers. See also *House Journal and Bills*, 87 and *Hearings*, 131–32.

In mid-September, Governor Glasscock again attempted to arbitrate the dispute. The miners agreed to the governor's terms, but the operators, especially those on Cabin Creek, refused to meet union representatives.[78] Worried over the violence and the disruption of business, some prominent citizens of Montgomery, near Paint Creek, met with Glasscock. Soon after the conference, Luther S. Montgomery of the *Montgomery News* reported to the governor that as many as five hundred persons had attended a meeting at the Opera House in that city and "agreed to all give up our arms and try to bring an end to the strike."[79] Pleased with the news, Glasscock wrote that he believed that it "was the beginning of the end of the present trouble."[80] Satisfied with the turn of events, Governor Glasscock found time to go to Huntington to rest for a few days. As he wrote to future Governor Henry D. Hatfield:

> I am going down to Huntington this evening to spend two or three days with Dr. Guthrie in order to get a little rest and I sincerely hope that the strike situation will be such within the next week or so that I can get away whenever I want to. I have never gone through anything like this before in my life and I hope I shall never again have to witness such a struggle between two contending parties. It has been day and night, Sunday and every other day with me for two or three months now and I feel like I am entitled to a little rest if I can get it but at the same time I know that it will not do for me to go very far away from Charleston until the situation gets better than it is to-day.[81]

With his strength restored, the Governor inspected the strike zone again in October. By the middle of that month, there were only seven military companies in the field, and the general expectations were that the others would be sent home the following week. However, Glasscock had hardly begun demobilization when trouble broke out yet again. A type of guerrilla warfare commenced near Kingston, in Fayette County, which killed three mules and wounded a number of persons. A serious incident also occurred on Cabin Creek, where the operators were bringing in "transportation men" to work the mines. This prompted the striking miners to fire upon the trains carrying the strikebreakers and the special police. An angry Glasscock fumed when

---

78   Glasscock to John Holmes, 11 September 1912, Glasscock Papers.
79   Luther S. Montgomery to Glasscock, 27 September 1912, Glasscock Papers.
80   Glasscock to L. S. Montgomery and B. S. Hastings, 28 September 1912, Glasscock Papers.
81   Glasscock to H. D. Hatfield, 3 October 1912, Glasscock Papers.

he learned that the companies were hiring a "great many worthless and irresponsible people."[82] Believing that a state of "anarchy" was in progress, Glasscock once again proclaimed martial law, establishing a military commission for the second time, which the governor instructed to act more vigorously in order to deter lawbreakers.[83] The second military court dispensed quick military justice even sentencing men to jail for offenses committed during the time when military law did not exist.[84]

By early November, the strike situation improved at Dorothy, on Coal River, and the two sides reached a settlement. One of the mine owners informed the governor of the successful negotiations and praised the work that he and Adjutant General Elliott had done to prevent violence. In turn, Governor Glasscock replied that if all the owners had treated their workers as fairly, "we would never have had the trouble that we had in this state."[85] It was clear, that the chief executive placed a large share of the blame on the management because of their inflexible stand on negotiations. Nevertheless, with the guard once again on duty, the violence subsided and Glasscock quietly removed martial law on December 12.[86]

On November 27, 1912, Governor Glasscock eagerly accepted the Mining Investigation Commission Report, hoping that its findings and recommendations would shed light on the causes of the strike and ways to end it. According to investigators, trouble erupted when the United Mine Workers attempted to organize miners on the two creeks, as part of its statewide effort. In examining the evidence, they reported two important facts that had caused the violence: (1) "desperate efforts and often unwarranted and unlawful acts of the United Miners to force the Union into the disturbed districts" and (2) "the equally desperate, unwarranted and unlawful acts of the operators and their agents to keep the union out."[87] In other words, neither side escaped blame.

In other areas, the commission stated that the mine guard system was strife promoting and "un-American." The investigators suggested that a better system of

---

82   Glasscock to I. V. Barton, 6 December 1912, Glasscock Papers. Glasscock was also of the opinion that most of the trouble could have been avoided if he, as governor, could have removed or suspended local officials who had not done their duty. See Glasscock to Lee Cruce, Governor of Oklahoma, 23 November 1912, Glasscock Papers.

83   *House Journal and Bills*, 87–89; *Hearings*, 396; Glasscock to H. D. Hatfield, 18 October 1912, Glasscock Papers.

84   Lee, *Bloodletting in Appalachia*, 35.

85   John H. Jones to Glasscock, 5 November 1912; Glasscock to John H. Jones, 11 November 1912, both in Glasscock Papers.

86   *House Journal and Bills*, 87–88.

87   Donahue, Walker, and Blue, *Mining Investigation, 1912*, 8–9, 10.

hiring reputable guards should be instituted. Since the police force on both creeks was inadequate, the companies did have a right to protect their property, but the commission felt that the use of watchmen, subject to the supervision of the state authorities, should be sufficient. These employees should also be required to take an oath and held liable for their acts, and the governor should be given the power to remove them from their position, if necessary.[88]

After a prolonged and personal inspection, the commission concluded that the "general surroundings" of the miners on Paint and Cabin Creeks were very good. The "Jenny Lind" houses, small and compact, were comfortable and while the rent was a little excessive, it was not exorbitant. Of course, the companies stated that they had built houses for the convenience of the miners, because many of the mines were located in isolated areas. Not discounting the expense and effort, owners could often make a profit for their trouble. After the initial investment of $300.00 to build a four-room house and renting it at six dollars a month, the structure would be paid off in four and one half years. The remainder would be profit.[89] In the investigators' opinion, the homes of the miners were " . . . above average of miners' homes in most places." At a fair estimate, "most of the lots on which they stand are forty by two hundred feet, and the dwellings are as comfortable as those of the average farm hands or for those who live by other manual labor." Perhaps, by way of comparison with the slums of the nation's urban areas, a concern of many progressives, the investigators took pains to point out that the lots provided space for growing vegetables, a practice that would improve health.

In the area of medical care, the families paid $1.00 a month for access to company doctors, medicine, and surgical needs, while single men contributed $.50, which seemed reasonable. An additional charge of fifteen cents a month provided miners the service of the Sheltering Arms hospital, located at Hansford not far from the mines, "a first class hospital, thoroughly up to date, and supported partly by endowment, partly by voluntary contributions and also by amounts received from pay patients."[90]

The Sheltering Arms, founded by the Diocese of West Virginia of the Protestant Episcopal Church, was established mainly for treating coal miners and their families in the Kanawha-New River region. A forerunner in what was known as a list patient hospital, it depended to a large degree on the monthly contributions of the miners.[91]

88   Donahue, Walker, and Blue, *Mining Investigation, 1912*, 3.
89   Gartin, "The West Virginia Mine War," 18.
90   Donahue, Walker, and Blue, *Mining Investigation, 1912*, 3–4.
91   Otis K. Rice and Wayne E. Williams, *The Sheltering Arms Hospital* (Charleston: West Virginia

This hospital is an example of how the entire community became involved in the labor strife. Earlier in the conflict, striking miners fired on two Baldwin-Felts mine guards traveling down Paint Creek. While one was killed, the other was wounded and managed to hide, later escaping on foot to the Sheltering Arms. Attempting to be impartial in the treatment of the sick and injured, the guard was treated, but fearing repercussions and harm to the injured man upon his release, a plan was devised to provide for his safety. Learning the schedule of the C&O train, which passed near their location, they placed the guard in a coffin and transported it to the depot. From there the "corpse" was saved and sent on his journey home.[92] The commission then turned to wages. It reported that the average annual wage of miners in West Virginia for the years 1905 to 1911, inclusive, was $554.26. The average annual wage of miners on Paint Creek and Cabin Creek was from $600 to $700. Furthermore, they concluded that the average wage on those two creeks was equal to if not better than that of the few unionized mines on the opposite side of the Kanawha River.[93] So far, the owners had fared well in the report.

On the other hand, the Investigation Commission criticized the company store for overcharging its customers. The store also sold the miner his powder, tools, and other necessities needed on the job and if the worker had any money left at the end of the month after deductions, he was often issued scrip to be used at the company store. If the miner desired to exchange the scrip for cash, there was often a 25% charge.[94] The committee members unanimously felt that these businesses charged more per article than was true in the open market, and they strongly condemned this practice, but added, "Not all of the companies, however, have been at fault in the same degree." Some owners, of course, thought their goods were of a higher quality. The commissioners also added, using a favorite tenet of the Progressive Era, "the light of ample publicity would shine effectively for all concerned." Another serious offense committed by the

Educational Services, 1990), vi.

92   Rice and Williams, *The Sheltering Arms Hospital*, 51.

93   Donahue, Walker, and Blue, *Mining Investigation, 1912*, 4–5. The committee also showed figures from the federal *Bureau of Mines and Geological Survey*, that for the year 1910 the miners from West Virginia made on average $573.94; Illinois, $497.71; Pennsylvania anthracite miners, $543.88; Pennsylvania bituminous miners, $572.72; Indiana, $715.32; and Ohio, $486.50. West Virginia miners appeared comparatively well on paper, but they worked a nine or ten hour day in most of the mines, while the northern miners worked an eight-hour day and had done so since 1898. See Lynch, "The West Virginia Coal Strike," 652–53.

94   Gartin, "The West Virginia Mine War," 18–19.

operators was the practice of "blacklisting" by which officials at one mine would warn other companies against employing particular miners because of their union activity.[95] The investigators criticized this as well.

In conclusion, the members of the Investigation Commission spared neither side in their summation. They stated the operators had a right to refuse recognition of the union. After all, acceptance would place them in a weaker position in competition with the northern coal producing states. On the other hand, they stated that the miners had a right to organize for their mutual benefit, a position difficult to reconcile. With good and bad, guilt and innocence on both sides, the investigators obviously encouraged compromise, a path not easily traveled during a labor dispute. However, they did recommend several pieces of remedial legislation. They suggested the creation of a workman's compensation commission, more power for the state board of health, and that the governor should have more authority over local peace officers. Finally, they called for a law similar to the Canadian Industrial Dispute Act of 1907, which used arbitration and a ban on work stoppage during negotiations.[96]

Unfortunately, the mining report did not lead to immediate remedies, but it did provide a locus on which further debate and discussion concerning industrial strife could center. Governor Glasscock hoped that a period of peace and calm discussion would follow on the heels of these findings, ultimately leading to remedial legislation in the 1913 legislature. To the chagrin of the governor and many others, peace in the coal valleys did not prevail. During December 1912, sporadic shooting occurred in the strike zone, but it did not warrant more troops. The situation worsened, however, in February 1913, when miners attempted to prevent strikebreakers from working.

On February 2 and 4, the mining camps of Acme and Ronda came under attack. This was followed by an incident at Mucklow, on Paint Creek, at about ten in the morning on February 7. In the latter attack, Fred Bobbitt, a bookkeeper from the Paint Creek Collieries Company, was killed.[97] Upon hearing that officials had tracked the perpetrators to a tent colony at Holly Grove, Governor Glasscock requested Kanawha County Sheriff Bonner Hill, along with a posse of six deputies, eleven "railroad

---

95   Gartin, "The West Virginia Mine War," 7–8.

96   Gartin, "The West Virginia Mine War," 18–24. This was much in line with Glasscock's own philosophy toward labor and management, that is, for the governor to remain impartial and the parties to seek arbitration for the dispute. See also Richard D. Lunt, *Law and Order vs. The Miners: West Virginia, 1907–1933* (Handen, Connecticut: Archon Books, 1979), 28–29. Hereafter cited as Lunt, *Law and Order.*

97   Bailey, "Grim Visaged Men," 123.

detectives," and Paint Creek coal operator Quinn Morton, to board a train to Paint Creek to arrest the killers. The train, called the "Bull Moose Special," was equipped with a machine gun situated in an armored car. When it arrived at the mouth of Paint Creek, informants claimed that the strikers at Holly Grove intended to fire upon it. Nevertheless, the invincible "death train," as the miners later named it, slowly continued its perilous journey into the strike zone. The people of the tent city knew the locomotive was coming, perhaps warned by local railroad workers in Huntington, so they prepared for action. Men, women, and children had gathered in a large mess tent where the inhabitants ate community style. In preparation for hostilities, the men created a "dugout" near the mountain, where the women and children would retreat at the first sign of danger. Inside the large tent, the gathered throng enjoyed the melodious twangs of a guitar, banjo, and fiddle, as they tensely waited for the death train At the first sound of the steam engine, music ceased, and rifles readied. Gunfire rang out, from whom nobody knows, and at the blast of the train whistle, the machine gun burst into action.

Some reports state that two shots were fired first at the train from the left side, which led to a burst of machine gun fire from the train. Others swore that at the blast of the train whistle, the machine gun first fired on the miners. Lee Calvin, a mine guard on board the death train, later testified in the Senate hearings that while leaning out the window and smoking on the right-hand side he saw shooting commence from the baggage car ahead of him.[98] Former Attorney General Howard B. Lee, not a strong sympathizer to the coal companies, stated that in 1945 the older former Sheriff Bonner Hill wrote him personally stating that "when the shooting began, he was standing in the aisle looking through the window, and the flashes from the guns fired from the outside were very plain, and he 'firmly believes that the first shots came from outside firing at the train.'"[99] Amazingly, only one man, Cesco Estep, was killed and one woman wounded. The "Bull Moose Special" continued to its destination. The watchword among the miners was "when the leaves come out," a sentiment captured in a 1913 poem written by a union sympathizer:[100]

---

98   David Alan Corbin, ed., *The West Virginia Mine Wars: An Anthology*, (Charleston, WV: Appalachian Editions, 1990), 36. Hereafter cited as Corbin, *The West Virginia Mine Wars*.

99   Lee, *Bloodletting in Appalachia*, 38–40.

100   J.W. Hess, ed., *Struggle in the Coal Fields: The Autobiography of Fred Mooney* (Morgantown: West Virginia University Library, 1967), 37–38. Hereafter cited as Hess, *Struggle in the Coal Fields*. See also Bailey, "Grim Visaged Men," 122–123.

It isn't just to see the hills beside me
Grow fresh and green with every growing thing;
I only want the leaves to come and hide me,
To cover up my vengeful wandering.

I will not watch the floating clouds that hover
Above the birds that warble on the wing;
I want to use this gun from under cover—
Oh, buddy, how I'm longing for the spring.[101]

Unable to wait until spring, miners seeking revenge attacked the mining company at Mucklow. Governor Glasscock again declared martial law throughout Kanawha County. Even before the leaves sprouted, parts of Raleigh, Fayette, and Boone Counties experienced hostilities. Violence, however, ceased with the arrival of six companies of the National Guard for the third time in eight months.[102] The only solution to the persistent problem seemed to be the use of force by the state. This final period of martial law lasted from February 10 to June 13, 1913, into the administration of the new Governor Hatfield.

Fifty-one arrests immediately followed, soon totaling one hundred and sixty-six strikers and miners, with most of the prisoners incarcerated in boxcars and shanties at Paint Creek Junction, the seat of the military camp.[103] Meanwhile, the *Charleston Gazette* reported with embellished language that a group of union miners had met at Smithers, on the Kanawha River, in a scene "that resembled a den of anarchists with total disregard for the value of human life."[104] The newspaper further alleged that miners had made threats against the lives of the governor and other state officials. Events culminated in the arrest of Mother Jones on the streets of Charleston outside the strike zone, quickly removing her and her companions to Pratt to stand trial in the military court. Many feared the worst as rumors circulated that the striking miners would march on Charleston and kill Glasscock. Although the people of the capitol city anxiously watched and prepared for further developments, the rumors proved false and calm once again prevailed.

---

101 Hess, *Struggle in the Coal Fields*, 37–38. Ralph Chaplin, who also authored labor's anthem "Solidarity Forever" and later became editor of the IWW's *Industrial Worker,* wrote the poem. See Foner, *Mother Jones Speaks,* 158.

102 *Charleston Gazette,* February 11, 1913; February 12, 1913.

103 Hoffman, *Fighting Mountaineers,* 120.

104 *Charleston Gazette,* February 14, 1913.

Mother Jones, along with Charles H. Boswell of the *Labor Argus* and two other companions, was charged with complicity in the riots on Paint Creek, which had resulted in a number of deaths. Jones and her fellow prisoners filed individual petitions with the State Supreme Court, praying that a writ of habeas corpus be issued in each case. They wished by this action to force the court to decide whether the military court had jurisdiction over the civil courts. The State Supreme Court, however, upheld the governor in his action, stating that Glasscock had the right to incarcerate the defendants in times of disorder, "regardless of the place where their arrests were effected, or by whom they were effected."[105] Judge Ira E. Robinson, who had sworn Glasscock into office, was the only dissenting voice on the bench, holding that the arrests were unconstitutional since the civil courts of the county were functioning. Nevertheless, Glasscock felt vindicated.[106] In a somber moment at an earlier visit, Mother Jones perhaps expressed the feelings of many of her followers when she reflected, "West Virginia, Medieval West Virginia! With its grim men and women. With its tent colonies on the bleak hills. When I get to the other side, I shall tell God Almighty about West Virginia."[107]

Exonerated or not, Glasscock produced no final settlement during his administration. Feeling he had no other choice in the face of violence and destruction and acting in the tradition of other federal and state chief executives, he enlisted the military power of the state to maintain order. Acting on the precedents set by other leaders, such as President Theodore Roosevelt, who considered using the military during the Pennsylvania anthracite coal strike of 1902, and on the progressive impulse to be fair to all sides, the embattled governor sought impartiality, encouraging the two opponents to arbitrate. Glasscock could take solace in the fact that the progressive periodicals were mild and sympathetic in their judgments. For example, the *Independent*, the *Survey*, and the *Outlook* took the view that both labor and management were guilty of wrongs and excesses, a neutral view with which the governor agreed.[108]

Even as a private citizen, Governor Glasscock could not escape the industrial turmoil. When the United States Senate sent a subcommittee on education and labor to Charleston to investigate existing conditions on Paint and Cabin Creeks, Glasscock appeared as a witness. In June 1913, the former governor stressed two factors, which he thought had hastened industrial warfare in West Virginia: (1) the chief executive's

---

105 *Charleston Gazette*, March 1, 1913.
106 Glasscock to C. R. Morgan, 23 December 1912, Glasscock Papers. Eventually these defendants were pardoned by Glasscock's successor, Henry D. Hatfield.
107 Gorn, *Mother Jones*, 169.
108 Gartin, "The West Virginia Mine War," 23–25.

inability to force local officers to do their duty, and (2) the obstinacy of the coal operators in refusing to arbitrate their difficulties through an impartial body.[109] The Senate Investigating Committee sharply focused on the actions of the embattled governor and criticized his use of military courts when civil courts were available. The former governor defended his actions explaining that the local authorities appeared unable to end the violence or even to raise a grand jury, which he had requested, in the face of obvious indictable crimes. Glasscock further explained that quickly sentencing lawbreakers to prison was for the moral effect. In fact, with peace restored, conditional pardons were granted to all prisoners.

The fact remained that, along with Mother Jones, two hundred and fifty offenders were tried by the military judicial system. The military court ruled over a wide variety of offenses including "larceny, adultery, disorderly conduct, intimidation of workers, disobeying sentries, perjury, doing police work in violation of the proclamation, and carrying concealed weapons."[110] Without presentment, indictment, or jury, sentences became final upon approval of the chief executive.

The governor's actions brought intermittent peace, allowing time to work for a settlement, but often resulted in a respite for the combatants to prepare for the next battle. If it had been possible for the military to assist the local officials in gathering evidence and raising a grand jury that would have been fair in its deliberations in a civil court, the criticisms would not have been so harsh.[111] Not satisfied with the senate investigation, socialists appointed their own committee chaired by Eugene V. Debs, who also criticized the actions of Governor Glasscock but was generally favorable to the newly elected governor.[112] Local socialists, in turn, berated Debs because they believed

---

109 *Hearings*, 515–27. See also Samuel P. Hays, *The Response to Industrialism: 1885–1914* (Chicago: The University of Chicago Press, 1957), 40. State and federal soldiers had ended many strikes previously. For example, the first great industrial strike occurred on the railroads in 1877 originating at Martinsburg, West Virginia. Democratic Governor Henry Mason Mathews at first used State National Guard troops to no avail before pleading with President Rutherford B. Hayes for federal soldiers, which finally quelled the strikers.

110 Cole, "Martial Law in West Virginia," 121.

111 Lynch, "The West Virginia Coal Strike," 648–49.

112 Frederick Allan Barkey, "The Socialist Party in West Virginia from 1890 to 1920: A Study in Working Class Radicalism" (Ph.D. diss., University of Pittsburgh, 1971), 137–147. Corbin, "The Socialist and Labor Star," 179–180. See also David A. Corbin, "Betrayal in the West Virginia Coal Fields: Eugene V. Debs and the Socialist Party of America 1912–1941," *Journal of American History* 64 (March 1978): 987–1009. In Corbin's view, the Debs investigation report was too lenient toward Hatfield and the UMW, calling it a "whitewash." Debs, on the other hand, believed his critics and

he was too conciliatory with Hatfield and the UMW, which appeared too eager to settle. This view was shared by Mother Jones and many of the striking miners, such as the young union leaders Frank Keeney and Fred Mooney, who were willing to carry the fight for official union recognition to the end. From that day forward, Jones harbored bitter feelings toward Debs and the National Socialist Party of America. Focusing the public's attention on the dissension among the various participants, Hatfield gained time to work diligently and quickly in the background to produce a heavy-handed "settlement."[113]

Taking into consideration the culture of the time, Governor Glasscock, who had previously taken a strong stand against violence, displayed considerable restraint in trying to bring the two sides together. Like General Sherman, he too felt his conflict could only be compared to "hell." Random acts of violence, aggravated by fiery rhetoric on both sides and fanned by passionate newspaper accounts, led to an explosive labor-management crisis, a crisis that many people called a civil war and even a class conflict. Some outside observers compared the struggle to something peculiar to "mountain culture," seeing the tactics as a type of guerrilla war or acts of terrorism that were similar to the feuds in the lawless period in southern West Virginia following the Civil War,[114] only on a much broader scale. To make it even more interesting to readers in out-of-state newspapers, in 1912 the voters of West Virginia elected a Hatfield as their governor, a name familiar from the famous Hatfield–McCoy feud. The Mine War of 1912–1913 certainly displayed all of the elements to validate parts of the various theories, including a struggle for a socialistic workplace. Although many miners were attracted to socialist ideas during the conflict, socialism never took firm root among the workers. Unfortunately for some of the combatants, there was pleasure and excitement on both sides during this life and death struggle between union and nonunion forces,

the West Virginia Socialists wanted the IWW to represent the miners. For a sympathetic view of Debs, see Roger Fagge, "Eugene V. Debs in West Virginia, 1913: A Reappraisal," *West Virginia History*, 52 (1993): 1–18. Lunt, *Law and Order*, 32–36, also defends Governor Hatfield. For a concise review of these charges and counter charges, see Foner, *Mother Jones Speaks*, 217–19.

113 Gartin, "The West Virginia Mine War," 23–25. In the "Hatfield Contract," the operators conceded a nine-hour workday, semi-monthly pay, the right of the miners to select a checkweighman, but little was said about union recognition. In fact, the situation was one of "status quo antebellum." In other words, if you were organized before the strike, then you would remain organized. If not, then you remained unorganized. Therefore, the miners on Paint Creek remained unionized, while the workers on Cabin Creek remained unorganized.

114 For the feuds, see Otis K. Rice, *The Hatfields and the McCoys* (Lexington: the University Press of Kentucky, 1978).

which ultimately led to the deaths of scores of people and thousands of dollars in destruction of property during a one-year period. Public opinion shifted from one side to the other, but as the strike progressed, more of the state's newspapers sounded anti-union.[115] At the same time, numerous socialists in the affected counties strongly condemned the mine operators and the Glasscock administration.[116] Of course, collective bargaining would not be truly legitimized until the passage of the National Industrial Recovery Act in 1933. The "Appalachian Agreement," appended to the code, and in effect, made "the UMW spokesman for the miners and the Federal government the enforcer of their working conditions."[117]

In the end, the use of military courts to solve the labor problem while the civil courts were open caused the governor to receive the strongest condemnation. Perhaps if there had been a way for Glasscock to act more swiftly and forcibly at critical times when the local authorities had not responded efficiently, there would have been no need for extensive use of the National Guard and, more importantly, the military courts. The editor of the *Huntington Advertiser* had it right when he suggested the creation of a state police force:

> It is costly and cumbersome, intended for emergencies only, and, rightly or wrongly, the use of the National Guard in labor troubles tends to produce a sentiment against the Guard and prevents the Guard from receiving the support of a large class of people to whom, in its legitimate function of a secondary national defense, the National Guard should strongly appeal.[118]

Keen observers quickly recognized that no labor–management conflict was ever like the one before or the one that followed, and there were no easy solutions. Glasscock knew he was dealing with an indeterminate process, a process that required the active attention of a chief executive aided by a governmental apparatus that provided work-

---

115 Sprague, "Unionization Struggles," 203, 210.

116 Corbin, "The Socialist and Labor Star," 169. According to Dale Fetherling, a Mother Jones biographer, Mother Jones "was a socialist, but not a Socialist." He adds, "she was an individual believer in collectivism." See also Pat Creech Scholten, "The Old Mother and Her Army: The Agitative Strategies of Mary Harris Jones," *West Virginia History*, 40 (Summer 1979): 365–74.

117 Richard M. Hadsell and William E. Coffey, "From Law and Order to Class Warfare: Baldwin-Felts Detectives in the Southern West Virginia Coal Fields, *West Virginia History* 40 (Spring 1979): 285. Hereafter cited as Hadsell and Coffey, "From Law and Order."

118 Bailey, "Grim Visaged Men," 114.

174

able rules and guidelines (which the state lacked) leading to order and continuity while resolving conflict. The governor had tried using words of persuasion, arbitration, meeting each side separately, issuing a Peace Proclamation, enlisting the aid of the community, encouraging local law enforcement to action, and finally, the last resort, martial law. He called for an investigation commission to gather information that allowed him to present its findings to the legislature. In the best tradition of Progressivism, Glasscock proposed legislation that would aid the central government in solving the present crisis and lend direction and continuity for future events. The process was not perfect, but it was proactive.

One important lesson learned from the mine wars on Paint and Cabin Creeks was that the use of the state's citizen soldiers to quell labor disputes was too controversial. In all, the guard did a good job under much pressure. Most of the young guardsmen were respectful of the human condition and the plight of displaced families, but some were not. A soldier killed only one miner, and that was by accident. Remarkably, only two soldiers died during their stay in the battle zone, and this was because of typhoid fever and ptomaine poisoning. Often when the miners interpreted an action by the soldiers as favorable, the owners perceived it to be harmful. The soldiers received much credit for their attempts to create better sanitary conditions on the two creeks, but were criticized by the strikers when they confiscated weapons, allowing watchmen or special police to carry theirs. Evidently, some of the National Guard assisted the mine owners in carrying out the evictions of the miners from the company houses, an act that angered the workers. In their attempt to prevent violence and to protect property, the soldier's actions sometimes engendered harsh feelings among the dispossessed families. On occasions when the guardsmen's tour of duty ended, some soldiers remained behind, employed by the companies as special police, an action strongly condemned by the UMW.[119] Learning many lessons from the conflict, the National Guard would never again be used to preserve peace in a strike zone in West Virginia.[120] Governor John J. Cornwell, a Democrat whose term ran 1917–1921, experienced problems similar to Glasscock's under his administration. As a validation of Glasscock's recommendations to the Senate hearings, stressing his inability to force local officials to promptly respond to urgent problems, Governor Cornwell sought and received legislation to establish a modern state police agency in West Virginia, the fourth oldest in the nation. As Cornwell explained, "Sheriffs are tax collectors and not police officers. While making

---

119 Bailey, "Grim Visaged Men," 111–125.
120 Bailey, "Grim Visaged Men," 125.

no wholesale criticism of sheriffs' offices it is only too true that little cooperation can be had from some of them by the Governor or other State authorities. . . ."[121]

The conflict between labor and management would continue into the Hatfield administration, though it was temporarily settled in the summer of 1913 with an uneasy agreement with the miners' union. The rank and file membership, however, unhappy that more was not received in the "forced" settlement, continued the struggle until a final agreement was reached later in the year.[122] In the opinion of the states comprising the Central Competitive Field, however, the West Virginia strike was a failure. Within a decade, the Mountain State's nonunion miners would be the core of the industry, forcing Pennsylvania, Ohio, Indiana, and Illinois to go open shop.[123] Governor Glasscock had worked diligently to arrange a compromise, but his efforts were in vain. Perhaps he had become a symbol of the impasse itself, with his impartiality distrusted by both sides. The accession of Henry D. Hatfield, a new chief executive who was perceived as more forceful, helped to ease tensions and resolve the dispute temporarily. Governor Hatfield received much praise for ending the strike, praise that should have been shared with the previous governor who had laid much of the groundwork. Thus ended the 1912–1913 labor conflict with no clear-cut heroes or victories but many victims.

121 Merle T. Cole, "Birth of the West Virginia State Police, 1919–1921," *West Virginia History* 43 (Fall 1981): 1–4.

122 Surprisingly, coal production for 1912 was 59,581,774 gross tons, a record breaking year. See the *Charleston Gazette*, January 8, 1913.

123 Sprague, "Unionization Struggles," 213.

THE 1913 LEGISLATURE:
ONE LAST CHANCE

"I am more anxious now to lay down these responsibilities . . ."[1]

A S THE DATE NEARED for the January convening of the 1913 legislature, Governor Glasscock worked on a number of bills that he hoped would ease the tension in the coalfields. First on the agenda, however, were the organization of the two houses and the election of a new United States Senator, which together promised to be time-consuming. Since there were so many important measures to consider, Glasscock called the legislators in a special session on January 2, a week before the regular term began, in order to prepare for the heavy load ahead.

A weary Glasscock knew the 1913 legislative session would be his last chance to pass reform programs. The progressives also recognized that the conservatives would attempt to maintain the status quo and protect business and development in the state. The reformers, however, felt momentum going into the session; they had rebounded from the severe 1910 defeat of the party, and they had reformed and reorganized the structure of the party itself. The voters of the state had also given most of their votes to Roosevelt and the Bull Moose Party in the 1912 presidential election. Progressivism with its impulse to action seemed to be in the air and the governor was determined to continue the march forward so that business could be regulated and fair elections would truly reflect the wishes of the people. The reformers did not desire to destroy the economic and political systems; they wanted to harness the energies of both and allow them to function in orderly, predictable, controlled processes.

As the lawmakers arrived in Charleston, Governor Glasscock worried that he had made a mistake in appointing Davis Elkins, son of the late Senator Stephen B. Elkins, to continue his father's term of office. This gave the younger Elkins some advantage

---

1 *Charleston Daily Mail,* March 4, 1913.

as a successor to Democratic Senator Clarence Watson, whose term would expire in 1913. Actually, there was very little difference in the political philosophy of Elkins or Watson; both were conservative, and both were acceptable to the business community. But Glasscock felt that the people of the state wanted a more progressive leader. The governor, who now viewed Elkins as a "pronounced reactionary,"[2] confided to Judge John W. Mason that the Elkins appointment was an error for which he was responsible "and if I am I know of nothing I can do except to ask forgiveness for my past mistake and make sure that I do all that I can to see that there is no repetition of that mistake."[3] Of course, the best remedy was to support a Progressive candidate, which Glasscock did in the person of William S. Edwards. This would be the last time that legislators would elect a United States Senator, for soon it would be in the hands of the people exercising their choice through a primary election.

The various political contenders arrived in Charleston and either directly announced their intention to seek the coveted position or very coyly devised subtle strategy with their supporters in the legislature and outside the marble halls. This was a spectacle with all the elements of a high drama—pathos, defeat, victory, and often bribery—and it was very much out of the hands of the voters.

The reform Republicans felt they had good reason to insist that the majority of the voters of the state were in sympathy with the Bull Moose Party and deserved the right to choose the next United States Senator. They contended that the recent Roosevelt majority of 22,000 votes in West Virginia should be a mandate for the election of a Progressive senator. During the election of 1912, twenty-five counties had supported Roosevelt in contrast to seven for Taft. The same trend was also evident in the State Senate, where the Progressives carried twelve districts and the "regulars" only three. Of course, Edwards believed the honor should fall to him, since "I am the only candidate presented by the Progressive organization, for the senatorship."[4] In addition to Edwards, the reformers liked former Congressman W. P. Hubbard, who was not very active in the early stage of political maneuvering. Each contender carefully made

---

2   Gerald Wayne Smith, "Nathan Goff, Jr.: A Biography" (Ph.D diss., West Virginia University, 1954), 381. This would prove to be the last West Virginia legislature to elect a United States Senator, because of the Seventeenth Amendment to the U.S. Constitution, which placed the election of U.S. Senators directly in the hands of the people. Ironically, the first U.S. Senator directly elected by the people of the state in 1917 was Howard Sutherland, a Stephen B. Elkins lieutenant who defeated Democrat William E. Chilton. See Ambler and Summers, *West Virginia, The Mountain State*, 392.
3   Glasscock to John W. Mason, 29 November 1912, Glasscock Papers.
4   *Charleston Gazette*, January 1, 1913.

plans and strategy in an effort to woo his fellow lawmakers while also appealing for public support through the press.

From the beginning, it was obvious that Elkins and Edwards would be the main contenders, and the outcome would indicate the relative strength of those two opposing groups. Elkins, who had attended Harvard, quit school and enlisted as a volunteer when war broke out in 1898. Upon his return home, the young veteran worked for his father and learned the fickle ways of West Virginia politics. Confident that he would once again occupy his father's seat in the U.S. Senate, he had reason to be hopeful because the Republican Party had regained its strength after the debacle of 1910 and appeared to be in the good graces of the people once again. In fact, the results of the election of 1912 surprised even the most optimistic party member. When the ballots were counted, the GOP had nearly made a clean sweep of the legislature. The Democratic majority in the House was overthrown and eleven of the fifteen senatorial districts fell to the Republicans. In the House the "Old Guard" held a majority of twenty, while the Senate was deadlocked at fifteen to fifteen. This was even more surprising since out of the fifteen holdovers, eleven were Democrats. The majority in the lower chamber made the difference upon which Elkins hoped to capitalize.[5]

Davis Elkins attempted to assume leadership of the conservative wing of the state Republican Party after the death of his father. This, however, did not prevent him from claiming a certain affinity with the reformers. In a letter to the legislators, Elkins obviously attempted to straddle the fence when he stated, "What this state and nation are today is due to the Republican party. I am not in favor of any third party, but believe our party should be reorganized along progressive lines," which was perhaps a contrite admission that it was time for the conservatives to parcel out loaves of bread instead of stone. He announced candidly that he supported the main principles of the Progressive Party, which simply stated were "popular vote and doing of what the people want, than what a few wealthy people want."[6] With his comments, Elkins attempted to weaken his opposition, knowing that winning an election always came before making public policy.

Like Elkins, William S. Edwards also had roots in the Mountain State, maintaining his family's coal interests and actively participating in politics. Edwards, truly a Progressive politician, favored by a majority of those members, was also a close friend of Governor Glasscock and former Governor Dawson. The prominent Edwards family had made their wealth in the coal industry in the Great Kanawha Valley and, aware of

5   *Charleston Gazette*, January 28, 1913.
6   *Charleston Gazette*, January 3,1913; January 9, 1913; January 25, 1913.

their civic duties, returned to society a portion of their wealth and time. Edwards' father, Colonel William H. Edwards, had opened the first coal mine on Paint Creek and built the first coal railroad there about 1854.[7] Later, he also opened a mine at Coalburg, where the family's fortunes grew. The Edwards family worked to improve their community, especially to provide good educational facilities for the children of West Virginia. For example, Colonel Edwards had served as president of the Cabin Creek District Board of Education for twelve successive years. His son, William, first entered the legislature in 1892, where he continued his family's interest in education.[8] Of course, from atop his legislative perch, he could also protect his family's interests in the Kanawha Valley.

Besides the support of Glasscock, Colonel Edwards also had the endorsement of former Governor W. M. O. Dawson, who conducted his campaign in the legislature. In the early phase of the session, many observers felt he was slipping in his bid for the senatorship in comparison with the powerful Elkins. But the colonel was yet to unleash the forces of the Progressives throughout the state. After a period of relative inaction, Edwards' stock rose because of Progressive voter pressure applied on their representatives in Charleston; the reformers made it clear that they would not compromise but were willing to wage "war to the hilt."[9]

Business leaders preferred Isaac T. Mann, a wealthy coal magnate from the southern part of the state, with extensive mining operations throughout that region. Like Edwards, Mann did not circulate as much in the legislature as the energetic Elkins. To his advantage, however, Colonel Mann had the adept backing of Elliott Northcott of Huntington, the U.S. Minister to Venezuela on a temporary leave of absence. Granting Davis Elkins the front slot, most observers analyzed the political scene as a very close race for second place between Mann and Edwards.[10]

From the beginning, various notables slipped in and out of the political ring. Judge John W. Mason, a perennial office seeker, to whom Mann had announced his intention of running for the senatorship in November of 1912, responded that he was also seeking the position. Indeed, Mason observed, he would be happy "to round out my public career with a term in the United States Senate."[11] Judge Mason, however, had

---

7   Otis K. Rice, "Coal Mining in the Kanawha Valley to 1861: A View of Industrialization in the Old South," *The Journal of Southern History*, 31 (November, 1965): 403.

8   *Charleston Gazette*, January 19, 1913.

9   *Charleston Gazette*, January 5, 1913; February 6, 1913.

10   *Charleston Daily Mail*, January 2, 1913.

11   I. T. Mann to John W. Mason, 16 November 1912, John W. Mason Papers, West Virginia University Library.

little chance of securing the office and was a weak contender. Digging deeply into the Republican past, the party's faithful raised the name of former U.S. Senator Nathan Goff as a possible successor to Watson and, in fact, many believed that there was a strong undercurrent for this "darkhorse." Yet the judge did not actively campaign, a tactic he had used in the past, and largely remained in the background.[12] This was often the strategy of some politicos on such occasions as the legislature at that time and remains a tactic used at party conventions today.

A tight race seemed certain, and there was never a shortage of possible candidates as the aspirants slipped in and out of Charleston, each having his day in the press. The name of former U.S. Senator Nathan B. Scott was widely touted even though upon his arrival at the capital city he tried to squelch rumors of his possible candidacy. In a blunt statement he commented, "No, I am not [a candidate]; have not been and do not intend to become a candidate for the office of United States Senator."[13] On the other hand, former Governor A. B. White conducted an active campaign, informing Judge Mason that "If elected I shall be delighted; if you or some other good man is preferred I assure you I shall not complain."[14]

The lines of battle were drawn, but the extra session passed with few results. Governor-elect Hatfield worried that the Democrats would not assist in organizing the legislature, "for the reason that if we are given this privilege we will be in position to elect a United States Senator."[15] The House organized, leaving the senators mired in debate. With its paucity of results, the public and the press chastised the lawmakers for their no-compromise attitude and criticized the governor for having called the special session in the first place and wasting the taxpayer's money. Knowing that this would be his last opportunity to fulfill his political promises,[16] Glasscock urged action. Mindful of the criticism, the Senate finally chose Democrat Samuel V. Woods of Barbour County as its president,[17] and by January 23, during the regular term, both houses finally settled down to business.

From Governor Glasscock's message to the legislature, there was no doubt that he desired to see West Virginia become one of the most Progressive states in the union.

12 *Charleston Gazette*, January 3, 1913; January 4, 1913.

13 *Charleston Gazette*, February 4, 1913.

14 A. B. White to John W. Mason, 2 December 1912, Mason Papers.

15 H. D. Hatfield to Glasscock, 6 December 1912, Glasscock Papers.

16 *Charleston Gazette*, January 10, 1913; *Charleston Daily Mail*, January 9, 1913; January 14, 1913; January 15, 1913; January 16, 1913.

17 *Charleston Gazette*, January 24, 1913; see also *Charleston Daily Mail*, January 24, 1913.

In his biennial address, which not only called for new reforms but also contained a litany of formerly defeated bills, he placed before the lawmakers a broad and ambitious program, calling for change in many areas of society. Glasscock asked for action on the "Virginia Debt" question, recommending that the legislature appoint a bipartisan commission of fifteen members for the purpose of meeting with a like commission from Virginia.

In reference to taxation, the governor again suggested a levy on natural gas produced in the Mountain State in order to replace the $650,000 once received from the tax on liquor licenses. Governor Glasscock also proposed a duty on every kilowatt of electricity produced by water power, or a repeal of the law giving water power companies the right of eminent domain. In the area of education, he recommended a new building for the College of Agriculture at West Virginia University, and he noted the need of teaching "the household duties" to the young people of the state. The governor also asked for the creation of a professorship of coal mining at the university.[18] Perhaps because of the recent labor dispute, mine accidents, and the importance of coal production to the state, the mining department under the auspices of the College of Engineering would be given more prominence. On January 17, 1930, with the appointment of Professor C. E. Lawall as director of the School of Mines, coal mining finally achieved semi-autonomy, functioning independently, but in close cooperation with the College of Engineering.[19]

Taking a radical position among several states, Glasscock suggested the sterilization of patients in the insane asylums, recommending a law similar to the ones enacted in Indiana and New Jersey. He also called for the abolition of capital punishment, referring the lawmakers to like laws in the states of Michigan, Wisconsin, Rhode Island, Maine, and Kansas.[20]

In connection with the industrial strife in the Kanawha Valley, the beleaguered governor directed the attention of the legislators to the recommendations of the Mining Investigation Commission, which advised the abolition of the mine guard system, requested more power for the chief executive over local peace officers, and championed the enactment of a workmen's compensation law. The governor also asked for more authority for the State Board of Health, the erection of armories, legislation to enable the chief executive to appoint special police in lieu of private guards, and a law

---

18 *West Virginia Senate Journal, Regular and Extraordinary Session 1913*, 81–131.

19 Callahan, *History of West Virginia, Old and New*, 672. See also Ambler, *A History of Education in West Virginia*, 866–67.

20 *West Virginia Senate Journal, Regular and Extraordinary Session 1913*, 93–94.

to aid in preventing and settling strikes and lockouts. In concluding his comments on the labor situation, Glasscock estimated that it had cost the state $250,000, "by means of troops, etc."[21]

In other important areas, Governor Glasscock called for an anti-lobby law, enabling legislation to carry out the state prohibition amendment, a county salary bill, a public service commission, a primary election law, a corrupt practices act, increased power for the commissioner of agriculture, ratification of the income tax amendment to the United States Constitution, support of women's suffrage, and a convention to update West Virginia's constitution.[22] In total, it was a comprehensive package and Progressive to the core. The governor presented the 1913 legislature with a full menu of reforms, knowing well that it would be a selective process, but hopeful because the mood of the people was progressive, and he would be assisted by an energetic Governor-elect Hatfield with his recently earned political chips.

As the labor crisis on Paint and Cabin Creeks continued, the lawmakers began the passage of laws, proving it to be a banner year for reform legislation. By the end of the session, the legislature approved more than half of the administration's measures and amended several others. A total of eighty-two bills and three joint resolutions cleared the House and Senate during the regular term. Overall, Glasscock was pleased with the results. In particular, he commented, "One of the best laws enacted by the legislature was that creating a Public Service Commission."[23] It passed both houses in amended form, but was still strong enough to receive the endorsement of the governor. The commission supervised, regulated, and controlled all public service corporations, including hydroelectric companies. The legislature did not tax the companies for every kilowatt of electricity generated as Glasscock had asked, but House Bill 195 did remove the right of eminent domain from private interests, which the governor suggested as an alternative.[24] Another law that pleased Glasscock was House Bill 25, an act to preserve competition among common carriers in the state of West Virginia, protecting intrastate commerce from restraint and monopoly.[25]

----

21 *West Virginia Senate Journal, Regular and Extraordinary Session 1913*, 93-94

22 *West Virginia Senate Journal, Regular and Extraordinary Session 1913*, 81–131.

23 *West Virginia Senate Journal, Regular and Extraordinary Session 1913*, 147–58; see also *Charleston Gazette*, February 26, 1913.

24 *West Virginia Senate Journal, Regular and Extraordinary Session 1913*, 660–61, 688–89, 834–35.

25 *West Virginia Senate Journal, Regular and Extraordinary Session 1913*, 217, 382, 557–58, 752, 754.

Among other important legislation were the Wertz, Bloch, Yost, and Slemaker bills. The Wertz act dealt indirectly with the labor crisis, forbidding deputy sheriffs from acting in the capacity of mine guards.[26] The bill passed with the approval of most mine operators for fear of something extreme. In effect, it had little value in ending the hated mine guard system, because it lacked a penalty clause for violators. The hated Baldwin-Felts Detective Agency continued to prosper and serve the coal operators until the mid-1930s.[27] The Bloch Bill embodied the workmen's compensation act; strongly desired by labor, it only passed the Senate in amended form by one vote.[28] Governor-elect Hatfield worked diligently for its passage, one of the first in the nation, modeled on a German act that provided aid for injured miners in the Ruhr Valley. In broader areas, the Yost Act carried into effect the state prohibition amendment.[29] In the business sector, the Slemaker Blue Sky law regulated and supervised investment companies doing business within the state, in order to prevent the selling of worthless securities.[30] In an effort to get it right this time, the legislators also passed a law creating a state road bureau, changing later to a commission in order to receive federal aid in 1917. On the local level, the Gray Silver Bill promised assistance to the farmers and fruit growers of the Mountain State and provided for a crop pest commission.[31] Finally, the legislature passed a joint resolution creating the Virginia Debt Commission, with state Senator William MacCorkle as chairman. This action was necessary as Virginia was growing impatient, and most lawmakers approved of paying "any just amount that this state owed."[32] In all, with the introduction and passage of several regulatory acts with their concomitant bureaucracies and administrative rules, proactive Progressives believed the Mountain State was moving forward into the future.

The primary election law once again eluded the reform governor. Likewise, the proposal to tax natural gas produced in the state, which many conservatives feared

26   *West Virginia Senate Journal, Regular and Extraordinary Session 1913*, 430, 579, 836, 838.

27   Corbin, *Life, Work, and Rebellion*, 114–15. See also Hadsell and Coffey, "From Law and Order," 281–82, 286.

28   *Journal of the House, 1913*, 523–25, 560–62, 759–62, 824–25.

29   *Journal of the House*, 300–10.

30   *Journal of the Senate*, 4–11.

31   *Journal of the Senate*, 129–37.

32   *Charleston Gazette*, February 7, 1913; see also the *Journal of the Senate, 1913*, 613, 760, 764, 784, 786–87, 798–99, 850–51; Ambler and Summers, *West Virginia, The Mountain State*, 325–26. On July 1, 1915, the Supreme Court decreed that West Virginia owed Virginia a total sum of $12,393,929.50, including interest. By the sale of bonds and the creation of the Virginia Debt Sinking Fund, West Virginia liquidated the debt in 1939.

would be excessive, failed. In the case of the former, the lawmakers evidently had their own reasons for wanting to retain the election of United States Senators to themselves and the selection of other candidates largely in the hands of party leaders. In reference to the latter, Governor Glasscock had always tried to entice the legislators to pass a levy on natural gas, with the proceeds of the tax to be used for beneficial services such as free text books, as he had done in 1911, or to replace the loss of revenue as a result of the prohibition amendment. Yet to the surprise of many, the small gas people from West Virginia's thirty-nine gas-producing counties actively lobbied against its enactment. These owners and their attorneys protested before the House Committee on Taxation and Finance during the hearings concerning the proposed law. They argued that the big out-of-state competitors supported the measure in hopes that the tax increase would drive many of the smaller owners out of business, paving the way for the larger corporations to purchase the bankrupt holdings and establish their monopolies. With the numerous attempts to place a severance tax on West Virginia's natural resources, exploitation rather than careful development would remain in the hands of corporate interests headquartered in the large metropolitan areas outside of the state.[33]

From the beginning, it was evident that a number of special interest groups would be very active for the duration of the legislative session. After all, the governor intended to promote real reform for the Mountain State. Glasscock called these groups the "invisible government." Displeased by their lobbying, he urged the legislators to enact an anti-lobbying law, which they failed to do. The West Virginia Child Labor Committee opened its activities early. This group pressed for an eight-hour working day and the abolishment of night work for all under sixteen years of age.[34] Also on hand were the representatives of the United Mine Workers,[35] who recommended and endorsed the workmen's compensation law; the initiative, referendum and recall; the abolition of the mine guard system; a uniform child labor bill; and the passage of the "qualification law," which would raise the standard of employment requirements for miners. The UMW also concerned itself with the importation of foreign laborers, which it opposed, and the right of miners to organize freely.[36]

33   *Charleston Gazette*, February 5, 1913. See also, John Alexander Williams, *West Virginia and the Captains of Industries*, 249–250.

34   *Charleston Gazette*, January 7, 1913; January 14, 1913.

35   *Charleston Gazette*, January 15, 1913. The members were also critical of the way Governor Glasscock had handled the strike situation.

36   *Charleston Gazette*, January 15, 1913; January 17, 1913.

The legislative halls and committee rooms were a beehive of activity, and the lobbyists were par excellence in their attempts to influence legislation. In reference to the water power bill, House Bill 195, Governor Glasscock stated that he believed "the most powerful and probably the most intelligent lobby that ever represented any interests before the legislature was here to oppose any real progressive legislation upon this important matter." He further commented that they confused members of government by the issuing of alleged statistics and facts;[37] the bill passed by one vote. The story was the same for the workmen's compensation act, which came under heavy arguments when the House Committees on Judiciary and Taxation held joint sessions on the proposed law.[38] The misrepresentations of the lobbyists, however, confirmed Glasscock's belief in the importance of the wisdom of the people and the necessity of a free press and adequate education facilities. He would have agreed when Governor La Follette stated, "Machine control is based upon misrepresentation and ignorance. Democracy is based upon knowledge. It was clear to me that the only way to beat the boss and ring rule was to keep the people thoroughly informed."[39]

While the lawmakers were busy enacting legislation during the regular session, the selection of a United States Senator remained at an impasse. From the beginning of the term, nationwide attention had focused on the West Virginia legislature to see which party would emerge triumphant. On the national level, Democrats had nearly captured the upper chamber of Congress and a number of states that were still electing senators drew the attention of the nation.[40] At this time, close scrutiny fell upon the state's new Governor-elect Hatfield. He had been conspicuously silent during the first weeks and his inaction only added to the flurry of speculation. Word circulated, however, that he would probably support Davis Elkins, since the latter had donated so much money to Hatfield's campaign.[41] The prospect of electing a senator, indeed, looked bleak, and there was little time left in the regular session. The aspirants exerted much pressure upon the lawmakers, and their supporters showered the legislature with telegrams and petitions. It was a well-orchestrated movement combined, almost daily, with personal endorsements from well-known individuals.[42]

---

37   *Charleston Gazette*, February 28, 1913.

38   *Charleston Gazette*, February 7, 1913; February 13, 1913; February 28, 1913.

39   Russel B. Nye, *Midwestern Progressive Politics*, 206

40   *Charleston Gazette*, January 25, 1913.

41   *Charleston Daily Mail*, January 14, 1913; January 15, 1913; January 16, 1913; *Charleston Gazette*, January 2, 1913; January 21, 1913.

42   *Charleston Daily Mail*, February 3, 1913; *Charleston Gazette*, February 6, 1913.

It appeared likely that the fight for the senatorship would remain on the floor. The Progressives demanded that representatives from the counties where Roosevelt had won a majority to elect their candidate from that open body. Yet it was not that simple. Even though Roosevelt had beaten Taft in the state, more "regular" Republicans had been elected to the legislature than Bull Moosers. For that reason, Davis Elkins demanded a GOP caucus to nominate a candidate. Whatever method was chosen, most perceptive observers predicted a protracted struggle. If the reform Republicans declined to enter a closed session and then name their own candidate, there would be a three-cornered fight on the floor between a Democrat, a Republican, and a Progressive. If the Progressive wing decided to enter a Republican caucus, a deadlock was certain among Elkins, Edwards, and Mann.[43]

A break seemed to appear on January 15 when Elkins received indirect support from the Governor-elect. Late that evening Hatfield strongly encouraged the Republicans to caucus in order to nominate a candidate, placing Hatfield, Elkins, and Mann in agreement on such action. In spite of the prestigious endorsements, word circulated that twenty-four members of the House had signed an accord not to go into caucus with their fellow Republicans.[44]

On February 4, the legislature finally held a joint vote, with no person receiving the necessary majority. The process continued over the next several days with Elkins, Edwards, and Mann each sharing the lead at different times.[45] This voting pattern continued until Delegate S. U. G. Rhodes of Mingo County dramatically announced the change of his vote from Mann to Edwards. With the switch, there seemed to be a perceptible change in the political wind. The move, however, was not beneficial to Edwards or Rhodes; within two hours of the incident, Delegate Rhodes and four other legislators were arrested for selling their votes to the Edwards people. Allegedly, Delegate Rhodes had agreed to deliver seven votes for the sum of $50,000 in support of Colonel Edwards. The other defendants were state Senator Ben A. Smith of Mason, Delegate Rath Duff of Jackson, Dr. H. F. Asbury of Putnam, and Davis Hill of Mason. Two others were later charged with misdemeanors.[46]

As the story unfolded, it was reported that Edwards had earlier gone to the detective agency of William J. Burns in New York, where he asked for aid in devising a plot to catch

43 *Charleston Gazette*, January 3, 1913.
44 *Charleston Daily Mail*, January 14, 1913 and January 15, 1913; *Charleston Gazette*, January 15, 1913.
45 *Charleston Daily Mail*, February 5, 1913; *Charleston Gazette*, February 5, 1913.
46 *Charleston Daily Mail*, February 11, 1913.

those lawmakers that could be bribed. The Burns operatives later arrived in Charleston and planted dictographs in the rooms of the several hotels. Allegedly, on February 11, during the legislative recess, the detectives bribed Rhodes and his cohorts. Given marked bills, the defendants were persuaded to meet in a room on the fourth floor of the Kanawha Hotel, presumably to rendezvous with Colonel Edwards. Upon entering the small cubicle, Sheriff Bonner Hill and Kanawha County Prosecuting Attorney T. C. Townsend (Glasscock's former tax commissioner) arrested the defendants. The accused were later released on $5,000 bond each.[47]

Apparently, William Edwards, also a victim of circumstances, suffered from his effort to apprehend fraudulent legislators. Of the five bribe-takers, four were already committed to him; only Rhodes had changed his vote. After the incident, a definite change occurred in the voting patterns of the lawmakers. On February 12, the Edwards following slipped from sixteen to seven. The main beneficiary of the scandal was William P. Hubbard, who climbed to a vote of twelve. Elkins also received added, if not tainted, support when Dr. Asbury denounced Edwards in the legislature and changed his vote to Davis Elkins.[48]

During the subsequent trial at Webster Springs, the state contended that upon hearing rumors of bribery, Governor Glasscock and Colonel Edwards had hired the Burns detectives, assigning them to the Attorney General's office. Edwards also stated that he had informed Prosecutor Townsend that he would approve any attempt to apprehend the criminals. The colonel further commented that although he suspected Delegate Rhodes of bribery, he had no idea who else might be involved. It was a trying experience for the Coalburg statesman, since he was the state's witness against those who had formerly been his friends. Edwards, sincere and honest in his effort to curtail corruption in the governmental solons, was still a weary man. He had lost the battle for the senatorial seat and the friendships of some of those who had supported him.[49]

Trying each defendant separately, sentencing took place in late summer. On August 4, Judge W. S. O'Brien of the Circuit Court ordered Delegate S. U. G. Rhodes, Rath Duff, and H. F. Asbury to six years each in the penitentiary. State Senator B. A. Smith received five years and six months, and Delegate David Hill was given five years. In this unprecedented action, the five legislators were also disqualified for life from holding any public office or any position of trust, thus ending a disgraceful period of the West

---

47   *Charleston Gazette*, February 12, 1913.
48   *Charleston Gazette*, February 13, 1913; February 14, 1913.
49   *Charleston Gazette*, July 5, 1913; July 11, 1913; August 2, 1913.

Virginia legislature. Although many hailed William S. Edwards for his selfless sense of duty, he felt embarrassed personally and politically because of his involvement.[50]

The joint vote of the legislature continued in vain. The Republicans at last secured the consent of enough of their members to hold a caucus, meeting several times unsuccessfully.[51] Finally, on February 20, Hatfield called upon his cohorts for a "valiant effort" to elect a senator. If necessary, he insisted that they hold an all-night session, admonishing, "It is not time for the Republican Party to die or be crucified in West Virginia."[52] The GOP heeded the warning and in the early hours of the 22nd, the caucus elected Judge Nathan B. Goff. Acceptable to the majority of his party, the judge was the obvious choice. He was the peacemaker, a role he did not particularly relish. In the early morning, the Republicans informed Goff, who was then presiding over the Fourth United States Circuit Court in Richmond, Virginia, of their action. The judge accepted, stating, "I had not wished this nomination. It is unexpected, but if the people of my state demand this service from me I cannot decline."[53] How ironic that the elderly Goff, an "old-line" Republican and Civil War veteran, from whom Stephen B. Elkins had wrested state leadership for the West Virginia GOP, was recalled to active service to save a fractured Party. It was ironic, too, that the legislators elected the judge rather than Elkins's son.

Judge Goff's decision ended one of the most exciting and raucous sessions in the annals of the West Virginia legislature. Clearly, many desired change in state politics. Glasscock's old gubernatorial opponent in 1908, A. C. Scherr, probably best summed up the feelings of Glasscock and the Progressives in regard to the 1913 election of a United States senator by stating that if any of the "unscrupulous machine" (referring to the conservatives) should be elected senator, "I see our finish."[54] In the political quagmire that existed, Judge Nathan Goff was one of the few persons who could unite the party. A weary governor wrote sincerely when he sent Goff his "heartiest" congratulations, "We need you and I am sure you will meet every reasonable expectation."[55]

On March 4, 1913, Glasscock spoke briefly at Governor-elect Hatfield's inauguration. In his remarks, the outgoing governor again called for a primary election law, which had eluded him during his administration. He stated that there was no reason why "a few

---

50 *Wheeling Intelligencer*, August 5, 1913; *Charleston Gazette*, August 5, 1913.

51 *Charleston Daily Mail*, February 11, 1913; February 14, 1913; February 20, 1913; *Charleston Gazette*, February 15, 1913; February 18, 1913.

52 *Charleston Gazette*, February 21, 1913; *Charleston Daily Mail*, February 21, 1913.

53 *Wheeling Intelligencer*, February 22, 1913.

54 A. C. Scherr to John W. Mason, November 19, 1912, Mason Papers.

55 Glasscock to Judge Nathan Goff, February 21, 1913, Glasscock Papers.

of us should sit down in an office and say who shall be nominated."[56] He also urged the passage of a county salary law, declaring that there were many public officers receiving far more remuneration than they deserved. In conclusion, Glasscock spoke out against bribery and corruption in government and added that it would be the regret of his life that industrial troubles came during his term in office, but he could do nothing else than stand for law and order. The governor ended his career on a Progressive stand, content that he had done his best, but relieved to lay down his burdens, as he explained to his receptive audience:

> . . . much as you people may welcome the new governor, happy as you may
> be; I am the happiest citizen of West Virginia not that I am ready to lay down
> the cares, worries, anxieties of the office, I was desirous to be governor. I
> went around asking for your votes, but I am more anxious now to lay down
> these responsibilities than I ever was to assume them. I hoped, worked and
> prayed for many things that did not come to pass; some of them did.[57]

Without a doubt, Governor Glasscock relished the idea of becoming citizen Glasscock once again, leaving behind the recriminations of public office and returning to Morgantown, surrounded by friends and family where he resided at 356 Spruce Street. He never again actively participated in political affairs, except to give wise counsel. During the first part of his administration, party conservatives had enjoyed much influence with Glasscock, especially while Stephen Elkins was alive. Yet once the governor saw several of his key bills killed, he became a more active reformer. By the end of his political career, Governor Glasscock was a confirmed Progressive. Taking into account the many disruptions during the last year of his term, Glasscock fared well with the legislature, although there remained much unfinished business on the Progressive agenda for the new governor to complete.

By the end of his administration, William Glasscock, along with former Governor W. M. O. Dawson, had definitely earned the right to call himself a Progressive. He was aided by the fact that his party, the Republican Party, usually maintained a majority during the Progressive Era, and unlike several of the border states, such as Maryland and Kentucky, race relations generally ran much more smoothly. Glasscock could point with pride to the fact that he had accomplished many reforms begun earlier to

---

56 *Charleston Daily Mail*, March 4, 1913.
57 *Charleston Daily Mail*, March 4, 1913.

a lesser degree by Democratic leaders and to a larger degree by Republican governors. Henry D. Hatfield, who was not ardently progressive but was politically astute enough to recognize the mood of the people and demand reforms, assured Glasscock, "I am willing to exert my energy in any way that is thought best to give to the people what they want in the way of any of these progressive measures."[58] Hatfield, now the nominal head of the state's Republican Party, continued the trend with accomplishments in the area of mine safety and health and the attainment of the elusive state primary. West Virginia, marching to its own cadence in stride with its culture and history, certainly had the credentials to enter the Progressive ranks. It would stand among other Progressive states, if not stand out as one of the most reformed in the region. Mountain State Progressives knew they had not accomplished everything for which they had hoped, and many problems continued to hamper a state that needed infrastructure and development to provide jobs for its citizens. West Virginia would still have to deal with labor–management problems, taxation and devising ways of equitably distributing returns from its natural resources, and methods of diversifying the state's economy. The early reformers, however, did establish the beginning of a "new order" that was certainly not perfect but more in step with modern principles of efficiency, continuity, and recognition that democracy was indeed a participatory process.

58   Henry D. Hatfield to Glasscock, 26 November 1912, Hatfield Papers.

EPILOGUE

"I assure you it is no soft snap to be Governor"[1]

THE GOVERNOR'S LETTERS AND PAPERS declined drastically in volume during the winter of 1912–1913. The industrial problems in the Kanawha Valley did ease up during January 1913, only to worsen in February. During the legislative session of 1913, Glasscock saw several good pieces of legislation enacted in addition to the election of a Republican to the United States Senate. Nevertheless, he looked forward to March 4, the expiration of his term of office. He expressed his feelings about the position of governor to a cousin:

> I assure you it is no soft snap to be Governor, and I am glad that the 4th of next March will relieve me from my present duties, and if I ever get into another position it will be after I have forgotten the trials and troubles and tribulations of my present administration.[2]

Governor Glasscock never forgot. On March 4, 1913, he declared himself the happiest man in the state, because he was now relieved of the arduous duties associated with labor and political strife. Upon retirement, Governor Glasscock resolved not to play an active role in state politics again, except to go as a delegate-at-large to the Republican Convention held in Cleveland in 1924, where he supported the vice presidential candidacy of Charles G. Dawes. Otherwise, he mainly kept his self-imposed promise, satisfied to observe on the periphery, offering advice and counsel when asked.

---

1   Glasscock to Mrs. R. A. Phelps, 26 August 1912, Glasscock Papers.
2   Glasscock to Mrs. R. A. Phelps, 26 August 1912, Glasscock Papers.

Financial problems also preyed on the governor's mind as he stood before the crowd of well-wishers watching a new governor sworn into office. He had previously written to his brother in Bellingham, Washington:

> I am in receipt of your letter of the 18th instant and wish to the bottom of my heart that I could accept your invitation and spend a few weeks with you, but I cannot do so. I am in such financial condition that it is impossible for me without doing an injustice to my family to take any vacation at this time. I have spent four years of the best part of my life trying to serve the public, and at a great financial sacrifice. I have paid no attention during that time to my financial affairs and they are now in such condition that I must now look after them, and for that reason I feel that I must get back to Morgantown as soon as possible and get to work. My term of office expires next Thursday, and by the latter part of the week I intend to be in Morgantown, and in less than two weeks from the time I am writing this letter I shall be found in my office trying to take up where I left it more than four years ago. For many years I made considerable money and if I had kept out of politics would now be in an almost independent position, but as it is I can see nothing in the future but hard work and economy. During these last four years I have contracted some debts that must be attended to, and I have no hope of a vacation this year, and by-the-way, I got none last year either. I thank you very, very much for the invitation and if it were possible for me to do so I certainly would accept. I would like to go away from home for a while and be entirely free and independent, but as stated above it is impossible for me to do so.[3]

During his stormy tenure in office, Glasscock experienced intense anguish, not to mention excruciating pain. Evidently, the governor's frustrations with his inability to solve certain problems resulted in physical ailments. These, in turn, incapacitated him, leaving their marks for life. His close friends reportedly stated that the beleaguered former governor never completely recovered from the stress of high office. His daughter-in-law, Mrs. William E. Glasscock, Jr., commented that in his later years his knuckles and feet were misshapen and his body bent forward when he walked. Glasscock suffered severe pain, but he was always "kind and courageous" and devoted to his family. With

---

3   Glasscock to S. A. D. Glasscock, 25 February 1913, Glasscock Papers.

his son, who was also an attorney, living close to his father in Morgantown, the former governor found it easy to dote on his family, especially his first grandchild.

At his home, Glasscock enjoyed twelve productive years after his service to the state. Toward the end, the health of Glasscock and his wife deteriorated, with more concern paid to Mrs. Glasscock, who had become seriously ill. During the winter, the two had traveled to Battle Creek, Michigan, to Florida, and back to Battle Creek, seeking medical aid for Mary and relief for his "old malady."

Along with worry over his wife's health, the trips proved to be a tremendous strain on the former chief executive, especially after he contracted influenza in Battle Creek. He never fully recovered. By early April 1925, both husband and wife, attended by a nurse, convalesced in their Morgantown home. Unexpectedly, one week after their return from Michigan, on Easter morning, an urgent call summoned William E. Glasscock, Jr. to his father's house to see him for the last time. The governor was dying.[4]

Glasscock's rapid demise shocked the community because his health seemed to be improving and he had even taken an automobile ride about Morgantown on Friday, April 10, just two days before his death. When he retired on Saturday evening, the former governor assured the nurse that he was all right and that she should give all of her attention to his wife. By Sunday morning, the former chief executive hovered between life and death. Mary insisted that attendants move her from her sickbed to be with her dying husband in the final moments of his life.

William E. Glasscock died April 12, 1925. His wife, to whom he was completely devoted, followed him in death three months later. In his will, he honored his partner in life:

> If I have succeeded in anything I owe that success to my wife. She has been faithful in all things and has always been willing to do more than her full share to secure our success and happiness. I have never been able to pay her the debt I owe her loyalty and faithfulness.[5]

An apt obituary commented on the governor's death, "Mr. Glasscock's death came as a shock to the entire community. In church and civil affairs he was regarded as

---

4   Mrs. William E. Glasscock, Jr., interview by Dr. Gary J. Tucker, August 15, 1975. Also see Morgan, *West Virginia Governors*, 79.

5   William E. Glasscock, will dated February 17, 1921, Monongalia County Court House, Morgantown, WV.

institutional rather than individual."[6] Tributes and memorials in the state's newspapers clearly showed that William E. Glasscock was considered an honest, decent man of religious character. As former Secretary of State H.G. Young stated, "He was a good man and a great deal stronger governor than was thought by some people who did not appreciate the problems with which he had to deal."[7]

Since Mrs. Glasscock was too ill to attend a public funeral, a private ceremony was held at the Glasscock home. A later service was conducted at the First Methodist Episcopal Church attended by an overcapacity group of mourners. West Virginia University ceased all school activities that afternoon as did the county government and both houses of the state legislature. Acquaintances and fellow politicians lauded the governor as a man who was always available to offer aid and support to his many friends. Governor H. M. Gore, 1925–1929, said, "In a personal way he was my friend and I feel that I have lost a wise counselor and constant friend."[8]

Through pain, discomfort, and political turmoil, William Glasscock lived a full, well-rounded life and was interested in people, society, politics, and religion. He traveled widely and at times played important roles on the national scene, such as the 1912 presidential election and the U.S. Senate investigation of the labor conflict. From early adulthood, Glasscock suffered much pain periodically, yet he progressed through life successfully, ultimately becoming the chief executive of West Virginia. In a personal way, it is doubtful that Glasscock's accomplishments equaled the pain and anguish that he suffered while in office.

His life would have been much different had he remained in the comfort of his hometown engaged in a lucrative law practice. Although William Glasscock became West Virginia's thirteenth governor, it was not a position he actively sought. Had it not been for a number of unusual circumstances, plus the friendship of U.S. Senator Stephen B. Elkins, it is likely that he would not have been chief executive. In that office, however, Glasscock endeavored to direct the passage of legislation that would benefit a majority of the people.

As the Glasscock administration concluded, the people of the state and the nation witnessed the waning of the Progressive Era. When war clouds formed over Europe, the

6   *Huntington Herald Advertiser*, April 13, 1925, clipping in William E. Glasscock Papers, West Virginia Department of Archives and History, Charleston, WV.

7   *Charleston Daily Mail*, April 13, 1925.

8   *Charleston Daily Mail*, April 13, 1925, and *Morgantown Post*, April 13, 1925; April 14, 1925; April 15, 1925.

attention of the country shifted from domestic problems to foreign affairs and before long, to military preparation for WWI.

Though political priorities were changing, the Progressive trend did not completely end with Glasscock. In 1915 West Virginia Governor Henry D. Hatfield finally won the passage of the coveted primary law, the establishment of a State Department of Health with power to enforce public health laws, and the submission of the women's suffrage amendment to the voters, continuing the progressive work begun under the administration of Governor A. B. White. By 1916, a noted historian stated, "West Virginia had as much progressive legislation on her books as most of her northern and western sister states."[9] In fact, although the governorship went to Democrat John J. Cornwell in 1916 (mainly because corporate leaders had turned against Hatfield due to his reform efforts),[10] some progressive legislation continued, such as the creation of a bi-partisan seven member (including the state superintendent of schools) State Board of Education, with supervision over the entire public education system.[11] The dynamics of change would ebb and flow throughout Appalachia and its beautiful hills, barriers to transportation and communication in older times that could no longer protect the inhabitants from the social and economic aspects of development and political struggles. By 1920, however, the Progressive period in the Mountain State ended, as it did in most of the other states. Governor Glasscock, at peace in Morgantown and proud of his accomplishments, was most assuredly happy to be home as another round of labor disputes christened the 1920s.

9   Burckel, "Progressive Governors in the Border States," 406.
10   Rice and Brown, *West Virginia: A History*, 216.
11   Ambler, *A History of Education in West Virginia*, 390–391.

BIBLIOGRAPHY

PRIMARY MATERIALS

Manuscripts

Johnson N. Camden Papers, West Virginia University Library, Morgantown, West Virginia.

Henry G. Davis Papers, West Virginia University Library, Morgantown, West Virginia.

W. M. O. Dawson Papers, West Virginia University Library, Morgantown, West Virginia.

Stephen B. Elkins Papers, West Virginia University Library, Morgantown, West Virginia.

A. B. Fleming Papers, West Virginia University Library, Morgantown, West Virginia.

William E. Glasscock Papers, West Virginia University Library, Morgantown, West Virginia.

_____, State Department of Archives and History, Charleston, West Virginia.

Henry D. Hatfield Papers, West Virginia University Library, Morgantown, West Virginia.

Mary Jones Papers, West Virginia University Library, Morgantown, West Virginia.

John W. Mason Papers, West Virginia University Library, Morgantown, West Virginia.

Joseph T. McGraw Papers, West Virginia University Library, Morgantown, West Virginia.

Ira E. Robinson Papers, West Virginia University Library, Morgantown, West Virginia.

William Howard Taft Papers, Library of Congress, Washington, D. C.

A. B. White Papers, West Virginia University Library, Morgantown, West Virginia.

Books and Periodical Articles

Lynch, Lawrence. R. "West Virginia Coal Strike." *Political Science Quarterly*, XXIX (December, 1914), 626–663.

MacCorkle, William A. *The Recollections of Fifty Years of West Virginia.* New York: G. P. Putnam's Sons, 1928.

"The Private War in West Virginia." *Outlook,* June 28, 1913, 403.

Official Records

Blue, Fred, P. J. Donahue, and S. L. Walker. *Report of West Virginia Mining Investigation, 1912.* Charleston: Tribune Publishing Co., 1912.

Glasscock, William E. *Speech Delivered by Governor Glasscock Before the State Board of Trade, Huntington, West Virginia, October 12, 1909.* Charleston: Union Typographical Label, n. d.

———. *The State of West Virginia: An Address Delivered by Gov. Glasscock at Seattle, Washington, July 29, 1909.* Charleston: News Mail Co., 1909.

———. State Papers and Public Addresses of Wm. E. Glasscock, 1909–1913. n. p., n. d.

———, and Henry D. Hatfield. *Messages and Documents, Session of 1913–1915, William E. Glasscock and Henry D. Hatfield.* Vol. I. Charleston: Tribune Printing Co., 1913–1914.

———. *Manual of the State of West Virginia for the Years 1907–1908, Issued by C. W. Swisher, Secretary of State.* Charleston: The Tribune Printing Co., 1907.

Harris, John T., ed. *West Virginia Legislative Hand Book and Manual and Official Register, 1916.* Charleston: Tribune Printing Co., n. d.

———, ed. *West Virginia Legislative Hand Book and Manual and Official Register, 1924.* Charleston: Jarrett Printing Co., 1924.

———, ed. *West Virginia Legislative Hand Book and Manual and Official Register, 1926.* Charleston: Tribune Printing Co., n. d.

U. S. Bureau of the Census. *Extra Census Bulletin, Coal Production of the United States.* No. 10. Washington: Government Printing Office, 1891.

———. *Special Reports of the Census Office, Mines and Quarries, 1902.* Washington: Government Printing Office, 1905.

———. *Thirteenth Census of the United States, 1910, Agriculture, Reports by States.* Vol. VII. Washington: Government Printing Office, 1913.

———. *Thirteenth Census of the United States, 1910, Mines and Quarries: 1909, General Reports and Analysis.* Vol. XI. Washington: Government Printing Office, 1913.

———. *Fourteenth Census of the United States, Taken in the Year 1920, Mines and Quarries, 1919.* Vol. XI. Washington: Government Printing Office, 1923.

U. S. Congress. *Hearings Before a Subcommittee of the Committee on Education and Labor, United States Senate.* Sixty-third Congress, First Session, Part I. Washington: Government Printing Office, 1913.

West Virginia Department of Mines. *Annual Report, 1916.* Charleston: Tribune Printing Co., 1916.

West Virginia Legislature. *Journal of the House of Delegates and the Senate, Extraordinary Session, 1911.* Charleston: News-Mail Co., 1911.

West Virginia. *Report of the Adjutant General, 1911–1912.* Charleston: Union Publishing Company, 1912.

_____. *Journal and Bills of the House, Session 1913.* Charleston: Tribune Printing Co., 1913.

_____. *Acts of the Legislature, Twenty-Ninth Regular Session, 1909.* Charleston: News-Mail Co., n. d.

_____. *Acts of the Legislature, Thirtieth Regular Session, 1911.* Charleston: Union Publishing Co., n. d.

_____. *Acts of the Legislature, Thirtieth-First Session, 1913.* Charleston: Tribune Printing Co., n. d.

Interview

Mrs. William E. Glasscock, Jr., Morgantown, West Virginia, August 15, 1975.

Newspapers

Charleston Gazette. Charleston, West Virginia, 1909–1913. Daily.

Daily Mail. Charleston, West Virginia, 1909–1913.

Fairmont West Virginian. Fairmont, West Virginia, 1908. Daily.

Morgantown Post-Chronicle. Morgantown, West Virginia, 1908–1911. Daily.

Moundsville Daily Echo. Moundsville, West Virginia, 1908.

Parkersburg Sentinel. Parkersburg, West Virginia, 1910–1911. Daily.

Wheeling Intelligencer. Wheeling, West Virginia, 1908–1913. Daily.

Wheeling Register. Wheeling, West Virginia, 1908–1911. Daily.

SECONDARY MATERIALS

Ambler, Charles H. *West Virginia Stories and Biographies.* New York: Rand McNally and Co., 1954.

_____. *A History of Education in West Virginia*. Huntington: Standard Printing and Publishing Co., 1951.

_____, and Festus P. Summers. *West Virginia: The Mountain State*. 2nd ed. Englewood Cliffs, N. J.: Prentice-Hall, Inc., 1958.

Atkinson, George W. *Bench and Bar of West Virginia*. Charleston: Virginian Law Book Co., 1919.

Bailey, Kenneth R. "A Judicious Mixture: Negroes and Migrants in the West Virginia Mines, 1880–1917." *West Virginia History* 34 (January 1973): 141–161.

_____. "'Grim Visaged Men' and The West Virginia National Guard in the 1912–1913 Paint and Cabin Creek Strike." *West Virginia History* 41 (Winter 1980): 111–125.

Barb, John M. "Strikes in the Southern West Virginia Coal Fields, 1912–1922." master's thesis, West Virginia University, 1949.

Barkey, Frederick Allan. "The Socialist Party in West Virginia from 1890 to 1920: A Study in Working Class Radicalism." PhD diss., University of Pittsburgh, 1971.

Barns, William D. *The West Virginia State Grange: The First Century, 1873–1973*. Morgantown: Morgantown Printing and Binding Co., 1973.

Beachley, Charles E., comp., *History of the Consolidation Coal Company, 1864–1934*. New York: Consolidation Coal Company, 1934.

Burckel, Nicholas Clare. "Progressive Governors in the Border States: Reform Governors of Missouri, Kentucky, West Virginia and Maryland, 1900–1918." PhD diss., University of Wisconsin, 1971.

_____. "Governor Albert B. White and the Beginning of Progressive Reform, 1901–05." *West Virginia History* 40 (Fall 1978): 1–12.

Burton, David. *Theodore Roosevelt*. New York: Twayne Publishers, Inc., 1972.

Callahan, James M. *History of West Virginia, Old and New*. Vol. I. New York: The American Historical Society, Inc., 1923.

_____. *Semi-Centennial History of West Virginia*. Charleston: Semi-Centennial Commission, 1913.

Casdorph, Paul Douglas. "Governor William E. Glasscock and Theodore Roosevelt's 1912 Bull Moose Candidacy." *West Virginia History* 28 (October 1966): 8–13.

Cole, Merle T. "Martial Law in West Virginia and Major Davis as 'Emperor of Tug River.'" *West Virginia History* 43 (Fall 1981): 118–144.

Cometti, Elizabeth, and Festus P. Summers. *The Thirty-Fifth State*. Morgantown: West Virginia University Library, 1966.

Conley, Phil. *History of the West Virginia Coal Industry*. Charleston: Education Foundation, Inc., 1960.

Corbin, David Alan, ed. *The West Virginia Mine Wars, An Anthology*. Charleston: Appalachian Editions, 1990.

_____. "The Socialist and Labor Star: Strike and Suppression in West Virginia." *West Virginia History* 34 (January 1973): 168–186.

_____. "Betrayal in the West Virginia Coal Fields: Eugene V. Debs and the Socialist Party of America 1912–1941." *Journal of American History* 64 (March 1978): 987–1009.

Crawford, Charles B. "The Mine War on Cabin Creek and Paint Creek, West Virginia in 1912–1913." master's thesis, University of Kentucky, 1939.

Cyclopedia of Monongalia, Marion, and Taylor Counties, West Virginia. Philadelphia: Rush, West and Co., 1895.

Davis, Allen F. *American Heroine: The Life and Legend of Jane Addams*. New York: Oxford University Press, 1973.

Fagge, Roger. "Eugene V. Debs in West Virginia, 1913: A Reappraisal." *West Virginia History* 52 (1993): 1–18.

Fast, Richard E. and Hu Maxwell. *The History and Government of West Virginia*. 3rd ed. Morgantown: The Acme Publishing Co., 1906.

Fetherling, Dale. *Mother Jones, The Miner's Angel*. Carbondale: Southern Illinois University Press, 1974.

Foner, Philip S., ed. *Mother Jones Speaks*. New York: Monad Press, 1983.

Gartin, Edwin V. "The West Virginia Mine War of 1912–1913: The Progressive Response." *North Dakota Quarterly* 41 (Autumn 1973): 13–27.

Goodall, Elizabeth J. "The Charleston Industrial Area: Development, 1797–1937." *West Virginia History* 30 (October 1968): 358–412.

_____. "The Virginia Debt Controversy and Settlement," Pt. I, *West Virginia History* 24 (October 1962): 42–74; Pt. II 24 (April 1963): 296–311; Pt. III 24 (July 1963), 332–351; and Pt. IV 25 (October 1963): 42–68.

Gorn, Elliott J. *Mother Jones: The Most Dangerous Woman in America*. New York: Hill and Wang, 2001.

Graebner, William. *Coal-Mining Safety in the Progressive Period: The Political Economy of Reform*. Lexington: University Press of Kentucky, 1976.

Hadsell, Richard M., and William E. Coffey. "From Law and Order to Class Warfare: Baldwin-Felts Detectives in the Southern West Virginia Coal Fields." *West Virginia History* 40 (Spring 1979): 268–286.

Harbaugh, William Henry. *Power and Responsibility: The Life and Times of Theodore Roosevelt*. New York: Farrar, Straus and Cudahy, 1961.

Hays, Samuel P. *The Response to Industrialism: 1885–1914*. Chicago: The University of Chicago Press, 1957.

Hess, J. W., ed. *Struggle in the Coal Fields: The Autobiography of Fred Mooney*. Morgantown: West Virginia University Library, 1967.

Hofstadter, Richard. *The Age of Reform*. New York: Vintage Books, 1955.

Jones, Mary Harris. *The Autobiography of Mother Jones*. Chicago: Charles H. Kerr and Co., 1925. Reprint, 1972.

Karr, Carolyn. "A Political Biography of Henry Hatfield." *West Virginia History* 38 (October 1966): 35 63.

Keeney, C. Belmont. "A Republican for Labor: T. C. Townsend and the West Virginia Labor Movement, 1921–1931." *West Virginia History* 60 (2004–2006): 1–18.

Knott, Stephen F. *Alexander Hamilton and the Persistence of Myth*. Kansas: University Press of Kansas, 2002.

Lambert, Oscar Doane. *Stephen Benton Elkins*. Pittsburgh: University of Pittsburgh Press, 1955.

Lambie, Joseph T. *From Mine to Market: The History of Coal Transportation on the Norfolk and Western Railway*. Washington Square, N.Y.: New York University Press, 1954.

Lee, Howard B. *Bloodletting in Appalachia*. Parsons, W. VA.: McClain Printing Co., 1969.

Leopold, Richard W. *Elihu Root and the Conservative Tradition*. Boston: Little, Brown and Co., 1954.

Lewis, Ronald L. *Transforming the Appalachian Countryside*. Chapel Hill: The University of North Carolina Press, 1998.

_____. "Black Presence in the Paint-Cabin Creek Strike, 1912–1913." *West Virginia History* 46 (1985–1986): 59–71.

Lunt, Richard D. *Law and Order vs. The Miners: West Virginia, 1907–1933*. Handen, Connecticut: Archon Books, 1979.

Lynch, Lawrence R. "West Virginia Coal Strike." *Political Science Quarterly* 29 (December 1914): 626–663.

Malone, Dumas, and Basil Rauch. *The New Nation: 1865–1917*. New York: Appleton-Century-Crofts, 1960.

Malcomson, Virginia D. "William E. Glasscock, Governor of the People." master's thesis, West Virginia University, 1950.

McCormick, Kyle. "The National Guard of West Virginia During the Strike Period of 1912–1913." *West Virginia History* 22 (October 1960): 34–35.

McGerr, Michael. *A Fierce Discontent: The Rise and Fall of the Progressive Movement in America, 1870–1920.* New York: Free Press, 2003.

McKinney, Gordon B. *Southern Mountain Republicans, 1865–1900.* Chapel Hill: University of North Carolina Press, 1978.

Morgan, John G. *West Virginia Governors.* Charleston: Newspaper Agency Corp., 1960.

Mowry, George E. *Theodore Roosevelt and the Progressive Movement.* New York: Hill and Wang, 1960.

Munn, Robert F. "The Development of Model Towns in the Bituminous Coal Fields." *West Virginia History* 40 (Spring 1979): 243–253.

Nye, Russel B. *Midwestern Progressive Politics: a Historical Study of Its Origins and Development, 1870–1958.* East Lansing, MI: Michigan State University Press, 1959.

Pepper, Charles M. *The Life and Times of Henry Gassaway Davis, 1823–1916.* New York: The Century Co., 1920.

Perlman, Selig and Philip Taft. *History of Labor in the United States, 1896–1932.* New York: Macmillan, 1935.

Pringle, Henry F. *The Life and Times of William Howard Taft.* Vol. 2. New York: Farrar and Rinehart, Inc., 1939.

_____. *Theodore Roosevelt: A Biography.* New York: Harcourt, Brace & Co., 1931.

_____. *Theodore Roosevelt and the Progressive Movement.* Madison: University of Wisconsin Press, 1946.

Rice, Otis K. *Charleston and the Kanawha Valley.* Woodland Hills, California, 1981.

_____. "Coal Mining in the Kanawha Valley to 1861: A View of Industrialization in the Old South." *The Journal of Southern History* 31 (November 1965): 393–416.

_____, and Stephen W. Brown. *West Virginia, A History.* 2nd ed. Lexington, KY: University Press of Kentucky, 1993.

_____, and Wayne E. Williams. *The Sheltering Arms Hospital.* Charleston: West Virginia Educational Services, 1990.

Scholten, Pat Creech. "The Old Mother and Her Army; The Agitative Strategies of Mary Harris Jones." *West Virginia History* 40 (Summer 1979): 365–374.

Smith, Gerald Wayne. "Nathan Goff, Jr.: A Biography." PhD diss., West Virginia University, 1954.

Sprague, Stuart Seely. "Unionization Struggles on Paint and Cabin Creeks, 1912–1913." *West Virginia History* 38 (April 1977): 185–213.

Steel, Edward M., ed. *The Correspondence of Mother Jones*. Pittsburgh: University of Pittsburgh Press, 1985.

Summers, Festus P. *Johnson Newlon Camden: A Study in Individualism*. New York: G. P. Putnam's Sons, 1937.

Summers, George W. *Pages from the Past*. Charleston: Charleston Journal, 1935.

Tams, W. P. *The Smokeless Coal Fields of West Virginia: A Brief History*. Morgantown: West Virginia University Library, 1963.

Tucker, Gary J. "William E. Glasscock and the West Virginia Election of 1910." *West Virginia History* 40 (Spring 1979): 254–267.

Turner, William P. "From Bourbon to Liberal: The Life and Times of John T. McGraw." PhD diss., West Virginia University, 1960.

_____. "John T. McGraw: A Study in Democratic Politics in the Age of Enterprise." *West Virginia History* 45 (1984): 1–40.

Vann Woodward, C. *The Strange Career of Jim Crow*. New York: Oxford University Press, 1966.

"West Virginia's Thirteenth Governor." *The West Virginia Review* 21, no. 10 (July 1944): 11.

Wiebe, Robert H. *The Search For Order: 1877–1920*. New York: Hill and Wang, 1967.

Williams, John A. *West Virginia and the Captains of Industry*. Morgantown: West Virginia University Press, 2003.

_____. *West Virginia, A Bicentennial History*. New York: W. W. Norton & Co., Inc., 1976.

_____. "New York's First Senator from West Virginia: How Stephen B. Elkins Found a New Political Home." *West Virginia History* 31 (January 1970): 73–87.

_____. "The New Dominion and the Old: Ante-bellum and Statehood Politics as the Background of West Virginia's 'Bourbon Democracy.'" *West Virginia History* 33 (July 1972): 317–407.

INDEX

College of Engineering, 182

Commissioner of Agriculture, in 1913 legislature, 183

Conley, W. G., 77

Consolidation Coal Company, 30, 104

Cooper bill, 28

Cooper, Dr., of Hinton, on Glasscock's health, 90

Cooper, John T., primary election bill, 45

Cornwell, Governor John J., 175-76

Corporations, unrestrained actions of, 11, 15-16; more heavily taxed, 17, 19; call for equal treatment of, 30; 31, 41, 77; Democrats as friends of, 87, 99, 104; large natural gas, 185

Cox, Frank, of Morgantown, 55, 56, 60, 61; on lynching, 143

Croly, Herbert, 127

Davis, Henry G., early association with U.S. Senator S.B. Elkins, 8, 9, 12, 14-16; 1901 election, 19, 49

Dawes, Charles G., 192

Dawson, C.G., acting Moundsville Penitentiary warden, 68

Dawson, Governor W.M.O., 13; elected governor, 18; 1908 election, 37, 38; attempt to increase taxes on production of coal, oil, and gas, 41; 1910 midterm election, 82; on Governor Glasscock's health, 90, 91; on Va. Debt controversy, 109-10; on racism, 143; 1913 legislature, 180; on Theodore Roosevelt's 1912 campaign in WV, 133; WV Progressive Party Convention, 139-40

"Death train", 169

Debs, Eugene V., 140, 172-73

Deer Park, Md., 12

Democratic Party, the "Democracy," 15, 105; during the 1870s, 12; businessmen democrats, 19

Denham, Sherman, 25, 116, 119

Dillon, C.W., of Fayette County, 125-26

District Unit Plan, 119-20

Dixon, Sam, of Fayette County, 125

Donahue, Right Reverend P.J., member of the state strike investigation commission, 160

Dry Branch, on Cabin Creek, 161

Duff, Delegate Rath, 1913 legislature, 188

Eaton, Capt. Harry A., of Cabell County, 65

Edwards, W.H., 180

Edwards, W.S., of Kanawha County; for Theodore Roosevelt, 130; WV Progressive Party Convention, 139; in 1913 legislature, 180, 188

"Elkins governors," 13, 16, 17

"Elkins machine," 14-16, 20, 98, 101

Elkins, Davis 27, 51, 54, 84-85; appointed U.S. senator, 100; 119, 124, 179-80, 187-88

Elkins, Stephen B., background, 5, 7; WV politics, 11; elected to U.S. Senate in 1895, 12; 1901 election to U.S. Senate, 16; on 1908 election, 20, 26, 33; 1909 legislature, 40; on primary election law, 43, 44, 51; on WVU presidency, 71; on price of natural gas, 75, 76; serious illness, 96, and death, 100, 01

Elliott, Adjutant General C.D., of Parkersburg, on 1908 election, 21, 67; on Gov. Glasscock's health, 89; 1908 election, 26; on 1910 election strategy, 91; 1911 legislature, 103, 110; Republican Party reform, 103,

GARY JACKSON TUCKER, PhD, has been a teacher of history and administrator for many years. He is a graduate of WVU Institute of Technology, BA; the University of North Carolina at Greensboro, MA; and WVU at Morgantown, PhD, all in history. Although Dr. Tucker is an author of numerous historical articles, *Governor William E. Glasscock and Progressive Politics in West Virginia* is his first book. Retired from the Wood County school system, he presently teaches history at WVU's Parkersburg campus.